Global Runner

Global Runner

World Record Marathon Adventures of Maddog

John Wallace

"I am tired of airplanes and need a rest from travel."

Table of Contents

Prologue: On Silver States, Sharks, and Stingrays

Marathon #1—Country #1, Silver

State Marathon, Reno, Nevada

September 1982

It's Sunday, September 19, 1982. Reno, Nevada. Or more precisely, if you care about these things, the Bower Mansion on Washoe Lake, twenty miles south of Reno on Highway 395, just beside a rock with graffiti on it. Dozens of runners are approaching the start line of the Silver State Marathon. There's a blonde-haired, thirty-eight-year-old male runner on the right side of the start line. He's wearing a Silver State Strider singlet. Race number 324 is pinned to the front. He's a hometown boy.

He looks fit and feels good, but he's nervous. He doesn't know anyone at the start line. He doesn't know much about running a marathon. It's his first time. He started running a few years ago to lose the weight he gained when he quit smoking. He's run a few short races in Reno—5K and 10K events— but got discouraged with those short distances when his oldest son—Chris, eleven years old with no training—whomped his butt in a recent "fathers and sons" five-mile race. John, for that is his name, has decided to run longer distances, as he always feels his best and most comfortable when he runs eight- to ten-mile runs on the weekends. He has always felt that something relaxing and wonderful kicks in after four or five miles out on the road.

But why run a marathon? Destiny? A midlife crisis; trying to prove that thirty-eight is not the end of his life (or, giggle, manhood)?

When he announced to his family and friends just a few months earlier that he would run a marathon, he had absolutely no idea how to train for one. But now he's ready. No, not really, but as ready as he'll ever be for his first marathon. Who ever really feels ready for their first marathon?

He's standing at the start line, unaware that this will change his life. He had read somewhere that a 3:30 marathon (eight-minute-mile pace) is recognized as a challenging and important target for most marathoners, so that has become his goal.

It's 6:00 a.m. The race starts. Immediately the adrenaline starts flowing. So too does the inexperience. He goes out at a 7:30 minute per mile pace—to give himself lots of margin, he thinks—he's expecting to slow down a bit in the last six miles. But he can't help himself. He follows the lead group, running the first mile at a sub-seven-minute-per-mile pace.

He soon realizes he can't keep up with these top runners and backs off.

He reaches the halfway mark—13.1 miles—in one hour and thirty-eight minutes, doing great, feeling great. He's on schedule. But he senses that he can't sustain the pace and so drops off to an eight-minute-per-mile pace. At mile 18 his legs are rubbery and very heavy. It's a struggle now. It's hurting to run an eight-minute-per-mile pace. By mile 20, his legs have turned to cement. He can't believe how much it hurts just to keep his legs moving at what he thinks is an unbelievably slow nine-minute-per-mile pace. But he tells himself he is tough and can handle this for another six miles.

At mile 22, he runs into an eight-foot-high, eight-foot-wide brick wall stretched across the marathon course. This is his first experience with "the wall."

It is not pleasant. His body has been hit with a giant sledgehammer. But he must finish. His family is waiting for him at the finish line. So too, he thinks, is his manhood. He tries to run again. Nope. His body shuts down. Refuses to move. He tries to walk and run but the pain is excruciating, the fatigue unbearable. He starts cursing and screaming at himself. He looks up to the sky and prays, "Please, please God, just help me finish this race—alive—and I promise I'll never do anything so stupid ever again." He's desperate.

But he begins to walk, his body now allowing this simple motion without unbearable pain. He tries to run again, but he hasn't accumulated enough prayers to withstand the pain. By mile 24, his body is bored with relentless pain and so cuts him some slack. He starts to walk and run, pain and curses still with each step, but he's moving faster and prayers are no longer needed. At mile 25 he realizes that if he can run the last mile lightly, he can still finish under that ridiculous time of 3:30. *Why is that so important?* He has no idea right now. More pressing matters are on his agenda.

Finally, he crosses the finish line. It's a time of 3:28.

To the loud and exuberant cheers of his family he replies, in a hushed and beaten voice, "I will never, *ever* run another marathon as long as I live!"

Twenty-six and a half years later, on a small island in the Pacific Ocean 4,386 miles away, he runs his 316th marathon, having averaged about a marathon run every month over those three decades of running. Three decades of marathon running.

He's not just possibly the biggest liar on the planet, but he has also set an astonishing world record—a marathon run in each of a hundred countries.

What the hell happened?

Why does someone who hurt, cried, screamed, wheezed, and prayed his way around his first marathon end up running a marathon in one hundred different countries?

And how does he do it?

Fast Forward

Fast forward to February 2009. It's the Moorea Marathon in Moorea, French Polynesia. Country #100 for John "Maddog" Wallace.

I chose the French Polynesia Islands as the hundredth country because it's a place I've always wanted to visit, and I'll have Nicole, my wife—who is my sports manager and personal translator—along for the trip. And, at the last moment, a good friend from Sarasota, Florida, Frank "MadMonk" Ouseley, decides to join us. The day we arrive is Nicole's birthday, so we celebrate at a fancy French restaurant, and I give her a lovely black Tahitian pearl as a present. And also as another way of saying thank you (again) for all the years of putting up with my obsession.

The race organization has granted my request to wear bib #100 for the race. I also had a special running singlet made for the occasion that read "*Pays #100*" on the front and "John's 100th Country" on the back, for which I get lots of comments before and during the race.

I am excited and thrilled to be at the start line at 4:30 a.m. The temperature is 80°F with humidity to match. We start in the darkness and relative cool, but as the sun rises, the heat and humidity soar. Maddog, for that is my race name, wilts like a prize flower. I finally cross the finish line in a time of four hours and fourteen minutes (4:14) to lots of cheers, including my own. A photographer from the German issue of *Runner's World* takes a photo of me at the finish line.

The final two miles of the race are the hottest and longest two miles I've ever run. All I could think about was getting to the finish line alive! Even after twenty-six and half years of running marathons being alive at the finish line still feels good.

When the race announcer calls my name and tells the crowd of my accomplishment—the first person in the world to complete a marathon in a hundred countries—it really starts to sink in. It sinks in even more when two pretty Polynesian women drape a finisher's medal and lei around my neck. But it only really, really sinks in when my family, friends, and I go out celebrating that night. At the finish line I've been too focused on dealing with my heat exhaustion and dehydration to be thinking about whether I'd done something special or not.

On our final day on Bora Bora, we take a boat tour around the island and snorkel in the lagoons with stingrays and sharks. It's a bit intimidating at first when you put yourself in the water with the stingrays and sharks, even though guides assure you everything is okay because they're used to people. The sharks are small reef sharks, and I think they're more scared of me than I am of them, and I'm not even wearing my running gear. They're only looking for food and most likely don't like the look of me. I know I wouldn't.

Stingrays are different. They brush up along your body and when they eat the food from your hand they suck it up like a powerful vacuum cleaner. If your mind wanders and you don't pay attention, you may end up with a big hickey on your neck that will need explaining when you next see your wife. It's the stingray's tail you want to avoid, though—you don't want to be stung by those. Death is not healthy. And it certainly compromises your ability to run marathons.

And so there I am, in the water of the Pacific Ocean, feeding these sting-rays. For no apparent reason, my mind whizzes back to 1982 and my days of smoking. That's before I started to run. What if I never ran? What if my future took a different turn? What if I were dead now? Hard to write this book for sure, but I never would have visited over one hundred countries. I'd never have had all the adventures. I never would have met thousands of people and made friends with people around the world. I certainly wouldn't be swimming with sharks and stingrays right now. You wouldn't be reading this book.

And then, just as this velvety, mushroomy-feeling stingray is about to glide into me, it hits me. I've not got this world record because I love running. It's because of all the experiences—the people, the places, the food, the beers, and the wildlife brushing up against me. I've led an extremely privileged life. The more I've done, the more I want to do. Running marathons has given me a healthy—all right, obsessive—excuse to travel.

And now I'm underwater in the middle of the Pacific Ocean face-to-face with a big lively mushroom who couldn't care less about my epiphany. As much as running a marathon is a metaphor for life, running marathons in more than one hundred countries is a metaphor for *my* life.

My goal of running marathons in one hundred countries didn't depend on me *beating* my personal best times; instead, it gave me my *best* times. Each country gave me amazing, incredible experiences and memories.

Living life. Cool. Ordinary guy lives life full-on. A mad dog. I see it clearly now. I finally get it.

Ouch. And a hickey.

Writing This Book

I didn't want the book to be boring or too long. Or boring and too short, for that matter, so I've made it into bite-size pieces. And since a hundred adventures and countries would be too many and too long, I selected those that were the most interesting and memorable to me. We start with the early 1980s—my beginnings—the end of the dark phase of running's evolution, when runners registered and planned for races without the aid of, can you believe it, the Internet—which is more than thirty years ago, and whoa! All of a sudden my feet are tired.

Staying traditional with counting, we move into the 1990s and then the 2000s. The penultimate section captures the past few years as I've reluctantly slowed down. I've worn my feet down to hardened stubs. My head is willing, but my finger points toward me as my body says, "No, no, no, no, no!" If you're still with me at that point, I try to tie it all together in a summary chapter.

Along the way, I'll tell you about my most memorable and embarrassing moments as I've run my way through three thousand pairs of running shoes—well, not really, but it sounds good—and give you graphic details of injuries, the best and worst of exotic foods, the best and worst marathons in the world, and where to find the friendliest people in the world. I have become an expert on airlines, independent inner-city walking tours, world beer, and teaspoons, since I picked one up in (almost) every country in which I ran a marathon.

Yes, that's right, teaspoons.

I had an uncle who, in his nineties, was writing his life story. Every now and then he would e-mail various sections of it to the family so we could catch a glimpse of what life was like "back then" as he was growing up. Pretty interesting stuff. One day we all got an e-mail from him saying that, on reading what he'd written, he'd come to the conclusion that his life really wasn't that interesting after all. He had decided to stop putting the book together. We e-mailed and asked him to reconsider, but we never did see a book.

Without getting too morbid, I've decided to write this book and see it through to the end, no matter how ragged it looks or how I feel. That's what marathoners do. I've taken a bit of a leap in assuming that the interesting (in my mind, at least) bits are of interest to others. That's a bit of the mad dog in me. I'd be thrilled to hear from you if you think it worked.

And less thrilled to hear from you of course, if you think it hasn't worked. That would be a pity, and I'll apologize in advance, because I'm not about to write another one.

Marathon #27—Country #3, Rio de Janeiro Marathon, Brazil

June 1988

Since I've only run marathons in the United States and Canada, I've decided to expand my horizon and run in other countries. Nicole and I have always wanted to visit Rio, so I'm thinking, *Why not?*

Next thing you know, we are checking into our hotel on Copacabana Beach a few days before the race. We're anxious to explore this amazing city and not get mugged while we do so.

What a beautiful city! We take a city tour that includes the downtown attractions such as the Metropolitan Cathedral and Cinelandia Square, and Copacabana, Ipanema, and other beaches of Niterói. It seems every kid on the beach has a soccer ball that seems to be attached to their feet with invisible string. It's no wonder Brazil is the world champion. We make our way to the Urca neighborhood, where we board a cable car that takes us up Sugar Loaf Mountain (Pão de Açúcar). There are stunning views of the city, right from Guanabara Bay to Rio's other famous mountain, Corcovado. We also get breathtaking views of Copacabana Beach, the Santa Cruz Fortress, and the beaches of Niterói.

No time to dillydally and ooh-ah, though, as we've got plenty more to see. We head off to Corcovado Mountain, where we take a scenic cog train ride through the Tijuca rainforest and up to the city's most iconic landmark—the statue of Christ the Redeemer (Cristo Redentor). At an elevation of 2,300 feet

(700 meters), the 1930s statue itself stands 98 feet (30 meters), with a wing-span of 92 feet (28 meters). It's one of the New7Wonders of the World.

The next day we take an escorted tour of some of the favelas (slums) of Rio. I'm a bit wary of this, given the pervasiveness of crime and the poverty of these favelas, but I'm grateful for the firsthand look at these dismal conditions. We're very lucky! We follow this with a walk along the Copacabana and Ipanema beaches, avoiding soccer balls, two-year-old soccer stars, beautiful Brazilian models, and muggers. It's an odd assortment for sure, made even odder with American and Canadian tourists trying to take it all in. There is also the thing we call the ocean. It's all quite spectacular and a sensory sensation. Almost overload.

We stand out of course, in part because it looks like we have money. We've followed the advice not to wear jewelry and protect our wallets, but I can't help myself and have brought our video camera along, which is why a police officer stops us on Ipanema Beach. My Portuguese is not good—some would say nonexistent, in fact—but he's clearly not happy, and his gestures suggest that he thinks I'm an idiot. He warns us that flashing such wealth is asking for trouble! I sheepishly put the camera away for the remainder of the walk.

It's Saturday, marathon day. The race starts at 5:00 p.m., which is a new experience for me. I'm not sure what to eat, I'm wondering if I should rest, and I'm thinking about how my body will react to starting in the heat of the day and finishing in the dark. At least I'm smart enough to leave the video camera in the hotel. Not that I'm scared of seeing the police officer again or anything.

The race starts and finishes in Copacabana. It's achingly hot and humid. Holy crap. A whole race like this?! Oh well, away we go…

Around the ten-mile mark, the course heads up onto an elevated freeway, where there is no protection from the sun. The heat is even more brutal. I've foolishly set a goal to run a sub three-hour race, but I think now that that's too ambitious. And dangerous, too, because if I focus on it, who knows what I'll do to myself to reach that goal. That's the mad dog in me, you see.

Past the halfway mark the sun starts to set, and the temperatures begin to cool a bit. But I've knocked the stuffing out of myself. I'm dehydrated and struggling. At twenty miles I'm in big trouble. The left side of my body feels numb, and my left arm is tingling. I'm feeling nauseated and dizzy. Not good. I know I'm dehydrated, but now I'm wondering, *Yikes, am I having a heart attack? Maybe suffering heat stroke?* I slow down and watch a turtle pass me. Eventually I struggle across the finish line with a time of 3:05, which is pretty respectable, especially in this heat, but I'm not really focused on much at all.

I walk immediately to the medical tent for help. Nobody speaks English so I engage in reckless—some would say desperate—sign language to explain my symptoms and problems. Perhaps I'm actually doing charades. Hard to tell.

Luckily, one doctor understands some of my antics—maybe the crying— and is obviously experienced with treating runners at a finish line. Before the nurses can stick an IV into me to address the dehydration, he gives me a glass of orange juice. I drink it and immediately start to feel better. I drink another glass; the tingling in my arm stops, and the nausea goes away. It seems I've been suffering from low blood sugar, and the sugar in the juice helps restore my levels. This is the first time I've suffered these symptoms, but I've got a funny feeling it won't be the last.

I thank the doctor, get off the bed, and walk outside to find Nicole. She may even be worried. I find her, or rather she finds me, and we walk over to an outdoor café and order two large Cokes. I gulp these down as if they're in shot glasses, and almost instantly I feel like I'm back to normal.

Sunday comes, and we treat ourselves. Tired of Rio's hustle and bustle and feeling a bit jaded from 26.2 miles of running the previous day, we decide to hire a car and driver to take us down the coast to the small village of Paraty. It's remote, rural, and very pretty. We enjoy a peaceful day exploring Paraty and the coast.

It's been a great trip. Although I can't say I enjoyed the race, I've now run in three countries and on two continents. I'm not 100 percent sure, but this traveling and running gig is feeling a bit addictive! I could get used to this.

Marathon #52—Country #5, The

Original Marathon, Greece

October 1990

It's been a tough slog for the past several months, because I injured my plantar fascia on my left foot shortly after finishing the London Marathon in April. I've been miserable, cranky, annoyed, and miserable for several months. The injury only makes it worse. God knows what I would be like without the cross-training—biking and swimming at the YMCA—I've done over the past six months.

I'm still not in good running shape, and my foot hasn't healed properly, but I'd already bought a marathon trip/package from Marathon Tours, so we were coming here—Greece—even if I couldn't run the race. It's a great deal even if you aren't running: tours of Athens and five days on the island of Mykonos after the race.

The original marathon commemorates the legendary run of the soldier Pheidippides to Athens from a battlefield at a site near the town of Marathon, Greece, in 490 BC, bringing news of a Greek victory over the Persians. The run was approximately 26.2 miles, but that varies depending on which historian you read or drinking buddy you talk to. Legend has it that Pheidippides delivered the momentous message "Niki!" (victory) then collapsed and died, thereby setting a precedent for dramatic conclusions to the marathon. I'm not aiming for anything that dramatic, as I don't really consider dying to be a good way to finish a race. Especially when you've got five amazing days left on a tour package on a Greek island.

We've arrived a few days before the race so we can explore Athens to take in all the history (spanning 3,400 years) and tourist sites. All? After our first day, I realize that that is a tall order indeed.

Our tour, which is a group of runners—mostly from the United States—guided by a rep from Marathon Tours, starts at the Temple of Olympian Zeus (6th century BC), one of the largest in antiquity and close by Hadrian's Arch (AD 131), which forms the symbolic entrance to the city. From there, walking along Dionysou Areopaghitou Street (on the south side of the Acropolis) we pass the ancient Theatre of Dionysus (5th century BC) where most of the works by Sophocles, Euripides, Aeschylus, and Aristophanes were performed. Continuing on, we reach the ruins of the Asklepieion (5th century BC) and the Stoa of Eumenes (2th century BC), and from there, the Odeon of Herodes Atticus, which was built in AD 161 and is nowadays the venue of the performances of the Athens Festival. I'm name-dropping, of course, but somehow I feel entitled to do so, as we're really here. Actually saying the words is different though—and pretty ugly if I'm talking and eating at the same time.

From the Odeon, or as they say in Greek, the Odeon, we climb to the sacred rock of the Acropolis, the site of some of the most important masterpieces of architecture and art, the most renowned of which is the Parthenon temple. Also impressive—we're lost for superlatives, really—are the Propylaea, the temple of the Athene Nike, and the Erechtheion, located close to the Parthenon. There's a great view of the city as well.

About three hundred meters from the massive rock of Acropolis stands the impressive Acropolis Museum, one of the most important contemporary works of architecture in Athens. It's made of steel, glass, and concrete and houses four thousand priceless finds from the Acropolis monuments that represent its history and function as the most important religious center of ancient Athens. Many years ago the British stole some of the original artifacts, and they're at the center of a long-term dispute between the United Kingdom and Greece to this day, which happens to be a Thursday.

Coming down from the Acropolis, we arrive at the Areios Pagos, the most ancient law court of the world. Opposite it is Philopappou Hill, with its beautiful cobbled little roads that are dangerous to run on, and the Roman monument by the same name at the top. Close by is the Pnyx, where the citizens of ancient Athens used to assemble and exert their democratic rights. Walking farther along the pedestrian road we arrive at the ancient Agora, which was the commercial, political, and religious center of ancient Athens. From there, via Ermou Street, we visit the Kerameikos, the largest cemetery of the ancient city, with some amazing tomb sculptures and stelae. The Iridanos River, sacred in antiquity, runs through the archaeological site. It's a veritable mental and visual explosion of antiquity today. Incredible. But that's not all that Athens provides.

The "core" of the historic center is the Plaka neighborhood (at the eastern side of the Acropolis), which has been inhabited without interruption since the first Thursday of antiquity. Walking through the narrow labyrinthine streets lined with houses and mansions from the time of the Turkish occupation and the nineteenth-century Neoclassical period is like travelling with a time machine, only much less complicated.

In the temporal space of just a few hours and the physical space of a few square kilometers, we see countless monuments and buildings of times past— the Lysikrates Monument, erected by a wealthy donor to theatrical performances, the Roman Agora with the famed Tower of the Winds (first century BC), Hadrian's Library (AD 132), scores of bigger and smaller churches, true masterpieces of Byzantine art and architecture, and remnants of the Ottoman period (Fetihie Mosque, Tzistaraki Mosque, the Turkish Bath near the Tower of the Winds, the Muslim Seminary, and so on). There are also some interesting museums (Folk Art, Greek Children's Art, Popular Musical Instruments, Frysira Art Gallery, etc.), lots of picturesque tavernas, cafés, and bars, as well as shops selling souvenirs and traditional Greek products.

And tourists. We are not alone. We are many, and we come with lots of dollars. Most likely because we can buy old stuff, very old stuff, stuff that looks really old, tourist stuff that is so new it's tacky compared to the old stuff, old stuff disguised as antiquities, and T-shirts. It seems that no matter where we walk in Athens, there are ruins lying around, as ruins tend to do, and tourists walking, taking photographs, eating, drinking, wondering if it's ruins or road works, and buying souvenirs.

The history is overwhelming, and we don't have a hope in hell of taking it all in in just two days.

Thank God—or maybe many gods since it's Athens, after all—that Sunday, marathon day, finally arrives. It's a mental holiday for me. I don't even have to work out how to get to the start line—way out of Athens in the town of Marathon—because our tour company buses us there. The course is relatively flat (elevation 33 meters) for the first 16 kilometers, then climbs steadily to 250 meters before dropping more than 150 meters over the final 10 kilometers to finish in the original Olympic Stadium. This, in fact, is where the very first Olympic marathon was run.

Once again I'm overwhelmed. There are thousands of runners from over eighty countries speaking many languages and dialects. Sensory overload again, which includes my amazement seeing European and Japanese runners smoking a "last cigarette" at the start line before the race starts.

Not knowing what my body—and injury—are capable of after six months of not racing, I start out slow. I'm feeling okay, but the weather gets hotter as I climb the next 16 kilometers to crest the hills at 32 kilometers in 2:48:31 and a split of 29:04. By the time I start my descent, the temperatures are above 80°F, and my foot is hurting.

There's hardly any traffic control over the final 10 kilometers as we enter Athens and run to the Olympic Stadium. I'm having to bang on car hoods to force drivers to stop at intersections. By the time I enter Olympic Stadium, I'm in serious trouble. Not because some road-raged drivers are chasing me, but because my plantar fascia is screaming in pain. I'm feeling nauseated and dizzy, and my left arm is tingling. It's the second time I've suffered these symptoms, so at least I know what the problem is and what to do. As soon as I struggle across the finish line (in a time of 3:38), I go directly to the medical tent.

Or I try to, that is. Instead I have my own Pheidippidean moment and collapse in the middle of the infield.

Uh-oh.

I'm puking, and I can't stand up. It's a mess. I'm a mess. Luckily a German runner comes to my aid and asks if I need help. The collapsing and puking probably gave that away. "Yes," I reply, "I need a cup of Coke to restore my low blood sugar level." He quickly returns with a cup of Coke, which I gulp down in a blur. I'm feeling better almost immediately. I ask for a second cup, and away he goes and returns again just as fast as the last time. By the time I finish the second Coke, I'm feeling much better. I thank my guardian angel and limp out of the stadium on my injured foot to find Nicole. We find an outdoor café where I order two more Cokes. I would make a great Coke commercial.

My body feels better, thank the Greek gods—or, well, the German—but I discover it's been masking my foot which now is in real pain. I've reinjured the plantar fascia. I'd kick myself, but that would make my foot worse. It's obviously not healed and I'm faced with having to spend the rest of the trip limping around like some guy who has hurt himself running. But I've completed the race, I'm still alive, and it's still a major thrill to have raced this most famous of races.

The next day we head to Mykonos Island (named for the grandson of Apollo, Mykonos). According to mythology, Mykonos was formed from the petrified bodies of giants killed by Hercules. We're staying in the capital, Chora, and I'm speculating as to which body part we're staying in, because around us are lots of pedestrian shopping streets lined with brand-name stores, charming cafés, old stuff, stylish restaurants, and tourists. Although I'm hurting and limping badly, we still manage to visit the church of Panagia Paraportiani, the town hall, and the castle situated above the harbor. As if being on a Greek Island isn't enough, we also visit Alefkántra or "Little Venice," which is an eighteenth-century district dominated by grand captains' mansions with colorful balconies and stylish windows. We relax at an outdoor café to admire a view of the quaint windmills standing imposingly on the hillside above. Despite the physical pains, it all feels really good right now, and I realize I'm sitting here with a smile on my face and feeling very content.

It's off-season and a bit cool on Mykonos. Sadly, the nude beaches are empty, but I've still got this smile on my face. Nicole suggests I could strip off and hobble around the beach naked, and it wouldn't be empty then, but I remind her that I'm too injured to bring her fantasies to life. As day turns into night, as it often does, we hit the shops to negotiate end-of-season deals. I treat myself to a leather jacket, and Nicole buys a hand-knitted wool jacket (we still have these jackets).

Even though we spend a delightful few days on the island, with me still recovering and Nicole putting up with my whining, when we return home my orthopedist puts me on pain-killers and anti-inflammatories to control my foot injury.

A few weeks later I foolishly try to run a 5K race and really aggravate my injury. And my doctor. He suggests a lobotomy. Instead, I suggest an MRI. He agrees but thinks some work on my brain would really help the healing process. The MRI reveals a ruptured plantar fascia. It also shows that it's been ripped from the bottom of my foot. The doctor tells me the injury requires surgery and one year of rest—*no* running for one year.

No running?

Things are racing through my mind. *I can't stop running, but really, I have no choice. I've got to take the long view. I can still exercise and keep up my fitness through cross-training. I realize I have no option, really. My body simply is telling me I can't run.*

Maddog actually listens this time.

And so for an entire year I cross-train (swim and bike). Each month I test my foot and each time it says, "No, you can't run yet." The doc proves to be right. It takes a whole year to heal. In the fall of 1991, concerned that I'd break my streak of consecutive years of running a marathon, I start training for my hometown marathon. With only three months of training, I run the White Rock Marathon and finish in 3:24. Maddog is back! And wiser.

Marathon #110—Country #6,

Antarctica Marathon, Antarctica

February 1997

It's not every day you wake up and run a marathon in Antarctica, but in February 1997, I planned to do just that. It started with that constant urge of mine to set goals and then go after them like a mad dog. My goal—a hidden agenda actually—was to run a marathon on all seven continents, a goal that I could work on while focusing on another nonhidden goal—all the provinces and territories in Canada. If I did it right, that would include the North Pole as well.

Marathon Tours of Boston was planning its second Antarctica Marathon in February 1997. Part of its promotion was the fact that this second marathon could be the last for logistical and environmental reasons. I decided to send in my deposit to reserve an entry. I asked Nicole if she wanted to come with me. Her response: "Are you crazy?"

Yes, probably, but that has nothing to do with going to Antarctica. To run a marathon. So I reserved a single slot and continued running marathons in Canada. Every so often I'd ask Nicole again about Antarctica, but I got the same response each time. Nicole's fear, it turns out, was the dreaded Drake Passage, where the three oceans—Pacific, Atlantic, and Antarctic—all meet. It's one of the roughest seas in the world. With a final payment due, I made one last pitch, this time including more information, like the key fact that one of the two packages offered included three days in Buenos Aires, one day in

Ushuaia, Argentina, and eight days on the ship. Thank you, Argentina. My wife would love to visit Buenos Aires, and so we both happily signed on for the trip, one of us a tad concerned about the Drake Passage. Oh well.

Marathon Tours contracted two ships to accommodate a total of one hundred runners and passengers. We assembled in Buenos Aires, where Marathon Tours placed us all in a first-class hotel and arranged an introductory cocktail party.

Originally called Puerto Nuestra Señora Santa María del Buen Aire (Port Our Lady Saint Mary of the Good Wind) when it was founded by Spanish aristocrat Mendoza in 1536, it was conveniently downsized for English-speaking folks to Buenos Aires. Not that "simple" is a word you'd associate with the city. It's been a populated site on the banks of the Rio de la Plata for tens of thousands of years, at first by nomadic hunter-gatherers. Today, several hundred years later, about three million people live in its huge, sprawling, beautiful, wild, crazy, often dangerous space. The social distance between rich and poor is massive. If they see a window open and hope to get something out of the car as you go by, children will throw themselves against your car as you drive by in the narrow streets. It is also home of the craziest drivers in the world (except perhaps for Sicily), where traffic lights are mere guidelines at best, and not very good ones at that. Driving is not for the fainthearted.

It is, however, a beautiful city with a European feeling and architecture (a nice change for those from America). There are many places to visit in the city itself, which we did, but after a few days Nicole and I escaped across the Rio de la Plata on a hydrofoil to visit the small town of Colonia de Sacramento, conveniently located across the river in Uruguay, another large South American country.

We follow up our stay in Buenos Aires with one night in Ushuaia, where we are also able to get in our last training run—up and down a glacier at the northern end of the town. We board our ship (our home)—the *Akademik Ioffe*—for the next eight days. It's a Russian ship that was built and hardened for travel in Arctic waters. She and her sister ship, which the other group departed on, were built and used as spy ships to track enemy submarines in the Arctic Ocean during the Cold War. But now they're working ships leased out for tourist expeditions to Antarctica. They are comfortable, the Russian crew are friendly, and the food is basic but good. The expedition staff, who will take us to shore and escort us around the continent, are Canadians, a long way from their own pole, and are very experienced and knowledgeable.

We steam out to the open waters and round Cape Horn to enter the dreaded Drake Passage. Apparently we're lucky, as the waves are only about fifteen to eighteen feet (they often exceed thirty feet). Still, for some people, one-foot waves are enough for motion sickness, and they're not able to leave their cabin for the two days that it takes to cross the passage. To keep our minds off the relentless roller coaster and to make us more knowledgeable, every day except marathon day the expedition staff provide us with lectures on Antarctica, including its history, early exploration, geography, and the flora and fauna of the continent.

And then, suddenly, after two days the sea goes calm as we approach the continent of Antarctica. We start to see small ice floes, and then on the third day at sea, we experience our initial landing on Antarctica!

There are no piers or docks in Antarctica; all landings are, as they say, wet. We scamper down a gangway and jump into Zodiacs, inflatable boats with outboard motors. The Zodiacs take us to the beach; we swing our legs over the side and step into the frigid surf. How do the penguins do this?

I have an opportunity to ask them when we visit hundreds of thousands of the little fellas and some seals. Around us are enormous ice caps and glaciers. The expedition staff takes us on tours in the Zodiac along the coast and around huge icebergs to explore glaciers calving into the ocean and to see more seals and some whales. The scenery is amazing. Awe-inspiring. Almost unreal. It's difficult to describe in words.

Our running a marathon here is simply an excuse to travel and experience new places. We go to hot springs in a cove off Deception Island. Who knew? And yes, we get into our bathing suits and sit in Antarctica surf, heated up by water boiling away from a volcano. Great cocktail conversation for the rest of our lives. Did I mention unreal?

Back on the boat that night, we steam along the coast to King George Island, the site of the marathon. I wake up because of a violent sudden shudder of the ship. Hair dryers, books, glasses—in fact anything not in our drawers—are flying around our cabin. Bad news—bad weather and bad seas! The next morning we arrived at the marathon site on King George Island, where seven nations maintain bases. One of them, Russia, is our host for the marathon this year.

By the morning, the weather is so bad and the seas so rough that the expedition staff declare it is too dangerous to attempt a landing. To make matters worse, our sister ship arrived earlier and managed to disembark its runners. We share the anguish as we realize they're going to start the marathon without us. There is almost a mutiny. We've all spent several thousand dollars to run a marathon here, and now we can't get off the ship! But wisely, some cool heads prevail when confronted with the fact that someone could easily die if we attempt to land. So we watch with frustration from the ship as our fellow runners on land start the marathon.

We're advised to have some lunch while the expedition staff monitors the seas and tries to reposition the ship in a bid to find a safer position to attempt a landing. There was hope. Even some smiles. Halfway into lunch the ship's horn blows, and the staff announces that we have five minutes to get ready. Thirty hectic and dangerous minutes later, we're all safely on shore. Confusion and turmoil, but we're there! Our fellow runners are almost two hours into the marathon but we don't care, because not so long ago it looked like we wouldn't be running at all.

The double figure-eight loop marathon course starts at the Russian base. The first loop runs out toward the Uruguayan base, through shoe-sucking mud that had been made worse by our fellow runners, and then across a glacial stream and up the Collins Glacier. We run up 1,100 feet to the top before returning down the same route to the Russian base. The next loop headed in the opposite direction on muddy, hilly trails out past the Chilean base to the Chinese base and then back. That's the half-marathon course; for the full marathon we do each loop twice.

I'm pinching myself—in part to see if I have any feeling because it's so damn cold—Antarctica, who knew—and in part because this is so cool. Some planning, some saving, some running, and here I am. I don't want to be anywhere else, and I'm happy to suck in all the challenges I am facing just to feel that way. Anything is possible. And if I'm not mistaken, not far away there are thousands of penguins laughing out loud at these crazy people. And the staff working on the bases must be wondering why people would want to do this.

To add to the fun, and it really is fun, there's no race support, no water stations, first-aid tents, and so on. We knew this, of course, so, we take four water bottles with us that the expedition staff has dropped off ahead of time at specific points along the course.

The weather is horrible, about –2°C, snowing and blowing gale winds. Nobody is sure how to dress for the race. Unfortunately, I overdress with PolyPro tights and top and a Gore-Tex suit over that to stop the wind. But I am not too teary-eyed, as safety *must* be first. I can't risk being cold in the event of an injury or worse.

By the time I make it to the glacier (about four miles), I'm cooking. And Maddog being Maddog, at the Russian base I strip off the Gore-Tex suit and replace it with a simple nylon jacket to stop the wind. The mud is a terrible problem—I've never run in mud before—and I'm afraid I'd lose a shoe with each step. But the mud was certainly not the most difficult challenge. That award goes to the glacier. The footing going up was slippery, but coming back down it was much worse, so steep and slippery that I lose control several times and have to resort to turning back up into the hill to regain control.

But nature throws in some other surprises. The staff has warned us to stay clear of all wildlife because they might regard it as their territory. No kidding. Several of us are chased off the course by sea lions, and we're constantly being dive-bombed by skuas, a seagull-like scavenger bird. Despite their massive size, the sea lions are incredibly fast over the first few meters. But they're not built for longer distances.

But we all persevere, and eventually all one hundred runners finish the race.

Although I told myself at the start of the race that Maddog wouldn't impose a time challenge because survival is after all, fairly important (taking off my Gore-Tex suit took more than five minutes), as I near the end of the race and realize I am close to four hours, I can't help myself; it becomes paramount that I beat the four-hour target! Mad, I know. This, I'm certain, makes me a better mud runner; I stop pussyfooting and just run through the damn stuff. I think I actually cross the line in 4:00:03 but a gracious timer gives me an official time of 3:59:59!

I'm thrilled, because this has been, without a doubt, the most difficult marathon to get to and then run, in my entire life!

Many runners are still out on the course after several more hours. But the ship's captain and the expedition staff allow everyone to finish, in spite of worsening weather and their concern about getting everyone back to the ship safely. The euphoria on the ship in the evening is amazing. We're exhausted and in pain, and the mental strain is equal to the physical pain. Even the non-runners were celebrating. My wife and several others volunteered to help with the race and stood outside in the cold for over five hours! They need medals to go along with the memories, too.

For the next two euphoric days, we visit many more sites on the islands and mainland of Antarctica. Now that the marathon is behind us, the glaciers and icebergs look even bigger and more awesome. On our last day here, we met up with our sister ship for a celebration and award party. Then it's time to head back across the Drake Passage, around Cape Horn, and back to Ushuaia. Again, luck blesses us, as the seas are not too bad.

When we left our ship in Ushuaia, my wife and I smile and say, almost as if it has been in a script, "I enjoyed it, I'm glad I did it, but I wouldn't get back on that ship if they gave me the tour for free!"

We all have stories to share from this experience and I want to share two others with you. One is a story of courage, and the other is of romance and humor. First the courage. There was a group of World Team members on our tour. World Team is a group of physically challenged athletes. One of these amazing people, a gentleman with a prosthetic leg, caught his good leg in a crevasse and sprained it severely on his first loop down the glacier. But he continued on and finished the marathon seven hours later!

The story of romance? A couple from our hometown, Dallas, Texas, had just gotten married the weekend before the trip, and the trip was their honeymoon. Unfortunately, the groom was prone to seasickness and became afflicted the moment we left Beagle Channel. He was the runner. We only saw the bride for the first three days when she left their cabin to get medicine, crackers, and drinks for her new groom. She was not a runner but had faithfully (true love?) trained to run her first-ever Half. He was very weak on race day due to dehydration and no food, lack of energy and so on. But he ran very slowly, and he was able to finish. The bride, on the other hand, felt good, and after completing her half marathon, decided to continue on and accompany her new husband—and she finished with him! But the next day she was so sore, she couldn't get out of bed. For the homeward journey, we only saw the groom when he came out to get her food and medicine. At least that was their story.

Marathon #117—Country #2, Midnight Sun Marathon, Canada July 1997

Normally, protocol specifies that the first marathon run in any country counts for that country, but I am using an author's privilege to count this marathon for Canada since it was one of the most memorable of the many I ran there.

Having run the Antarctica Marathon in February, it seemed only natural to have a crack at the Arctic as well. I found the Midnight Sun Marathon in the mining town of Nanisivik, about five hundred miles north of the Arctic Circle, on Baffin Island in Canada. Baffin is the largest island in Canada and the fifth largest island in the world. These days the island has a population of about 11,000 people and 14,000 polar bears. Kidding. But who knows, maybe it could were it not for global warming. In Inuktitut, ᐊᓂᓯᕕᒃ, the Inuit language, Nanisivik means the *place where people find things.* I wasn't sure what I'd find, but that was part of the reason to go there.

The race was organized and sponsored by the owner of a zinc mine in Nanisivik and there were rumors that the mine was going to be sold and the race discontinued. Although Nanisivik was at that time part of the Canada's Northwest Territories (NWT), the NWT was soon to be split into two, with the eastern portion, where Nanisivik is located, becoming Nunavut—in part recognizing that it was mainly populated by the Inuit. Since there were no races in the soon-to-be territory, and the likelihood of any races was slim, the US 50 States Marathon Club, which kept the records, decreed that anyone running Nanisivik could grandfather the race as the new territory of Nunavut. That sealed my decision, as I would need the race to complete all the provinces and territories of Canada.

I had to cry a bit to get Nicole to come with me, even more so when I discovered that only runners could fly on the 120-seat charter flight from Ottawa to Nanisivik for the race. Nicole had to register for the 10K race, which she did. I stopped crying. Since the flight left from our Canadian hometown, we could visit family before and after the race. I think this sweetened the deal, but the crying influenced her decision, I'm sure.

After a few days visiting family in Ottawa we fly to Nanisivik. My heart goes a bit jiggly when I look out the window of the 727 as we arrive in Nanisivik to see the long stretch of gravel that the locals call the runway. I don't want to look at Nicole, but I can tell she's nervous—she grips my wrist and cuts off the circulation in my hand.

After landing safely and prying Nicole off my arm, we're greeted by representatives of the race and the mine and escorted to our lodgings for our five-day stay. Runners are lodged in empty houses that were normally occupied by mining families. Many of the houses have no furniture other than beds and maybe a table. We're given either sheets and blankets or a sleeping bag. Not the Hilton for sure, but heck, this is the Arctic. I'm not scared or anything, but this is also the place that polar bears like to call home.

The race organizers did not notice that Nicole and I are a couple and have assigned us to separate houses for male and female runners. When I mention I'm pretty sure I've been married to this woman for thirty years, they reassign us to a dormitory that was used to house guests and miners for a short term. Marriage has its privileges; these guest rooms are nicer and have a common room with a small kitchen and satellite TV, so we have access to entertainment and news. All runners ate in the Dome, a large common building that housed a cafeteria, a small shop, pool/gym, and library. Single miners and some families eat in the Dome, so we get to meet many of the miners. With a total township population of about 250 in 1997, an influx of 120 crazy runners is an invasion.

With two days to kick around before the marathon, we have time to explore the area. No need for a tour bus, as there are few buildings, and no one is terribly keen on venturing anywhere too far. The region is barren, with only the bravest of vegetation growing higher than a blade of Texas grass. Some small lichen grows for the few summer months when the temperature climbs to an average of 31–41°F. July is Nanisivik's best month, when the lowest monthly snowfall for the year occurs—3.4 inches, a darn sight better than October when they get over fifteen inches.

At least there's constant sunlight because it's so far north. On our first walk we notice something else: an abundance of hills and a bitterly cold wind that constantly whips through our light jackets like a scythe. We are given a bus tour to Arctic Bay (population around 650), an Inuit village located on Admiralty Inlet about twenty miles west of Nanisivik. The race committee had requested that runners bring T-shirts and running shoes for the local Inuit people. I brought two garbage bags of running T-shirts (more than two hundred) that I give to the nurse at the health center. She's really pleased, although I make it clear that they were not just for her. She says she'll use them as bribes for the Inuit children (and parents) to visit the health center for checkups and vaccinations. Who knows, I may have created some runners out of this. Maybe more, had I washed the shirts beforehand.

We also discovered that the road between Arctic Bay and Nanisivik is the marathon route. The gravel road starts at sea level and climbed three badass hills to an altitude of fifteen hundred feet!

The day before the Sunday marathon, which the Inuit call Saturday, we were given a guided tour of the zinc mine. The miners work for six months (seven days/week) and then are given a one-month vacation (expenses paid) anywhere in the world! It sounded like quite the lure, but I wasn't sure I'd want to be underground all that time.

The 10K race starts at nine o'clock on Saturday night (twenty-four-hour daylight, remember). It's a tough hilly course that starts in the center of Nanisivik and goes five kilometers uphill before turning around to finish back in town. I think Nicole will find it hard, so I go with her as we walk/run the 10K course. It's a tough slog, all right, but we finish, with me a tad worried about what it's doing to my legs. I have to run the marathon less than twelve hours later. No polar bears either, not that we were looking for them.

On Sunday morning we were bused with the ultramarathoners to the start line in Arctic Bay for our eight o'clock start. Most of the town, the Royal Canadian Mounted Police in their full red dress color, and bagpipers greet us at the start. I feel special.

I feel cold. The temperature is 28°F. The light snow doesn't help, but it adds a very realistic arctic touch to it all, and I wonder how the race organizers managed to arrange for the snow to fall on this day, of all days.

If you care about these things, I'm wearing running tights, a long-sleeve T-shirt, a throwaway sweat shirt, and gloves. I'm still cold.

A friend of mine, Gordon Hartshorn, from Fort Worth, Texas, is also running the race. It is, he says, his favorite race. Gordon is wearing only his Texas race shorts and singlet! I offer him my sweat shirt, but he doesn't want it. They're tough, those Texans. Must be the steaks.

It will be Gordon's final race of a record seventy-four marathons in seventy-four consecutive weeks. Wow. It will also be his very final, final race, he says, because he's dying of prostate cancer. Gordon tells me this for the first time just before the start of the race. His son Mike is running with his dad.

This puts me in a weird space mentally, but the race gets tough as we climb 284 meters/940 feet to the top of the first hill, called "Pain in the Ass," and I have to refocus my thoughts. I keep coming back to Gordon in my mind, and it becomes a more special race for me too.

We continue up to the top of the second badass hill, called "Marathoner's Madness," at 498 meters/1,650 feet. After a short downhill, we then continue to climb to the top of the third badass hill, called "Terry Fox Pass," at 530 meters/1,750 feet. Then the course drops 108 meters/360 feet to Nanisivik at the 20-mile mark. Unfortunately I know what's next. The course drops 422 meters/1,400 feet over the next five kilometers from Nanisivik to the Ministry of Transportation docks on Admiralty Inlet. Then we turn around and run the same 422 meters/1,400 feet back up to the finish line in the center of Nanisivik! As I near the top of that final badass hill, I pass Gordon coming down. He was now wearing a mukluk—a fur coat—that an Inuit local had given him on the course, because he's suffering from hypothermia. He's in really bad shape but refuses to quit.

I cross the finish line in a time of 3:59:38, which at that time was my second-slowest marathon (twenty seconds faster than Antarctica). But I'm happy and proud, and time really doesn't matter that much in the grand scheme of things.

After crossing the finish line and putting on a warm-up jacket, I walk back on the course to meet up with Gordon. I meet him about halfway down the hill and walk with him and his son to the finish line. As we approached the finish line, Gordon takes off his coat and asks me if I'll take it since he wants to cross the finish line in his traditional race gear—the Texas race shorts and singlet. After he crosses the finish line, he thanks me for my support and friendship (we've run many states together in our quest to finish the fifty states). Choking back tears, I tell him I am proud and honored to be his friend. A month later, his son called me to tell me that his dad had passed away. If you want to read a story of courage in a runner, look up Gordon Hartshorn.

After the race, the mine sponsors a gala dinner of steak and beer in the Dome to celebrate the race and Canada Day. It's apparently one of the biggest (and best) social events of the year. We enjoy talking to the miners and learn how they cope with the desolation and remoteness of the mine and their job. I think they enjoy talking to us and discovering how crazy we are.

Just to put a final arctic chill on things, we take off on Monday to return to Ottawa, but the weather is so bad—snow and high winds—that we have to return to Nanisivik. We're forced to spend two extra days in this arctic paradise before we return to Ottawa. The local newspaper in my hometown learns of Maddog's exploits and requests an interview, which they write up as "Local Native Running a Marathon at the North Pole."

It turns out my decision to run Nanisivik while I had the chance was the correct one. The race was held the following year and then canceled when the mine was sold and closed down. Some diehard runners resurrected a race in Arctic Bay a few years later, but I never saw the need to go back after the region became Nanavut.

Marathon #130—Country #9,

Noosa Marathon, Australia

August 1998

I need one more continent to complete my goal of running a marathon on all seven continents, and so it's off to Australia. There is a joke that asks, "Why do seagulls fly upside down in Australia?" The answer: "Because the sky is more interesting." It's a bit harsh, but our free-spirited, koala-loving, prison-founding Aussies are good fun, and the country is spectacular even if it is huge and full of über-deadly snakes, spiders, jellyfish, crocodiles, and sharks, not to mention shrimps on the barbie and Foster's Lager.

I've been trying, unsuccessfully, to find a marathon in Sydney. But the Sydney Marathon seems to be held intermittently, and it has been canceled for this year. So I search for another marathon in Australia and somehow discover a marathon in Noosa Heads. What kind of name is that, mate?

The Noosa Marathon is a small but popular race held along with a much bigger Half-Marathon race in Noosa Heads, which is located near Noosa National Park on the Sunshine Coast in the state of Queensland. It's about 280 kilometers north of Brisbane, the state's capital.

Fortunately Nicole is able to schedule work meetings in Sydney for the week after the race. After arriving in Brisbane with our time zones tossed upside down and listening to how weird people's accents are down here, or "down under," we rent a car and drive south along the Gold Coast to spend a few days in Surfers Paradise to acclimate and recover from jet lag.

I acclimate by doing very little. Nicole acclimates using tried and proven shopping therapy. I have a crack at imitating the Aussie accent only to end up sounding like a dork, which sounds the same in both countries. On Saturday we head north along the Gold Coast to Noosa Heads, because let's face it, there's only so much spectacular beach and sun you can take, isn't there?

After picking up my race packet later on Saturday I checked out the course. It was hilly, but it doesn't look too bad. The weather is predictably hot and humid, but it doesn't really matter; I've been struggling badly in training and races for the past four months and I don't expect to run well. I'm injury-free, but I've been struggling with fatigue and at that point can barely break four hours in a marathon.

And so at the start line I have a sense of purpose—run this marathon and complete the continent goal. No more, no less. And no collapsing at the finish line. Or anywhere else for that matter.

The gun goes off. And so do I.

I reach 10 kilometers in fifty-two minutes. ^##%(&@*, I'm drained already. I reach 25 kilometers in 2:22 but I am totally fatigued and struggling badly. I reach 30 kilometers in 2:53, and at this point, I hit the wall. I carry on, but it feels like I'm running backward, if indeed I'm actually moving. I am done. Chewed up and spit out. I have nothing left. I'm walking, at least I think I am, in a straight line. Eventually, maybe five years later, I cross the finish line in 4:12—hurrah—a personal worst (PW) for a marathon. But I've now completed marathon #130 and in country #9. Most important, though, this is the seventh continent on which I've run a marathon. It isn't pretty, and neither am I, but I've accomplished what I set out to achieve.

After the race we drive back to Brisbane and fly to Sydney for Nicole's meetings. I've no other option but to be a tourist and revisit many of the sites we've already seen on our last trip to Australia. Sydney is such a beautiful city with its spectacular Opera House, the Sydney Harbour Bridge, and the top-less beauties on Bondi Beach. The women especially. In the evening we enjoy visiting the Quay and Rocks for drinks and dinner.

But I'm eager to get back home to visit my GP and other doctors to see if they can find out "what is wrong with me." Something's not right and I don't know what it is.

At home over the next few weeks I undergo many, many, many tests, including every blood test known to mankind. The results? Nothing! The doctors can't find any problem to explain my fatigue. I think they think it's all in my head, but I assure them I'm good in that department. Their only advice is to "'stop running and rest." Which to me is plain bizarre. And to Maddog, it's simply unacceptable.

One month later, I try to run a marathon in Connecticut. I'm fatigued at 10 miles. At 18 miles I become so dizzy and disoriented that I have to sit down on the road and cry because my body has shut down and I can't move. I think I'm having a heart attack. Eventually I get up and struggle to the finish line with yet another PW. Along with the medal, which is the last thing on my mind, I walk away knowing I have a serious medical problem.

This time I contact the Baylor Sports Clinic at the Baylor University Hospital in Dallas. They are renowned for working with professional and elite athletes to help them rehabilitate and improve their performances. I'm assigned a medical team to work on my case. They review all the medical tests that I've undergone in the past month. They review my training/racing logs for the past three years. They conduct their own battery of tests, including two intensive sessions on a treadmill where I'm connected to an EKG and a breathing apparatus that looks like scuba gear. I have IVs in my arms and legs so they can draw blood and muscle tissue while I exercise on the treadmill. They floss my teeth and wash behind my ears. They test and measure all the parameters of an endurance athlete.

When the tests are completed the team sits me down and asks that I take some time off from running and rest while they fully analyze the data. I'm stunned and a little disappointed. *Thanks for the advice, and the workouts, but it's still not acceptable to Maddog! Surely…surely…it can't just be rest that I need?*

Marathon #132—Country #10,

Cozumel Marathon, Mexico

November 1998

A few weeks after the completion of the tests at the Baylor Sports Clinic in Dallas, I met with my team of doctors to learn the results of their analysis and recommendations.

First the good news: The tests indicated that my health and fitness were in the top 0.1 percent of athletes in my age group. My fitness and body age are equivalent to that of a male athlete aged thirty-five. I am approaching my fifty-fifth birthday! And more good news. There was nothing wrong with me. There were no diseases or health issues.

Then the bad news: I was burned out.

What the hell does that mean? Am I a piece of toast? Am I a piece of burnt toast? They explained that because I was truly a Maddog, I had been over-training and over-racing my body for the past few years and probably longer. I had been pushing my body beyond its limits too long, and it was fighting for survival! The only way it could do this was to shut down whenever I continued to ignore its cries and push it beyond its limits. It did this by literally shutting down—refusing to run or move. They described the symptoms and resulting actions that I had been suffering for the past year. In the early stages of the problem and symptoms, whenever I suffered fatigue, Maddog would blame it on lack of training and hard work and train harder. This became a vicious and predictable cycle. When my body started complaining, I refused to listen to it and instead pushed it harder. After all, more exercise and more running will make my body stronger, right? Eventually something has to give or break. Usually these foolish actions resulted in an injury that would cause me to rest for months, during which time my body could recover. But with no major injuries during the past few years, I have essentially caused my body to break down!

What was the solution?

COMPLETE rest—**NO** running and **NO** exercise for one month! The team explained that if I were a normal person—a mere mortal—they would have allowed light exercise such as swimming and biking. However it was obvious that I was a Maddog, and if permitted to do those exercises I would probably swim five miles and bike fifty miles each day. Thus—**NO** exercise for one month! At the end of the month I **MUST** hire a professional coach to develop and supervise a "sensible" training program that would slowly build up mileage and speed and include lots of mandatory rest.

I understand what the team is telling me—but I don't believe it. I cannot accept it. I have been training and racing like this for years. I have friends/competitors who train and race harder than me, and they aren't burned out. I could not accept these results and recommendations.

Instead, I register for another marathon. The marathon will be in a few weeks in Cozumel, Mexico. I need one more test/marathon to prove their results could not be true.

So I booked a one-week vacation/marathon in Cozumel. Cozumel is an island in the Caribbean Sea off the eastern coast of Mexico's Yucatán Peninsula, opposite Playa del Carmen. That means that it is hot and humid.

The sports manager and I arrive a few days before the race to acclimate. My good friend Edson, from New York City, joins us for the race. Sunday is marathon day. It's hot and humid, as expected, and the course is flat and fast. But not Maddog! The race and my performance are a disaster. I pass mile five in 47:47 and a split of 9:26/mile. I reach the half in 2:01:48 and a split of 9:24. I know that the second half will be much slower, and I also know that the Baylor medical team is right. I am burned out.

But being Maddog, I still can't quit, so I struggle to reach 20 miles in 3:08:59 and a split of 9:43 and cross the finish line in 4:19:26. Not a PW but not a very good time or performance.

By the time I struggle across the finish line, I have accepted the truth as told by my medical team and vow that I will follow their advice and recommendations. I start my thirty days of rest the second I crossed the finish line.

I finish the remainder of our vacation and the year on rest sabbatical, contemplating what impact this terrible and significant prognosis and event will have on Maddog's running life and indeed on the rest of my life. Little do I realize that there will be two even more significant and important life-changing events to arise early in the coming New Year.

What were those events? They were significant enough to warrant their own report—and a chapter in Maddog's book.

Footnote: Only recently did I learn that Maddog was an unwitting pioneer in another aspect of running. My 'burnout' is now a more recognized, and common, problem among endurance athletes due to the popularity of ultras and ironman triathlons. It is now identified as Overtraining Syndrome (OTS). More athletes, today, are experiencing similar symptoms – and denial!

1999: A Year of Life-Changing Events

I began 1999 following advice and recommendations from the Baylor Sports Clinic in Dallas to recover from burnout in my running life. I was concerned that I might never be able to run competitively again. That was an important event in my life.

But little did I know that two more important life-changing events would also occur at the start of that year. That is a little white lie, since I knew one was about to happen. I had made an important decision at the end of 1998. I would retire from my job as an executive in marketing and sales for a high-tech company that manufactured telecom equipment. The retirement would be effective the first week of January 1999. I had beaten my goal to retire at age fifty-five by three months. Now what would I do?

That question was answered shortly when Nicole's company, Nortel, offered her a one-year foreign assignment in England. She was eager to tackle this challenge, and since I had nothing to do—other than rest—why not? I encouraged her to accept the transfer. While she worked her butt off, I could travel around Europe—and maybe even run a few marathons after I recovered from my burnout.

She needed to start the new job in March, so we agreed that she should go ahead, and I would stay behind to sell our house in Dallas and most of our belongings. We would not be returning to Dallas. She would retire when the assignment was over and we would move to our retirement home in Florida. We had planned for retirement and had purchased a house in Sarasota in the midnineties. Since it was furnished, we didn't need to move furniture. We could sell our Dallas home and put our personal belongings in storage and Nortel would pay all the expenses. What a great deal and good timing!

I was able to continue with my "rest and recovery" program while preparing the house for sale and packing. I had to complete my month of rest and begin a ten-week training program with a professional coach who trained pro and elite runners in Dallas. Nicole left for England in March, and I stayed to sell the house, pack, and complete my training program. I successfully completed those tasks and was ready to join Nicole in England in April. By then she had rented a new three-bedroom house in St. Michael's Mead, a new subdivision in Bishop's Stortford, about thirty miles north of London. Nortel paid all the expenses on the rental house and provided a company car and a monthly stipend to cover additional costs of a foreign assignment. Essentially we lived for free in England for one year and banked Nicole's entire salary. What a great deal!

I had contacted the Bishop's Stortford Running Club before arriving and was welcomed to join the club. I had completed my ten-week training program and was once again running but had no plans yet for racing. I quickly learned that running clubs are much different in England. As the members would proudly claim, "We are a bunch of drunks with a running problem." The clubs are much more social. The BSRC had a clubhouse with meeting facilities, a kitchen, and a bar with beer taps. On a typical meeting night, members would meet for a run or race and then convene in the clubhouse for a shower, followed by a potluck dinner and beer. I really enjoyed my year with the BSRC.

After a few weeks of running in England, I started to think that perhaps it was time to run a marathon again. And thus began a very challenging and valuable lesson on how to run marathons in foreign countries. I think it is important to explain and share these lessons and experience with you so you can understand how difficult it was—and take advantage of my experience.

First, recall that it was 1999, and the Internet was in its infancy and not very robust. Big races like London, Paris, etc. did had informative websites and the capability to register, but races in Third World countries did not have the expertise or budget to develop websites. So the big races were easy to find, get information about, and register for, but there were few of those.

The smaller races were a much more difficult challenge. The most common places to find info on those races were running magazines such as *Runner's World, Running Times, AIMS*, etc. Another source of info was race brochures handed out at race expos. Those publications provided race calendars and ads that listed the names, addresses and phone numbers for the race. Very few had e-mail addresses to make the process quicker and easier.

Let me explain the process. If I had time, I could write a race director (RD) and request information. But that process needed weeks to complete and seldom worked because there would be no response. So the next step I tried was to call the RD. Didn't work. If I called an RD in Greece, for example, he would answer the phone in Greek (or what sounded like Greek to me), and I would reply in English—and that was the end of the conversation. Next step, and the one I found to be the most successful and thus became my primary method, was to send a fax. I would write a concise fax in English requesting info and fax it. In most cases the RD could not understand or read English—but I usually received a response within a few days. How? The RD would give my fax to a race volunteer who understood English or—more likely—he would take it home and give it to his kids, who spoke English. They would translate my fax to their dad, the RD, who would provide a response that they would then translate into English, and then the RD would fax a response back to me. We would often exchange several faxes in this manner until I received all the necessary info. By then the RD and I were usually friends, and he would often assist me with travel logistics and even invite me to stay with him and his family.

The third method was word of mouth from runners I would meet at races. I would ask runners from other foreign countries if there were any marathons in their country and how to get information. Usually they would give me their e-mail address so we could correspond, and they would help me find and register for races. And in some cases, where there was no marathon in a country, I would ask local runners and their running clubs to organize one.

Using these methods, which I learned through frustration and experience, I was able to run thirty-one marathons in thirty-one countries (and accomplish my first world record) during our year in England. If I had perfected these methods earlier, I believe that I could have completed fifty-plus marathons in fifty-plus countries in that year. My biggest handicap was finding marathons and setting up the travel logistics. Even with the robust Internet that is available sixteen years later, I still have to revert to the other methods—particularly word of mouth, to find marathons in small Third World countries!

Marathon #133—Country #11, Prague Marathon, Czech Republic

May 1999

I've been living in England for one month and training and running short races with the Bishop's Stortford Running Club, but I have not run a marathon since my burnout in Mexico in November 1998. It's time to find out if I can go the distance.

I choose the Prague Marathon since it's a big, popular race in Europe and has a website that makes it easy to find and register. Nicole and I decide to go to Prague for a long weekend to run the marathon and play tourist. We arrive on Friday so that we have time to explore the city before the race. We take a city tour to enjoy all the tourist sites, starting with Old Town.

We conclude the tour back in Old Town Square (Starometske namesti) for dinner and drinks. Hotels in Prague are expensive but meals and beer are cheap.

Sunday is M-day! I wasn't sure what to expect from my old rested body. My longest training run has been eighteen miles, and I have no confidence that I'm in marathon shape. The course starts and finishes in Old Town Square and crosses the Vltava River many times. Shortly after the start we pass many of the city's tourist sites. We run along the Vltava River beneath the seemingly never-ending hilltop castle and cross over the historic Charles Bridge, dotted every few meters with its parade of haunting Baroque statues. In the race's first two miles alone, we cross the Vltava River no fewer than three times, over three bridges, each one presenting an expansive view of the city that stands physically and historically in the center of Europe.

I wisely start slow, and I'm happy when I reach 10 kilometers in 55:58 and a split of 5:25.

Around the 12-kilometer mark we run through the city center, getting lost in the knotty turns of the Old Town's narrow cobblestone streets lined with tightly packed Gothic houses that date to medieval times. Along Na Prikope Street we pass Wenceslas Square, the walkway and boulevard that is the site of almost every important moment of Czech modern history, including the country's declaration of independence in 1918, the Nazi invasion in 1939, and the popular demonstrations of the Velvet Revolution in 1989. I pass 15 kilometers in 1:22:34 and a split of 5:21/kilometer and the Half in 1:54:43 and a split of 5:23, which is really slow. I feel good, so I decide to lower the pace for the second Half.

I pass the National Theatre near 32 kilometers and reach 35 kilometers in 3:07:19 and a split of 5:03. I push the pace lower again to cross the finish line in the Old Town Square in 3:43:31. My finish time isn't great, but I'm happy. I did not experience any problems, and I ran a negative split in the second Half by seven minutes. Maddog is back! I have completed marathon #133 and country #11. It's my first marathon and country since moving to England. I know it will not be my last.

After a hot shower, Nicole and I wander around Old Town Square enjoying the sights and a few beers before we treat ourselves to a fantastic dinner with a bottle of wine for less than fifty dollars.

When we return home to England I send an e-mail to my family and friends to tell them about the marathon and our wonderful trip to Prague. And a great idea strikes me. If I'm going to travel and run marathons around Europe, I should write race/trip reports after each race so that I could keep my family and friends informed. *Yes, that is a good idea! I will start after the next marathon!*

That's one of the best decisions I ever made. Without those trip reports that recorded my thoughts, observations, and race statistics there is no way I could possibly contemplate writing a book about Maddog's marathon adventures! (Believe me—it was not easy going back and writing this report sixteen years later, but it was needed for the book!)

Marathon #134—Country #12,

Stockholm Marathon, Sweden

June 1999

Today I find myself being driven by Nicole to Stansted Airport in England. I'm off to Sweden for the Stockholm Marathon. First run in 1979, it finishes in the Olympic Stadium where the 1912 Summer Olympics were held.

I meet another marathoner on the plane. Naturally, we have plenty to talk about. More important, there is someone to listen to me. We catch the bus together at Arlanda Airport for a forty-minute drive into Stockholm central station. Immediately, off we go to the Olympic Stadium, where we pick up our race packages. I also buy a three-day pass for the transportation system. It turns to be a smart move since my hotel is out in the suburbs. I know the metro and bus system very well by the time I leave.

As soon as I drop my gear off in my hotel room, I'm out again to hit the town—the old town—to play tourist and have my pasta dinner.

Stockholm is very pretty. It's built on fourteen islands on the coast in the southeast of Sweden at the mouth of Lake Mälaren, by the Stockholm archipelago and the Baltic Sea. The area has been settled since the Stone Age, in the sixth millennium BC, and was founded as a city in 1252 by Birger Jarl. I wander around and around—not too concerned about time on my feet as the race doesn't begin until 2:00 p.m. the next day. First stop is Gamla Stan, the Old Town, one of the largest and best-preserved medieval city centers in Europe.

All of Gamla Stan and the adjacent island of Riddarholmen are like a living pedestrian-friendly museum full of sights, attractions, restaurants, cafés, bars, and places to shop. The narrow winding cobblestone streets, with their buildings in so many different shades of gold, give Gamla Stan its unique character. In the middle of Gamla Stan is Stortorget, the oldest square in Stockholm. Stortorget is the central point from which runs Köpmangatan, the oldest street in Stockholm.

It's addictive to explore stuff. How many times will I be in Stockholm? I'll make the most of my time. I remind myself that I'm here for a marathon, and that I do need to get to the start line at some point. So I'm at the stadium by noon. The temperature is in the midsixties, which is fine, but it does go up to the seventies by the end of the race.

The course is two loops around the major tourist highlights of the city. Brilliant. It rounds off the portion of my tour I haven't completed. There are thirteen thousand runners, so I start slow and avoid running into others or being trampled by runners who haven't seen the sights the day before. At 8 kilometers, I'm doing a five minutes/kilometer pace and feeling good, and I hold that pace until the halfway mark. I reach halfway in a time of 1:47. I push the pace, thinking I may break a 3:30 finish time.

But at 33 kilometers, the wheels start pinging off. I'm struggling to run under a 6:30/kilometer pace for the next 7 kilometers, but then, like a B-movie script, a beautiful Swedish woman (blond, of course) passes me. I pinch myself—really? Is she wearing a bikini? She is. Sure enough, she's still in one as I stop squealing like a girl because my pinch draws blood. I find myself inspired.

I focus on the bikini. It drags me the last two kilometers in 10:15. I sprint by the bikini, and the woman who wears it, on the final lap in Olympic Stadium. I finish in a time of 3:37. I'm six minutes faster than my Prague time, but I'm still not pleased with my performance. Fussy bugger. Maybe it was all the walking? I'm not in shape yet to run a sub-3:30! And had the bikini arrived later in the race, my time would've been much worse. Who knows what would've been possible if the bikini had run past me at 15 kilometers.

But the race is over, and despite some disappointment, I can relax and enjoy Stockholm. I'm a full-time tourist now, which means I can drink beer, eat whatever I want, and do whatever I feel like doing. So after a short rest and a shower, I go back to Gamla Stan and find a great restaurant on a little square. Everyone is eating el fresco, even at 10:30 p.m. We're only now watching the sun start to set. It doesn't get dark until after midnight.

OMG; it's sinking in how expensive Sweden is! The dinner specials cost between twenty-five and forty dollars. A beer is six to eight dollars! You could easily live a fairly sober life here. And although breakfast is normally included in the room price, you've got to be keen on pickled herring and deli sandwiches at seven if you want to feel like you're getting a good deal.

I've now got some sightseeing time for the next few days. I'm choosing between visiting some islands in the Stockholm Archipelago or using my ScanRail Pass (a very good investment that will save you hundreds of dollars) and heading north to make a loop around Sweden and Norway. I opt for the latter, a three-hour boat cruise through the lakes and canals to the Baltic Sea and then catching a 5:00 p.m. train north. For an upgrade fee, I can get a semiprivate sleeper coach on the night train. Bargain! As a hotel costs a minimum of eighty dollars, I get to use the train as a hotel for two nights. Plus I'm covering five or six hundred miles while I sleep!

I'm on the train travelling from Stockholm to Lulea, which is a city on the coast of northern Sweden with 46,607 inhabitants and is the capital of Norrbotten County. My roommate on the semiprivate sleeper can speak English, which I think is great until I discover that he's a staunch communist from Lulea. I get a history lesson on Sweden, Lulea, and politics. Occasionally, he takes off on tirades about Marx, Lenin, capitalists, and stock portfolios, so I decide its best to talk about the bargains of a train sleeper and pickled herrings rather than my retirement living on stock portfolios.

I'm put into a deep sleep courtesy of Mr. Das Capital; I might have missed a few key insights between pages 100 and 500, and I don't wake up until just before we arrive in Lulea at seven o'clock on Monday morning. I'm happy to leave the train and walk around for three hours, decommunizing myself and becoming one with Lulea.

After three hours of walking aimlessly around my newfound town, I decide to catch the next train to Kiruna, which is the northernmost town in Sweden, situated in the province of Lapland. From there, the train will take me over to Narvik in Norway. It sounds quite magical, flitting from one country to another, and in a way, the train ride turns out to be just that.

This train travels above the Arctic Circle, which we bump over as it is a very thick red rope laid underneath the train tracks. Who knew? The journey is advertised as the "Most Northerly, Most Beautiful, Most Wild" railway in the world. The first is probably true, but I'm not up on my world geography to know for sure. But I question the claim of "most beautiful," as some of the scenery from Calgary to Vancouver in Canada is just as spectacular, although not as scary.

When the train leaves Kiruna and heads to Narvik, it passes over, through, and around a mountain range that is about ten thousand feet high. Spectacular. Coming down the Norwegian side, we're hugging the mountain on our right while looking almost directly down the other side on the left into the waters of the fjord. Well, it's somewhere down there below the clouds. I'm thinking the larger people on the train would be better seated on the mountain side to ensure that we keep our balance. There are a couple of chubby tubbies a few seats in front of me. I smile and start nodding my head to the side as if to say, "Wouldn't it make sense for you two to sit on the other side of the train?" They stay seated and smile back, nodding their own heads the same way back to me, no doubt thinking I'm an idiot sent by my village on a world trip.

I keep looking out the window, but I don't see any train tracks. Or any land for that matter—it's a sheer drop of five thousand feet into the fjord. Finally, after about five days, the train drops down to sea level at Narvik, and I'm relieved that I don't have to change my underwear. It's 6:00 p.m., and we're about a hundred miles above the Arctic Circle.

Wow. People really live here.

Apparently, they don't mind if the train station is closed. Or if there is no taxi. Or bus. Not knowing my way around and being the only person who speaks English isn't that bad, but combined with the rain and cold (I'm guessing 35°), it's a bit bleak. I start walking, hoping to find a room and a pickled herring. Half a mile later I find a hotel—$125 for a room—and I keep walking. Two more hotels later and the farthest from the station, I find a room for seventy dollars. Compared to sleeping in the cold a hundred miles north of the Arctic Circle, a seventy-dollar room sounds pretty good, fish or not.

I'm hungry and a little whiny, but pleased the train took its time down the mountain, which it has no doubt been doing for decades. I'm thinking that since I'm in Norway, maybe a reindeer dinner is possible. The desk clerk, who fortunately speaks English, tells me reindeer is indeed possible if I go to the hotel back up the street. Maybe I should run first, because I haven't run for two days. I didn't bring any rain or cold weather gear with me, which may sound strange coming from a Canadian visiting a community a hundred miles north of the Arctic Circle. Too many years living in the United States perhaps. So I run in shorts and a T-shirt, and I pass several locals wearing ski jackets and two runners with full Gore-Tex suits on. Everyone's looking at me strangely. I'm cold. As much as I want to try reindeer, in an act of spontaneous thinking I stop at a local grocery store, buy two cans of beer (at five dollars per can), and convince myself it'll be a better option if, instead of eating reindeer, I drink these two cans of beer in my hotel room.

Minutes later I'm drinking beer as I watch the BBC News on TV. I can't get the thought of reindeer out of my mind. I shower and return up the street, more appropriately dressed this time, for a reindeer steak.

The steak, it turns out, only costs twenty-five dollars, which I figure is quite reasonable. Even more so when I discover the liter of rotgut house wine I decide to wash it down with costs ten dollars more. I've not eaten anything since breakfast, but rather than ask for the waiter's arm, I order a bowl of onion soup for twelve dollars. It's been an expensive dinner, but I needed the soup so I could wash the red wine down.

I'd have run back to the hotel but I'm sloshing around in wine, soup, and reindeer that maybe hasn't completely died yet. Maybe cooked reindeer is more expensive. At this time of year in the northern climes, daylight doesn't go away, so I close the drapes in order to sleep. I've got a bus to catch from the train station at 7:00 a.m. that will take me south to catch another train at the closest railway line.

I arrive at six o'clock; I'm early, but I don't want to miss one of just two buses that leave during the day. At seven, we depart on a five-hour ride to Fauske, which is as far north as the Norwegian railway goes. It's five hours of the most spectacular scenery I've ever seen. Like the Swedes, the Norwegians have mastered the art of travel in mountains. We're up, down, through, over, under, and possibly, at one point, just inches away from reaching China, all the time never faraway from stunning fjords. We never fall into the fjords. We even take a ferry across a fjord. Some of the tunnels are over three miles long. I decide that one day I'll return and take the bus route north out of Narvik, which will take me another three hundred miles north of the Arctic Circle. Maybe they'll have a marathon there as well as herring.

I don't spend much time in Fauske, departing on the train at 12:15 p.m. The scenery is still amazing, but the farther south we come, the more mundane it becomes, with flatter land and then farmland. My roommate in my semiprivate room is a young cyclist from Toronto who has been biking the roads along the coast by himself for the past month and is now heading home. He tells me that Dallas is leading the NHL Stanley Cup (hockey) series 2–1! We pass through Tronheim, and then I fall asleep until we arrive in Oslo at 7:00 a.m.

It's early, I've rested, and I'm pumped—ready to sightsee and feeling pretty big, knowing I'll get my accommodations sorted out well before the night falls this time.

They say we travelers must expect the unexpected, which doesn't really make sense, but neither does the fact that the tourist desk tells me there are no hotel rooms available in Oslo.

My crying spurs the operators behind the travel desk to find something for me. They come up with a solitary hotel room, presumably in a hotel, thirty miles out of Oslo for $250/night. I can't cry any harder than I am already, and a mock epileptic fit doesn't look like it will go down too well. Besides, I've never been good at acting, and I could look like a dork.

I decide to reserve the room, a good ultra away, just in case I can't find anything else here, in the capital of Norway, for goodness sake. Really?! For all I know, I could be sharing the room with Thor and Hagar and their Viking friends and animals.

I'm hungry now. Crying will do that, so I set out to find a fulsome break-fast. After an hour of walking aimlessly I realize such a breakfast is not pos-sible. I make do with a pastry and coffee.

Feeling closer to normal, I hop on a city tour bus to get the layout of Oslo.

Oslo, the capital of Norway, sits on the country's southern coast at the head of the Oslofjord and is known for its citywide green spaces and muse-ums. Many of these are on the Bygdøy peninsula, including the Norwegian Maritime Museum, the Vikingskipshuset, with ships from the tenth century, and the Norsk Folkemuseum, with artifacts from Sami and Viking cultures. We visit Vigelandsparken, a unique sculpture park that is the life work of the sculptor Gustav Vigeland (1869–1943), with more than two hundred sculp-tures in bronze, granite, and cast iron. The bronze statue of the little Angry Boy (*Sinnataggen* in Norwegian) is among the most famous sculptures, along with the Monolith (*Monolitten*) and the Wheel of Life.

Next we visit the Holmenkollen Ski Museum and Tower. The museum presents over four thousand years of skiing history, Norwegian polar explora-tion artifacts, and an exhibition on snowboarding and modern skiing. The observation deck on top of the jump tower offers panoramic views of Oslo

Although I like Oslo, I'm getting increasingly frustrated; time and time again I'm told by hotels that there are no rooms available. So I decide to leave Norway and take a train instead to Göteborg, Sweden.

My body, meanwhile, is screaming for a run. I've been a train junkie for what must be an unhealthy amount of time, and now I *must* do a run. Today! There are no showers in the train station, but it occurs to me I should find a health club and ask to pay a day fee just to use their locker room and shower. The attendant thinks I'm nuts, and maybe I am. That's another story, I say to him, but despite that he only charges three dollars, which is the cheapest thing I've found in all of Norway. I pound through a brutal eight-mile run along the Aker Brygge and through the royal farm. Feels good. After a quick shower, I rush to the train station for a ten-dollar Burger King burger and a five-dollar Coke. No herrings, not even on the side.

At this point I'd prefer to simply sleep in the station, maybe even on the tracks, but I must go on to Göteborg and find a hotel room. We roll into

Göteborg at 10:20 p.m. I'm relieved; there are lots of hotels near the station. First stop is a Renaissance Hotel, price $200! I keep moving. One block off the main square, there's a clean two-star hotel for eighty dollars. There's not much to the room, but I can at least stand in it and lean over onto the bed. Ah, a place to sleep!

Come morning, there's not much to do in the room—actually nothing, other than bend myself back upright, so I rise early, get into my running gear, and ask the clerk where to run. He recommends a bike path that takes me to a forest outside of town. There are a number of well-marked dirt running trails in what is a really thick forest. I pick a 10-kilometer loop and maddog my way through the forest. What a great run!

Back to the hotel and breakfast. I could eat several reindeer. Surprise! They have Swedish meatballs and scrambled eggs. I think I eat about eighty dollars' worth.

Another surprise. I catch yet another train, this time to Malmö. I arrive at 4:00 p.m. Malmö is a neat little place, a university town with lots of young people hustling about. I book into another two-star hotel at the tourist office and then walk around the central area. It's happy hour, and it seems that the whole town is at the outdoor bars and restaurants enjoying the special prices—beer is a steal now at only seven dollars. Although the whole town looks to head off to nightclubs, as they're really dressed up, I need to hit the sack by midnight.

I'm addicted, you see. The next day I get up early to catch—yes, you guessed it—the express train to Stockholm. It arrives in Stockholm at noon, with me on it. I start shaking off the addiction at this point. After a decent lunch in the Gamla Stan, I catch a bus to the airport, where I then board a plane home to Stansted. It's great to be back, although I'm missing the trains.

I've got five days to rest up before I leave again for Tallinn, Estonia!

Marathon #136—Country #14, Paavo Nurmi Marathon, Finland

July 1999

After running a marathon in Tallinn, Estonia, I catch a ferry across the Baltic Sea to meet Nicole at the airport in Helsinki, Finland.

We overnight in Helsinki, and I play the guide role before we catch a train to Turku, which is the oldest city in Finland, dating back to the thirteenth century. Archaeological findings in the area date back to the Stone Age, when the first marathon was held here.

Our first task, though, is to find the race registration office at the Paavo Nurmi Stadium to pick up my race number for the Paavo Nurmi Marathon. Paavo Nurmi was a famous middle-and long-distance runner who lived and trained in Turku while winning nine gold and three silver medals in the Olympics. In his top form in the 1920s, he went undefeated for 121 races. The marathon supposedly runs over his training course. He was a legend and appears on bank notes and has had sculptures made of him. Famous Finn athletes idolize him. He always ran with a stopwatch.

I meet up with Don Lang, one of my 50+DC Club colleagues, at the start line. He ran a race in Norway a few days ago. It's always great to see runners from home.

It's not only hot during the race but very windy. I strategically position myself during the race behind some runners to reduce the effects of the wind. At the 12-mile mark, I find myself with just one other—a female runner, whom I teach to alternate places and share the lead role running into the wind. We do this for about five miles until a group of men pass by and I, in retrospect, rather unchivalrously, tuck in behind them. By mile 21 the gods have judged me and the men storm away as my legs, now each apparently carrying ten-pound rocks, can no longer keep up with their sub-8-minute pace. I slow down.

I get to listen to the Ruisrock Festival (Metallica and others) that's playing on Ruissalo Island. The marathon course does two loops around the island, so we all get to share in the musical treat of Metallica and others while we run, which is inspirational to me only in the sense that I run faster to lessen the time I have to spend listening.

My female ex-companion passes me at about mile 25. I hear the gods laughing. Maddog shows up. It's a challenge. He puts on a sprint to catch up and then hangs on to her for the last mile. He sprints the final lap in the Paavo Nurmi stadium to beat her, finishing in a time of 3:39. He smiles. She probably doesn't like him. I'm sure I don't either.

Then it's into the shower quickly so I can meet up with Nicole. We walk along the Aura River, stopping for wine and beer or two. We find a restaurant that serves only wild game and food found in the forests and streams of Finland. Nicole has wild boar. I try wild bear; you don't find that in many restaurants. The sauces are made of wild berries like cloudberry and lingonberry. It's a great wild meal, and I don't utter a single complaint about the cost, even though it's more than we pay for two nights in our hotel.

Marathon #137—Country #15,

Middelkerke Marathon, Belgium

August 1999

We come to Middelkerke, about twenty miles from Bruges. I'm one of just three hundred running the marathon. I have a bad sinus infection, I'm taking antibiotics and pain-killers, and there is a wicked multidirectional wind on the coastal route. I'm not sure how they will affect my breathing and energy level. Turns out okay with a time of 3:39.

Nicole and I catch a train to Brussels; sample a few Belgian beers (there are over five hundred types), and people watch. We fly to Milan, Italy, where it's holiday rip-off season; we get a pizza, a ham sandwich, and two beers for lunch for eighty dollars.

Then it's off to Naples. Despite some natural beauty—much of it was built on the coast and on the sides of mountains—it's filthy. Garbage and trash is everywhere. We hire a private guide to take us around the city for a three-hour tour. Our guide, Giuseppe, is a war veteran about 150 years old. He has lived in Naples all his life and speaks little English. And, we think, he learned to drive soon after the wheel was invented. It's gotten busier on the roads since then, so to be sure that he's still on the road, he aims for the center line and never veers off it. It's up to the other cars to get out of his way. After a few brown stains on his upholstery, I realize he's been driving like this all his life. Bizarrely, we relax and let him do his thing.

After the tour we pick up a rental car and head south to Sorrento, stopping at Pompeii to find out what all the fuss is about with the volcano—Vesuvius—that erupted there in AD 79. A spectacular place, Pompeii. It was lost for about fifteen hundred years, covered in ash and dirt. During the excavation, archaeologists used plaster to fill in the gaps between the layers of ash that once were human bodies. You can see the exact positions of people when they died.

Sorrento is very pretty, built up into the side of a mountain one to two hundred feet above the Bay of Naples. We treat ourselves to a modern and luxurious four-star hotel built into the cliffs. We eat dinner at the hotel because the views are so spectacular. After dinner, I open a second bottle of wine while we plot our next day. Nicole calls our son, Chris, in Colorado.

He tells us my dad died two days earlier. It's a shock for the whole family. We refocus to figure out how to get back home to Canada in time for the funeral. First thing the next morning we drive to Rome and catch a direct flight to Canada. We make it in time for the funeral, but I see I'm the only one wearing Dockers and a polo shirt.

We head back to England and start planning our next trips. It's tough, but I realize life must go on. Life can be fragile and short; I'm even more determined to enjoy every moment I can.

Marathon #138—Country #16,

Moscow Marathon, Russia

August 1999

Moscow is a very difficult place to visit (or at least it was in 1999). But it teaches you patience and perseverance—fine attributes for the distance runner. Forget about learning the language, though, you'll have more chance of understanding the ancient dialect of the Komodo dragon than of understanding Russian.

I get my first OMG-Russia experience soon after I arrive in England to live. Using some information from *Runner's World*, I call the Moscow contact telephone number. Nobody speaks English at the other end—not unusual—so I send a fax requesting information. But the fax number doesn't work. Eventually, I come across an English entry form and send in the application.

Now I need a visa. I look over the processing requirements for a visa and realize I will need six years of intensive studying to satisfactorily complete the paper work. Or risk ending up in some undisclosed gulag with no option for marathon running for several years.

I need to be invited to Russia and sponsored by an individual or a company. I need to indicate where I would be staying every day and have a written confirmation that includes my visa application number, shoe size, favorite type of vodka, and an assessment of our ability to perform a Cossack dance. I'm sketchy on the language, but it looks like they also require the size of the underpants of our oldest child, too.

Then that data must be presented to the Russian embassy for processing, which takes ten to fourteen days. It's one of those vicious circles that are difficult to get around unless you have assistance inside Russia.

It's at this point that I realize travel agents are worthwhile. So I find one and hand over what I want to do and beg and cry as I ask them to make it happen. Their Russian representative "invites" me to Russia and handles all the paper work inside Russia. The London office then takes my passport to the embassy. Finally, I have a hotel reservation, airline reservations, and a visa. Comrades, here I come!

I fly to Moscow via Stockholm since there are no direct flights from England to Russia. Stumbling out of the Moscow airport after a nonthreatening customs experience, I'm immediately besieged by hundreds, or perhaps seven, taxi drivers wanting to drive me into the city. Nobody speaks English, though. I find a woman at a hotel-booking desk who speaks enough broken English to tell me there are no direct trains or buses to the city. But I could take a bus-and-metro combo. Such a combo, however, assures me of one thing, which is that I'll likely get lost. Sensibilities take over, immediately followed by my Scottish ancestry. I start negotiating (think *sign language*) with the taxi drivers, playing one taxi against another in a bid to get the price down. I get it down from sixty dollars to thirty. Feeling pretty proud of myself, Ivan and I head to the city, and in particular, the Rossiya (Russia) Hotel.

Ivan tells me, sort of, that it's not exactly an official taxi, but that he's moonlighting with his own car to make extra money. An hour later he drops me off in front of a huge building and utters something that sounds like Rossiya. The sign on the front is in Russian, and there are no clues as to what it actually means. But really, my options are limited. I get out and walk into a huge lobby with two reception desks. I go to the one on the right and get in line. I still can't see anything that tells me this is the Rossiya. As I wait for fifteen minutes, I can see that everything is done manually. No rush. No problem. I'm patient. Although I'm getting a little anxious when I catch on that neither receptionist speaks English.

Fortunately I have a hotel voucher from the travel agency that I hand over with my passport and visa. I try speaking English and get a look back that, roughly translated, intimates, "Are you crazy? I don't speak English."

After about five years Ulyana finishes manually checking some papers and, I assume myself, by looking at the unused computer sitting on her desk. Perhaps they are short on cords to plug it in. She makes two phone calls, abruptly hands me back all my documentation, and says, "West!" At least I think so. Charades time. With just seconds remaining on the timer, she gets me to understand that I am standing on the east side, and I need to go to the west side. Ah...the other side of the building. Really? So I go out of the building and walk around to the other side—which turns out to be a whole city block.

My eyes stumble when suddenly the Kremlin and the Red Square appear in front of me, directly across the street. At least I know I am in Moscow.

I'm at the west entrance now. Into the lobby I go and wander over to the reception desk to the right. Really. After fifteen minutes Comrade Katya points me to *other* reception desk across the lobby. I'm getting good at this now. I'm not understanding why the other reception desk is the only one that can admit me (especially as later I discover my room is directly above the desk). Anyway, I go the other side. A clerk finds my reservation and, gulp, processes it. High five.

I'm mentally cracking open a bottle of bubbly. The clerk takes my passport, which is scary, and hands me a small card that has Rossiya Hotel printed on it, as well as some numbers (my first confirmation I'm actually in the hotel). I wait for a key but she moves on to the next customer. Back in line I go.

But in an impulsive state of defiance, I turn and ask sheepishly where my room is and if I get a key. She understands enough English to explain the numbers on the hotel card represent my floor and room number, and I must turn the card in on the floor to get my key. I get off on the tenth floor where I find the floor matron, who looks like one of those Russian villains who beats the crap out of James Bond. Of course, she doesn't speak English. After more charades and sign language I finally wander into my room. Running the marathon will be easy by comparison.

I don't spend much time in my room because there is nothing to do, really. I throw my stuff on the bed and head out of the hotel. I wander across the street to explore Red Square. I find out later that the Rossiya is the largest hotel in Russia; it has about five thousand rooms and takes up an entire city block. Just to confuse travelers more, it's divided into five sections: East, West, North, South, and You're Lost, none of which are connected internally. It used to be *the* place in Moscow where all the VIPs stayed because of its proximity to the Kremlin. But it's not been updated for at least twenty years, and they lost many VIPs, who registered but strangely were never seen again.

You can't help being impressed by the architecture as you walk around Red Square. Saint Basil's Cathedral, which is on the south side of the square, is recognized as one of Moscow's landmarks and is over four hundred years old!

I'm thrilled to see another runner ambling by—he's wearing a Boston Marathon T-shirt—an American from Florida who has visited Russia many times and is now living in Rostov. A stroke of good luck, because he understands the Russian culture, and how to shop and get around, and he even has a rudimentary knowledge of the Russian language. We go to dinner together, and he helps me order, because, of course, there is no English version of the menu; the food is all Russian.

I'm feeling more at home now. After dinner, Earl takes me to a local convenience store to buy bottled water, soft drinks, and some snacks for the room. Although you can buy most of the basic items in the hotel shop, the prices are 400 percent higher.

Simply buying things in a store, however, is its own special experience, and it should really be up there with visiting the Red Square and other Soviet tourist attractions. In the store, all the items are behind a glass counter (with their Russian name and a price). I need to make a list of the items I want, and their prices, and then add up the prices and pay the cashier the total price. I then tell her the individual items that I need; she approves my list and gives me a receipt. I take the list back to the counter, and the clerk gets my items for me. To add valuable hours to your limited tourist experience, I'd recommend you go hungry and don't drink anything while you're here.

My new friend explains over dinner that you can't buy a train/bus/air ticket without a passport and a visa. If you drive anywhere, you're likely to be stopped and your papers checked. He says he is usually stopped at least once or twice a week in Rostov. Graft, coercion, and bribes, he says, are considered a normal way of life.

After dinner we part ways, and I decide to go to the hotel bar for a beer. I want to sample some Russian beer and know that I can't (all right, shouldn't) drink the next day because I have a rule not to drink for two days before a race. As I stand at the bar with my American uniform on—jeans, running shoes, and a marathon T-shirt—a Russian approaches me and asks where I'm from. We talk for a while, and I ask where he learned his English. On the black market, he replies. This changes my view of black markets.

And then my alarm bells start to ring. Could he be a "new Russian," like the Mafia? He asks—well, insists nicely—that I visit his bar with him, where the beer is 50 percent cheaper. Not wanting to piss this guy off, I reluctantly agree to go for a beer. The good news is it's just one hundred feet from the hotel lobby. There are thousands of such sidewalk bars in Moscow as well as little kiosks or huts every few hundred feet where one can buy beer, vodka, soft drinks, vodka, or vodka. Half of Moscow seems to always walk around with a beer in their hand. Or vodka.

My new Russian friend introduces me to a few of his friends, none of whom speak a word of English. I buy a few rounds (beer is $1.25/pint), and we share stories about the United States and Russia. Fortunately, my buddy is not Mafia, but he does pay them protection money every week! At 2:00 a.m. I wisely decide to stop drinking, or else it will be a bad day tomorrow on prerace day. Of course, I could've been even wiser and left at one o'clock, but there you go. It's all about experience, isn't it?

I wake up not understanding why I feel so bad. I discover that beer is 12 percent alcohol here. Most Russian beers are 8–12 percent, and one is even 17.5 percent. That stuff has got a kick to it, and it's kicking me silly. Nothing like a city bus tour to cure a hangover. Besides, I'm itching to learn more about the place.

One of my new drinking friends last night had told me there was an Intourist office in the hotel, which I found. Gold mine! The staff even understood me, and—tears to my eyes—spoke English. One of my first requests—and as it turned out, disappointments—is trying to get tickets for the Bolshoi Theater. Unfortunately the season doesn't begin until a couple of weeks after I leave Russia.

The Intourist office becomes my sole source of communication and information in Moscow. No one else speaks English, there are no signs or information in English (even the Intourist office had no brochure or written information in English), and all the TV stations are Russian, with English movies and the Euro-Sports channel, both dubbed. I've never felt so isolated. I'm feeling unnerved, almost intimidated, in Moscow.

After a broken-English city tour that shows us all the major attractions in Moscow (most are within a three-mile radius of the Kremlin), I go to the race HQ and pick up my race packet. Surprise. Several lines, but nothing in English. Fifteen minutes later, and I'm still figuring out what line I'm supposed to be in. Fortunately I've brought a copy of my entry form with me and handed it over. They gave me my number and race instructions (in Russian) and kept my copy (with the English instructions). Perhaps an underlying sense of humor pervades Russian society. I decide to attend the race pasta party because at least there will be other English-speaking runners there. You know, the normal pasta buffet where you gather around with your buddies. Instead, I was seated at a formal table with five non-English-speaking Russians and served at the table. It was a very quiet dinner.

So off to bed early and a commitment to myself to stay away from the hotel bar. And also time for *the nightly call*. Without fail, every night about thirty minutes after I retire to my room I get this call: "Englis, you Englis? You want beautiful Russian girl come your room, give you sex or massage?" It puts a smile on my face the first few times—the call that is—but by the final night they're calling several times. I tried not to be rude because, who knows, maybe I'd get a knock on the door from the Mafia? Given my distinct lack of Russian language skills I doubt the Mafia would be impressed by my charades performance. Or my crying.

The next morning, I rise early to be sure I had time to find the start line. Somewhere in the Red Square apparently. Of course my instructions are in Russian, so I can't be 100 percent sure of anything, really. But I didn't get a visit from the Mafia overnight, so, so far, so good.

There are thousands of police and military lined up in Red Square shoulder to shoulder on both sides of the race course for the first half mile. They look very ominous, since it is raining and they are all dressed in a dark-gray raincoats! Surely they're not running as well? I'm half expecting to see a convoy of missiles and tanks roll by.

They don't, but the race starts and we head out for the first 2 kilometers over the bridge by the Kremlin and around the city on the south side of the Moscow River and then back over the bridge and on to a boulevard along the Kremlin and Moscow River. What a buzz. They've blocked off a 10-kilometer route along this boulevard and there is a policeman stationed every fifty meters along the course with several at every intersection. There are more police than spectators along that route, which we have to run four times to finish back in Red Square.

The course is flat and fast and, since it's cloudy and raining for the first hour, heat is not a problem. The support isn't great—perhaps it can't get through the police lines. And we have water every five kilometers. I'm concerned again about the water—they're scooping it out of large containers, perhaps laced with vodka. Fortunately, I'm not paranoid. I was expecting—well, hoping for—bottled water, but when I look back, I see I was in pixie-world to be thinking that.

Nevertheless, I finish with a PR for the year (3:37:45), although I still haven't broken the 3:30 mark!

After the race I explore Moscow some more while I wait for my appetite to reappear. By four o'clock I'm hungry, so I head to McDonald's just off McRed Square, figuring it'll be easier to order fries and a Coke to satisfy my normal hunger for grease and salt after a race. By pointing at pictures and using sign language, I'm able to get my order.

Several thousand police and military personnel are gathering around Red Square, which is cordoned off, as are the streets around the square. Down one side street there are several army trucks full of raw recruits waiting in the wings to be called. Another marathon?

I detour for several blocks to get back to the Rossiya Hotel, following tens of thousands of muscovites going in the same direction. A new revolution perhaps. It eerily reminds me of that scene in the movie *Dr. Zhivago* where the protesters are mowed down in the streets of Moscow by horses and the military.

Relief. It's just a rock concert in Red Square to start a week of celebration for Moscow's 852nd birthday. Eight hundred fifty-second? Puts American history into perspective. The entrance to the concert is on the side street next to the Rossiya. I was worried that I wouldn't be allowed back into the hotel, but when I flash my hotel card, I'm allowed in. Good thing, too, because otherwise I would miss my nightly phone call. But before that, I sit at the outdoor bar in front of the hotel and watch the concert for a few hours—all in Russian, of course!

The next morning I have to decide between visiting the Kremlin or the Pushkin Museum, which is the second largest in Russia. I choose the Kremlin and spend a few hours walking around on my own. You can visit the cathedral square and the five-hundred-year-old churches inside the Kremlin, but you cannot enter the congress buildings. There are police every few hundred feet and lots of black suits with earphones coming out of their collars (KGB or whatever they are called now). If you live in Russia, you must get very good at standing.

And in the afternoon it was time to fly out and learn how to speak English again.

Moscow is very beautiful; there are lots of nice things to see and do. It's very inexpensive if you do the things the locals do and stay away from places frequented by tourists. But if you plan to go, brush up on your Russian or get a translator. My only regrets were that I couldn't see a ballet at the Bolshoi, as you know how much I like ballet, and I didn't have time to visit the Pushkin Museum. Then again, those are two very good reasons to go back!

Marathon #144—Country #22,

Dublin Marathon, Ireland

October 1999

The purpose of this trip is to run two marathons: one in Dublin and one six days later in Wales. I head to Ireland via the Irish Ferries terminal, boarding a hydrofoil that crosses the Irish Sea in less than two hours. High winds have whipped the Irish Sea up into twelve- to fifteen-foot swells. I've never seen so many seasick people in my life. About 80 percent of us are seasick within the first hour. The big breakfast doesn't seem like such a great idea now. I'm one of the lucky ones and can keep things down, but watching, listening, and smelling three hundred people throw up does make it challenging.

I've been to Dublin before, but this time I discover the Dublin Castle and Phoenix Park—the largest urban park in the world. The guide points us tourists to the many bullet holes in the buildings and statues from the many unsuccessful independence wars during Ireland's violent past. I missed all this history on my first trip.

The marathon itself is treated as a big event in Dublin. It has about six thousand entrants, of whom half are from the United States, many there trying to find their roots. The marathon course is a fairly flat loop through and around the city, but most of it is in the suburbs; it's kind of boring. I run easy since I've got another race in six days that will be much harder. I finish in 3:37, which in retrospect, was probably faster than I should've gone.

I decide it's time to treat myself like a king, so I head out of town and stay at the Kilkea Castle, the oldest inhabited castle in Ireland. It has been inhabited since it was built in 1180, and the exterior has essentially been untouched since then. It's now a luxury hotel, as tourists love this sort of thing, and I'm proof of that.

The tower I'm in is apparently haunted. Boo. After dinner I go to the bar for a nightcap and then retire early. I check my door as I usually do to double-lock it. But they don't have double locks or a safety chain, so I make sure the door is closed and locked. At exactly 2:45 a.m., I wake up and see my room door open and swing in about one-quarter of the way. I let out a sheepish hello. The door slams shut.

Then there's an awful thumping noise starting in the hallway or somewhere in the tower. After a few minutes, I'm getting annoyed; so I call the front desk to tell them someone has tried to enter my room and now there are loud noises in the hallway. After a few more minutes, the noise is still going, so I call the front desk again and complain more strongly. After a few more minutes the noise goes away, and I fall back to sleep.

The next morning on the way to breakfast I ask the front desk what they found the previous night. They explain that they sent someone to the tower, but he found nothing, or nobody, and no noise.

They also tell me that no employees were in the tower at that time, and no unauthorized persons had access to my room key.

A ghost? I don't know. Ghosts don't open doors, do they? Don't they just walk through them?

Marathon #145—Country #23,

Snowdonia Marathon, Wales

October 1999

After Ireland, off I go to Wales. It's the undiscovered secret of the United Kingdom, but I guess that, since I'm telling you this, that label is no longer quite accurate. It has everything the other countries do: mountains, ocean, people, history, ghosts (no doubt), and lots of sheep.

But it's also much cheaper to visit and less congested. I'm off to the Snowdonia National Park where the marathon is to be run. On the way to Llanberis I stop at LLANFAIRPWLLGWYNGYLLGOGERYCHWYRNDROBWLLLLAN TYSILIOGOGOGOCH. Which is easy to say if you practice. A lot. This is the longest town name in Britain and it means "Mary's church by the white hazel pool, near the fierce whirlpool, with the Church of Tysilio by the Red Cave." Obviously.

But regardless of the Welsh dislike for vowels, and the historical claim that they wrote the first-ever dictionary totally drunk, it turns out to be a fine marathon.

I meet fellow Canadian Wally Herman, who is running his eighty-seventh country! Wow. The weather has been crap these past few days, so it's going to be a tough race. It starts in Llanberis, climbs a thousand feet to the Llanberis Pass, and then drops a thousand feet down into Beddgelert. Love that name. At the top of the pass, the winds are gusting at 60 mph and I'm thinking I'll be blown off the mountain. From Beddgelert we climb up another five hundred feet to Pont Cae Gors before descending again. The final climb, mile 21–23, is the worst. We climb a thousand feet up a hiking trail to the top of a mountain. I run the whole way, and I'm looking forward to flying down the other side. But I get to the top and find the descent is so steep and the trail so treacherous that I lean back into the mountain and apply full leg brakes. I weave my way gently down the trail of slippery grass, mud, and loose rocks. One mistake, and I'll have an extremely quick descent time, in seconds, and I find myself thinking that life is kind of important after all. I finally arrive on the edge of town on wobbly legs and run the final mile through Llanberis to finish on the shores of Llyn Paradan. My time is 3:43, which I'm proud of, and I leave with a deep admiration of mountain goats, especially the Welsh ones.

Marathon #146—Country #24, Monte Carlo Marathon, Monaco November 1999

My Monaco marathon trip starts with my heading to Barcelona via the island of Mallorca. Spread throughout Barcelona are many buildings designed by a Spanish architect named Gaudi. Talk about weird. He must have been on psychedelic drugs when he designed these buildings, and I don't have words to describe them. I could try to describe them, but you must see them to believe it! His religious faith and strict vegetarianism were rumored to have led him to undertake several lengthy and severe fasts, and maybe that's why the buildings look the way they do. Whatever the case, he has a global following, despite being dead for about seventy-five years.

I only spend two days in Barcelona, and it's not enough. I then take a night train to Monaco, traveling by coach car to the French border, where I have an hour layover before catching a second train with sleeper cars. I'm the first to arrive in the four-sleeper couchette. An Australian comes in, followed soon after by two pretty young Spanish women. I'm surprised, but they're shocked to discover that they're assigned to a couchette with two men. They call the conductor and complain. But they only speak Spanish, and he only speaks French. So it seems only natural that the linguistically handicapped ugly American comes to the rescue. With my basic French and, okay, I'll be generous here, my limited Spanish, I become the translator

But the train is full, and there are no other sleepers available. So we all go to bed fully-clothed to ease the girls' minds. By two o'clock, the Aussie is snoring like a wombat that's eaten an accordion, and the girls are swearing (I don't know any swear words in Spanish, but I know they're swearing). By four, the girls give up, take their suitcases, and sit in the hall outside our cabin. By six, I've joined them—either that or I snuff the wombat—and we all enjoy the scenery as the train travels along the Côte d'Azur. Finally, I arrive in Monte Carlo at nine o'clock, step off the train, and run into my friend, Edson, from the 50+DC Running Club. A bit surreal.

Race day finds us at the marathon start line on the main road in Monte Carlo in front of the casino. For twenty-six miles and .2, we run east along the coast and up and down and up and down and…well, you get the idea, the coastal mountains. We run through Monaco into France, through France into Italy. This is the only marathon that runs through three countries. I count this country/marathon as Monaco. The scenery is awesome. With the cool weather I'm able to finish in 3:33, which is great, given the hilly, goat-ish course. After the race I end up eating a hot dog at a small carnival on the sea. Not the typical image of Monaco, but when you've just knocked off 26.2 miles, any food is good food.

Now it's time to make my way by train to Portugal for the next marathon!

Marathon #147—Country #25, Lisbon

Marathon, Lisbon, Portugal

November 1999

I dress down in the hope of securing a decent but inexpensive place to stay in Madrid, en route to Lisbon. The Madrid travel agent takes one look at me and tries to direct me to a hostel. When I say I want a two- or three-star hotel with an ensuite bath and at least one English channel on TV, she obliges me and quotes the bottom end of the price scale, looking at me as if to say, "Are you sure? How are you going to pay for it?" My ugly warm-up top has worked. It's one of the best investments I've ever made. It keeps me from freezing to death and probably saves me hundreds of dollars on this trip alone.

Madrid is big city that smells and tastes like pollution during the busy traffic hours. Fortunately, Retiro Park, which is the old gardens and hunting grounds of the kings, is only a mile from my hotel. So I jog over to the park and run the many dirt trails through the park, as I need to continue my training runs. I take a city tour immediately to learn the layout of the city but walk everywhere after that. After two days in the city, I feel I've seen everything. I'm getting tired of the big city, so I decide to escape to the countryside. I take a tour to San Lorenzo De El Escorial and Valle de los Caídos. El Escorial (the Royal Monastery) is considered to be the eighth wonder of the world. It was built by King Felipe II in 1562 to honor the Spanish victory over the French at San Quentin and to house the pantheon for all the Spanish kings. It's time to move on to Lisbon to meet my sports manager, (Nicole) who is bringing me fresh clothes and supplies.

I arrive in Lisbon at 8:00 a.m., and Nicole is arriving at one o'clock, so I go to race HQ and pick up my race package. I run into a friend from the 50+DC club in the street, and we decide to tour the city together and have lunch while I wait for Nicole. After she arrives, I show her around the old center of Lisbon, where our hotel is located. The next day we take a city tour. There are lots of attractions: the Castelo de San Jorge that overlooks the city and our hotel, Jeronimos Monastery, Torre de Belem, a fourteenth-century defense tower built in the Rio Tejo (Tejo River), a duplicate of the Christ Statue in Rio de Janeiro (but not as tall), and the Discoveries Monument. Portugal is very proud of its place in history as one of the dominant explorers and colonizing countries.

Sunday is race day. The Lisbon marathon starts just off the main commercial square in the old city, runs north into the hills and returns to the center of the city to go out along the Tejo River toward the Atlantic Ocean before turning around and heading back to the commercial square. This, however, is not how I do it. For the first time in 147 marathons, I'm misdirected off course by race officials. About 5 kilometers into the race, I'm being sent with twenty other runners off course with the 10K racers. It takes us about five minutes to realize that we're with the wrong group. A bonding moment. We retrace our steps, cut a few corners, and manage to rejoin the marathon pack. Subconsciously, I pick up the pace, even though I'm telling myself to gradually get back lost time. I pass the halfway mark three minutes ahead of my expected time, so I figure I'm heading for trouble. But trouble never appears, and I finish in 3:28, feeling mighty happy in spite of the screw-up.

Nicole has to return to England and work and take back a load of my dirty laundry. So I leave early the next day by train for Faro and the Algarve Coast. I'm about to check out my glorious and fabulously modern thirty-dollar hotel room and decide to go out onto the balcony to check out the view. It's raining lightly, so I close the patio door behind me. As it closes, I hear an ominous *click*!

I've locked myself out! I'm on the third-floor (top) balcony. I try to muscle the door open but give up and try to catch the attention of anyone on the street. I shout, "Hey, señor," but the few people who look up just scurry away. So I shout, "Hey, asshole!" Still no takers. What to do? I'm getting wet and cold, and I consider throwing the patio furniture down into the street to attract attention. Fortunately, the proprietor of a hair salon across the street comes out for a cigarette and sees me waving and shouting. She goes into my hotel, and a few minutes later I'm saved by the desk clerk.

The next day I catch a train to Seville for two days of R and R and then on to Valencia to catch a night ferry back to Mallorca for my next marathon.

Marathon #148—Country #26,

Calvia Marathon, Spain

December 1999

En route to Mallorca from Portugal, I visit Seville. I really like Seville. It's a very old city with narrow streets that wind around in all directions. I quickly learn how to get lost in Seville. A compass is useful, as is the wisdom of not leaving the hotel room without a map.

Seville is home to the third largest cathedral in the world, one of the most famous bullrings in the world, and in the section known as Macarena, where they all dance, they have the only remaining section of the original defense wall and the Macarena Church that contains the Virgen de Macarena, which, kind of oddly, they dress and parade through the streets each week.

My last evening in Seville is very pleasant and memorable. I'm walking back to the hotel after an "early" ten o'clock dinner and hear some music emanating from a small tavern. A group of ten local musicians are jamming on guitars and other string instruments that I don't recognize plus a piece of hollowed-out wood that looks like a coconut that's being beaten with a piece of wood. The bar only holds about twenty customers plus the musicians. I don't understand a word being said, but it's a great atmosphere and great music. They play until two, when they have to break up because some of them have to work the next day. Chatting with them, I find out they've been doing this every Wednesday for ten years. I buy them a round at about one o'clock, and the bartender gives me a look like "crazy gringo." I guess that's not the custom here. Thank god I don't know the macarena; it could get really embarrassing.

After one more day touring Seville, I take a night train to Valencia. I arrived at six o'clock in the morning, book a private cabin on the night ferry to Mallorca, and spend the day touring Valencia. After a wonderful sleep the ferry arrives at seven. It's too early to find anything open or anyone doing anything, so I sit in front of a rental car agency until nine, when the manager finally arrives. I get a car for $150 for nine days. And a one-bedroom apartment in Palmanova for only $35 per day! I'm happy.

The marathon is on Sunday morning—two half-marathon loops along the coast and into the nasty hills of the interior. I cross the Half in 1:43, and I'm not sure I can continue that pace through the same hills again. But I decide to go for it. I'm feeling good the whole way, "good" being a relative term, of course, and I cross the finish line with a negative split, in 3:29. It's my best run in three or four years. I'm proud knowing that I've run three marathons in three weeks and qualified for Boston in all three!

Now it's time to clean up and meet my sports manager and my son Jason at the airport. Jason has flown from Galveston to Gatwick, met his mom at the airport, and they continued on to Mallorca (with a load of clean clothes). We spend the week touring around the island. The north and west sides are the prettiest—great sandy beaches and high mountains and coastal cliffs. The roads are fairly good on the island but some of the drives through the mountains are pretty scary. The east and south sides are not as pretty, mostly scrubland with a few hills.

It's not summer vacation weather, but we enjoy a week of R and R together. Finally, after being on the road for more than a month, it is time to go back home to prepare for my next marathon.

Marathon #149—Country #27, Rome

Millennium Marathon, Vatican City

January 2000

Although the marathon organizers expected thirty thousand runners, there are only five thousand of us. Clearly, something's not working, or perhaps the pope is simply not the attraction he once was. Not that he's running, or I didn't see him if he did. But maybe the hotel prices, $500 per night to celebrate the millennium, have something to do with the low turnout.

In any case, there is much to see and do in Rome, especially in a four-day visit like we (Nicole, our son Chris, and I) have. You need at least a week to visit the city, so we cram in the week in many hours of hard-core touring each day.

Since there are going to be millions of people/drunks/thieves in central Rome for New Year's eve, I figure we should take as little as possible with us, because there's a good chance we'll lose it. I put all our valuables, passports, and extra money in the safe deposit in the hotel and take only enough cash to get us through the night, plus one credit card for backup. Rather than use my trusty money belt, I decide it's better not to look so obvious when getting money out for things, so I put our cash in my jeans pocket.

Wrong decision. The money never even makes it to Saint Peter's Square, our first destination. It's stolen before we get off the Metro. I know how it happened: the crush and rush of people and a guy with his hands all over me and Chris, and then *poof*, he's gone as soon as the doors open.

On New Year's Day, the pope tries to cheer me up at the start of the marathon in Saint Peter's Square with a blessing, but that doesn't get our money back. Not yet anyway. Have faith, they say. He gives a special blessing to the runners as well, although it's probably an afterthought.

Then we're off! It's sunny and cool—great running weather. The course is fairly flat and passes by all the main tourist attractions in Rome to finish next to the Coliseum. It should be a good day, but my right hamstring is hurting—a pulled muscle from a couple of weeks ago. I start slow, but at five kilometers I have to slow down. At eight kilometers, I'm visiting a medical station to get the hamstring wrapped.

Had the race not started in Vatican City, I would have dropped out at this point. But the rules of the 50+DC Club state that if the race starts and finishes in different countries we can pick either (but not both) to count as the country of the race. Even though I only run 200 meters in Vatican City, I intend to count the country as Vatican City since it is considered a country. And since there may never be another opportunity to do so, I feel I have to finish this marathon. So I jog, walk, stretch, and visit numerous medical stations all the way, but I finish (4:17). A much slower time than I'm used to, but I finish. Phew!

Now it's time to move on. Although we would have liked to spend more time in Rome, we're looking forward to getting out of the city and the crowds. On Sunday morning we pick up a rental car and head for Sorrento. We stop in Pompeii so that I can give Chris a quick tour of the ruins. It's much easier walking around in January than it was last August, when the temp was 100°.

We finally arrive at our hotel in Sorrento. The Bel Air is a four-star hotel built into the cliffs overlooking the Bay of Naples with fantastic views of Sorrento and Naples and a two-hundred-foot drop from the patio into the Tyrrhenian Sea. (Do I ever spoil my family—I am not used to this luxury on my travels!) Surprisingly, there are lots of tourists in Sorrento and Capri, but most are Americans on excursions from Rome. The next day we take a hydrofoil over to Capri, a funicular from the marina to the village of Capri, and a bus up a steep winding road to the village of Anacapri. Chris and I take a chair lift up to the top of Mount Solaro for some fantastic views of the island

and Sorrento across the bay. Capri is a very scenic island but you had better be in shape, because the roads on the island only go up or down!

When it's time to head home, we drive the scenic route along the coast through Amalfi to Solerno to pick up the motorway back to Rome. What a beautiful but scary drive! It is basically a single-lane road with multiple hairpin curves that become really challenging when you meet a tourist bus! Then you hit the motorway where you damn well better get out of the way if you are only driving 100 mph!

But all in all, a great trip with lots of history and lots of scenery.

Marathon #152—Country #30, The

Egyptian Marathon, Egypt

February 2000

Egypt is known for many things: the pyramids, ancient civilization, mummies, the Nile, and sand. And more sand. And more pyramids.

Today, though, I'm off to Egypt for a marathon in Luxor, which will be my twentieth marathon and country completed since we moved to London. This trip is at the top of my list for difficulty and frustration in setting up. Egyptian travel agencies are inefficient and incompetent, and when you try to recommend some solutions to improve their service and business, they just simply ignore you.

But after months of frustration, with phone calls and e-mails unanswered, I finally get everything arranged and confirmed. Nicole and I are off to Cairo via Amsterdam. We arrive in Cairo at 1:20 a.m., purchase our visa stamps, and clear customs. We're surprised to find my cousin Gary Troke and his wife, Sheila, waiting for us. They have a business in Cairo and have lived there for the past six years. The plan was to visit them on our way home, but an unexpected business issue requires that they go to the United States later that week, and they will not be back in time to host us. However, their son Carey will host us, and they offer us the use of their home and car and driver during our visit. They feel bad about the change in plans, and they want to spend some time with us. They drive us to our hotel at the airport where we had hoped to get about four hours of sleep before catching a connecting Egypt

Air flight to Luxor. But after a few drinks and lots of conversation, we end up getting only two hours of sleep. Had I known they would meet us at the airport, I would have canceled the hotel and saved $140.

We arrive in Luxor at 7:30 a.m. On our drive from the airport to the hotel, we see that half the vehicles on the roads are pulled by donkeys or horses! Donkey carts are the main transport for cargo, and horse carriages are as plentiful as taxis for carrying people. The taxis are all at least twenty years old, completely dented and held together with wire and rope. The only modern and well-constructed buildings in Luxor are the international hotels and a few government buildings. Even new apartment buildings look like slums and are ready to fall down. Although poverty and filth are everywhere, there are no beggars. Instead, the poor work and hustle the tourists, and we endure two days of relentless hustling by every taxi and carriage driver and every street vendor. The upside is that everyone is friendly and eager to provide services. If you take a picture of an Egyptian or his donkey, he will demand payment. If he takes your picture with your camera, he will demand payment. If the donkey takes a picture, you ask him to come to the United States and appear on a late-night TV show.

Our hotel is the Luxor Hilton, a supposedly five-star hotel located on the east bank of the Nile. Really, it's comparable to a thirty-year-old Holiday Inn. I say thirty years because that's my estimated age for our TV set and the hotel's telephone system, which is perhaps pulled or operated by more donkeys. Nicole has brought her computer along with the notion of being connected with the office in England; but, clearly, neither the donkeys nor the hotel has mastered the IT connections. It costs me a small fortune to check my stock market activities, and it occurs to me that being hustled by people on the streets iss more relaxing and less frustrating.

Luxor is located in what was the ancient city of Thebes. It contains two major temples. The Karnak temple, dedicated to the god Amon, is the largest temple in the world that is supported by columns. It's massive. The great hall contains 134 columns, all of which are about seventy-five feet tall with a top circumference of forty-five feet. Impressive by standards these days, but even more incredible to imagine the engineering feat, considering it was built thirty-six hundred years ago. No doubt the donkeys would have played a major role in the construction, too. We spend the first afternoon wandering around and listening to various tour guides.

The Karnak Temple is linked to the Luxor Temple via an avenue about one mile long that is lined on both sides with sphinxes. The entrance to the Luxor Temple is flanked by a giant statue of Ramses II and a tall obelisk. There used to be two obelisks but the second one is now in the Place de la Concorde in Paris. Ask the Greeks. They know what it's like to have ancient ruins taken by foreign countries.

The next morning we take a guided tour with some other marathoners to the west bank of the Nile. The Nile runs from southern Egypt—called Upper Egypt in ancient times because the water runs south to north—to the Mediterranean Sea. The Nile Valley is very fertile due to the annual flooding of the river. Both banks support lush vegetation and agricultural crops for about two to three miles inland all along the river. Once you get past that point, bring your buckets, because it changes immediately to desert.

Our bus joins a second bus to form a convoy that is escorted by an armed police vehicle to the tourist sites on the west bank. We pass through barricades about every two miles on the road. At the only bridge in the area, there are machine-gun towers at both ends. This very visible security is the Egyptian response to the terrorist attack two years ago in Luxor, where fifty-seven tourists were killed. Our first stop is the Colossi of Memnon, two giant statues of a pharaoh. Then we travel on through Medinet Habu and past the Temple of Ramses III to the Valley of the Kings. After I get over the surprise of seeing an armored troop carrier with a machine-gun turret guarding the entrance to the valley, (this is the location where the terrorist attack occurred), we proceed with some more history lessons.

During the middle and New Kingdom periods (2060–900 BC), the kings realized that the pyramids made great monuments but were easy to find and loot. So they decided to move their tombs to the Limestone Mountains on the west bank opposite Thebes. Here they dug huge tombs into the solid limestone mountains and then tried to hide them. It should have worked because the area is very rugged and desolate (it reminds me of Utah or Arizona), but the legend is that the workers and their descendants went back and looted the tombs in later years. This also killed the legends/stories that they always killed the workers to keep the location secret.

Because women could not be buried with the men, they chose one valley to bury the kings—the Valley of the Kings and another for the queens—the Valley of the Queens. We only have time to visit four or five tombs.

Then it was on to Deir El-Bahari with our police escort to visit the Temple of Queen Hatshepsut. This temple is built into the cliffs of the Limestone Mountains between the Valley of the Kings and the Valley of the Queens and faces due east toward Karnak Temple. At one time, a road connected them on both sides of the Nile. Since it was not acceptable for a queen or woman to rule Egypt by herself at that time, Queen Hatshepsut used to dress as a man and even wore the false beard used by the kings—and she ruled for twenty-three years.

Finally it's M-day! It's held on a Friday, which is their main religious day. They bus about a thousand runners—two hundred marathoners and the rest 10K runners—in a large convoy escorted by several police vehicles to Queen Hatshepsut's Temple. Since there are many foreigners and Egyptian dignitaries at the race, there are more police and machine guns visible than I've ever seen in my life! The course starts and finishes at the temple and consists of a 10K loop past most of the tourist sites in the area. So yes, we have to do it four times, and it gets boring. Plus we have to endure fumes from the tourist buses and dodge donkeys, donkey carts, and an occasional camel. The worst obstacle is the peasant kids who run beside us begging for money or gifts. But I feel protected, since there are armed police at every intersection and two armored pickup trucks with six police, armed with machine guns, cruising up and down the course

Unfortunately, I started too fast, and my right leg (hamstring) begins to hurt about 10 kilometers into the race. I slow down a bit but not enough, because by twenty miles I'm a "hurting puppy." My right leg hurts, my left leg hurts, my whole damn body hurts! I go into survival mode, just trying to finish without dying. But it's difficult to focus on willing the pain away when you have peasant kids still running along, begging for your headband, your watch, and even your running shorts! During the first three loops I could put on a burst of speed and leave them, but now there are no bursts left. I have to listen to their constant begging and almost trip on them several times. But finally the finish line is in sight, and I struggle over it in 3:49:38—a very disappointing time!

Nicole has hired our favorite taxi driver, Ali to bring her to the finish so that she can take some pictures and we can go back to the hotel immediately and not have to wait for the buses. That turned out to be a wise plan since I'm totally beat and in no mood to wait around.

After a good sports massage and hot bath, I'm ready to face the world again. We hire a felucca for a private sail and lunch on the Nile. We have a crew of two—a captain and a cook/waiter who grills us an excellent lunch served with wine and beer as we cruise along the Nile for two hours, a most pleasant and memorable activity.

It's time to return to Cairo. Egypt Air has a monopoly on air travel within Egypt, which is reflected in its attitude toward customers. After an hour of standing in line for our flight to Cairo and watching several Egyptians butt in line ahead of us (it's what you do here, apparently), Egypt Air announces the plane would be an hour or more late. This is only after a fiery redheaded American woman plays a classic linebacker move and charges across the ticket counter to demand information. She also holds her place in line, which shocks a few Egyptian men trying to push in, and teaches them some English words that normally wouldn't be repeatable even in the United States.

When we arrive in Cairo, Gary's driver is waiting to take us to their apartment, located in Maadi. I also confirm my suspicion that the Italians must have taught the Egyptians how to drive, because the first thing that you notice is that there are no rules! Every car in Egypt is dented. There are cars unique to Egypt called *Dents*. But the Egyptians throw a few more challenges into the game. In two days of driving around Cairo, a city of eighteen million people, I saw a maximum of eighteen traffic lights, and only two work. And everyone ignores those! At night the Egyptians drive with their headlights off! They believe that using their lights will kill the battery, so they don't turn them on but will flash them to warn another vehicle or pedestrian to get out of the way. It's quite unnerving at first, but they seem to handle it well.

Carey had booked a private tour guide for us during our stay. With a private driver and guide we're able to visit all of the major tourist sites in and around Cairo in the two days. So on Sunday morning, we're off! First stop is the Cairo Museum. Our guide took us to all the major exhibits and explained the history and culture of Egypt. I definitely recommend that anyone start their Egypt trip with a visit to the museum. We also visit King Tut's treasures. The gold mask and headdress fashioned in his likeness is a spectacular piece of craftsmanship, considering it was made three thousand years ago. The coffin that contained his mummy was built of solid gold. When you consider that King Tut was only a minor king in Egyptian history, it is sad to think of what treasures were buried with the other kings and have been lost forever to the tomb robbers. Our last stop is at a special room that houses many of the mummies of the kings and queens. They're interesting but kind of ugly and disgusting!

Then it's time to visit the pyramids at Ghiza. I always thought that the pyramids are far out in the desert, and they were when they were built, but now the city has been built right out to them. The three pyramids of Cheops, Chephren, and Mycerinus, and the Sphinx, as well as other smaller pyramids, can all be viewed from the comfort of a bar from across the street if you prefer.

The next, and last day, we set out for the pyramids at Sakkarah. The largest pyramid is the step-pyramid of Zoser. It has six levels and is the oldest pyramid in the world, circa 2700 BC. The necropolis or burial grounds at Sakkarah are the largest in Egypt. On the way to Sakkarah our driver gets lost and drives through the village of Sakkarah, and it's like stepping back a thousand years in time! The village has no paved roads, only a rough dirt path down the middle of the village with an open ditch on one side that serves as sewer, garbage dump, etc. On each side of the path are mud and mud-brick houses with roofs of straw or palm fronds. No electricity or water except for a central well. The village women carry water, stacks of vegetables, and sugar cane on their heads, and the men ride donkeys. And this village is only twenty miles from the outskirts of Cairo!

Marathon #159—Country #37,

Paris Marathon, France

April 2000

The planning for this trip started over a year ago. As soon as we confirmed we were moving to England, a few of my running buddies from Dallas said they would run the London Marathon if we were still here in April 2000. When we arrived in England, I discovered that the Paris Marathon is to be held the weekend before London so I challenge them to run back-to-back marathons with me.

These friends are part of a running group in Dallas called the "BrookBachRock" (BBR), which is an abbreviation for Brookhaven College, Bachman Lake, and White Rock Lake—the three locations in Dallas where we would meet for training runs. We've run together for over sixteen years, adding and losing various members throughout the period. This group of friends gave me the nickname "Maddog" for my tenacity and perseverance in always striving to be the first to cross the finish line in a race and even during training runs—much to their chagrin and pain!

Our initial plan was to submit our entries through the normal lottery for the London Marathon and use the Wallace Hilton as our base. Since London gets over two hundred thousand entries for only thirty thousand slots, they use a lottery system. Many local runners in England have to try their luck for years before they ever get accepted. We had expected/hoped that overseas entries might get special treatment, but no way! We combined our entries under one check, which meant all or nothing, and we were both surprised and disappointed when we received a rejection notice. But not to be daunted, we decided to buy our way in by purchasing a race package through Marathon Tours in Boston. The operators get guaranteed entry slots for overseas runners to combine with travel packages. The advantage is that they provide all the travel arrangements and guarantee an entry. The disadvantage is the added time and cost because you must accept their travel itineraries, and this factor causes Holly to drop out. But the others are still game and decide to use Marathon Tours to book both London and Paris for them.

My plan is to meet the BBR in Paris, run the marathon, and return to our home for a few days before they moved into the package hotel in London. Nicole has coordinated a business trip to Paris so we can take our car and make a final wine run also. In the final few days, there's a surprising but pleasant change in plans. Holly decides to come to Paris just for the Paris Marathon, and John brings his wife, Debbie, along, also for the Paris portion of the trip. So there are five members of the BBR (Maddog, John, Fred, Dick, and Holly) and three spouses (Nicole, Debbie, and Sue) in the final count when we meet in Paris a few days before the marathon.

To say it's a fun time would be putting it in very simple terms. Apart for the odd split of the group, we terrorize Paris together. We do the city tour thing and wander around the Louvre. Some venture off to explore the Eiffel Tower, Notre Dame Cathedral, and Montmartre. But we always meet up for dinner, which includes a great dinner cruise on the Seine on Friday evening. We all adopt the Maddog marathon diet—lots of food and copious amounts of beer and wine.

The marathon starts on the Champs Elysees next to the Arc de Triomphe. Fortunately, the hotel selected by Marathon Tours is right next to the arch, so we're able to walk to the start. The course passes through or by most of the major tourist sites such as Place de la Concorde, the Jardin des Tuileries, the Louvre, Place de la Bastille, and the Bois de Vincennes. We run past the Parc Zoologique and the Hippodrome de Vincennes, back along the Right Bank of the Seine past Notre Dame, the Grand and Petit Palais, the Tour Eiffel, and the Palais de Chaillot, and through the Bois de Boulogne, and the finish is on Avenue Foch next to the Arc de Triomphe.

With over thirty thousand runners in the narrow streets of Paris, the race is really crowded. It's difficult at times trying to stay together, but we work out a system to keep each other in sight, especially at the water stations and even for relief breaks. Our goal is to finish in 3:45. We run at an almost perfect pace, and even though all of us go through a lull at some point, we pull each other along to finish hand in hand in 3:45:12. Later, we continue where we left off—celebrating with lots of food, copious amounts of beer and wine, and big talk about the upcoming London marathon.

Marathon #160, London Marathon, England

April 2000

Since I've already run London (and England), I can't count the country a second time.

On the Saturday before the run, Maddog, John, Fred, and Dick reluctantly accept the fact that the weather is going to be miserable during the race. But we're pleasantly surprised on marathon day to see sunshine! By the time the race starts, we've stripped down to shorts and a singlet. Like in Paris, we're all running in a Texas-flag singlet, which brings many cheers from the spectators who recognize the flag.

The marathon course starts in Greenwich and passes many of the major tourist sites in London such as the Cutty Sark, Canary Wharf, and the Tower of London. We run over the Tower Bridge, along the Thames River, past the London Eye, Big Ben, and the Parliament buildings to finish in Saint James Park.

Again we pledge that it's all or none—especially for the second one. I'm quite aware that I'm escorting three (running) virgins on the second leg of their first-ever back-to-back marathons. Our primary goal is that everyone finishes—our secondary goal is to beat the 3:45 Paris time.

It take us just over two minutes to even get across the start line, but, more alarmingly, it takes almost ten minutes to run the first mile. There are so many runners at times, it's so congested, that it's almost impossible not to trip over others. There are at least thirty thousand runners, and the narrow streets squeeze us together; we're like a slow-moving mass of vertical sardines. The only difference is we're wearing running shoes, which are not so aptly titled at this moment. It's also really difficult for us BBR folks to stay together. There's no option for us but to run faster later in the race when the sardine pack thins out.

We make up some of our penalty time in the first half and continue the strong, even pace through the second half. We feel like we are flying! It's a big moment when the finish line comes into sight. All four of us cross the line hand in hand in 3:44:22! The three virgins accomplish a tremendous feat—they run the second leg of their first back-to-back marathons faster than the first, and they run a negative split in this second marathon!

After showers, big talk, and a short rest, Nicole and Sue join us, and we enjoy a bottle of French champagne to celebrate our success. Then it's off to the nearest pub to eat greasy food (to replace all the fat cells burned during the race, really) and wash it down with beer.

Marathon #163—Country #40,

Copenhagen Marathon, Denmark

May 2000

Nicole and I travel to Copenhagen for our last marathon and trip before we leave England and return home to the USA.

After touring around Copenhagen for one day, Nicole and I leave the city for a day to take in nearby sights. We pass the Eremitageslot—a royal hunting lodge built by King Christian VI in 1736—before arriving at the Kronburg Slot (slot = castle). Kronburg Slot overlooks the port of Helsingor at the narrowest point of the Oresund. Sweden is only 4.5 kilometers away. The castle was built in 1420 as a defensive fort, at which the kings of Denmark charged a toll or tax for all ships passing through the Oresund. It's more famous, though, as the setting for Shakespeare's Hamlet—the play was based on this castle and a Danish king. Live performances of Hamlet are performed each year in the courtyard of Kronburg Slot.

It's Sunday and thus marathon day. The course starts and finishes in the center of the city close to the Radhuspladsen—the city square next to the city hall. We start with sunny and warm weather (it turns to light rain by the end of the race). The course is flat, which is great, but I'm not liking this race. We only run about three or four miles through the historic and interesting part of the city. The rest of my run is through the suburbs and an industrial area near the docks. The entire second half is on bike paths and sidewalks next to the roads, which entails lots of stepping up and down—hard on the legs and dangerous when you're tired.

For about 16 kilometers, I find myself running with a gentleman from Copenhagen, two years younger than me, who is running his forty-first marathon this year in an attempt to set a world record for the most number of marathons run in one year. The record is one hundred and he hopes to run 105! I'm doing okay, time-wise and pain-wise, but then I hit that invisible brick wall at 36 kilometers. The last six kilometers are not fun! I tell myself, oh, I don't know, hundreds or thousands of times, "Just one more step. Just run one more step, John." Pathetic as it sounds, it works as I will myself to cross the finish line in 3:49. I'm not pleased with my time, but at least I've finished, I'm alive, and I'm injury-free.

A quick shower later, and Nicole and I head out to spend the rest of the day enjoying Copenhagen. The race's entry fee includes free entry into the Tivoli Gardens, so off we go. Despite many gardens, concert halls and stages, an amusement park, and several restaurants, we don't find that appealing or interesting. We have a small snack and a beer and leave, opting instead to wander down the Stroget to the Nyhavn.

The Nyhavn or "new port" was built in the seventeenth century and is now one of the major tourist sites in Copenhagen. It's very colorful, with lots of great restaurants. We enjoy an excellent dinner and wine while watching the beautiful women of Copenhagen stroll by. Well, I do, anyway. The view isn't cheap—it's Scandinavia, after all—but it's our last dinner and trip in Europe for a while, so it's worth it.

You see, we're heading back, for good, to Dallas. From there the movers will come to load our stuff from storage, and we'll depart the next day for Florida. It's been a fantastic experience living in England, and I've been spoiled being able to run megamarathons. I have completed thirty-one marathons in thirty-one countries during our year in England. My first World Record! And during my travels and marathons I have learned that nobody has ever completed a marathon in every country in Europe. I become obsessed with that goal.

Marathon #165—Country #41,

Eurasia Marathon, Turkey

November 2000

Planning for this trip began back in March while I was running the Turin marathon with my friend Edson. He indicated he would be running the Eurasia Marathon in Istanbul. We both need to complete a marathon in Turkey as part of our quest to run a marathon in every European country.

The Eurasia Marathon has the distinction of being the only marathon in the world that runs through two continents. The historic old city and business sections of the city are located in Europe; the residential sections are mostly located in Asia. The old city lies across an inlet called the Golden Horn across from the downtown area called Taksim where most of the tourist hotels and restaurants are located.

We're staying in Maslak. Although it's only about six miles from Taksim, the traffic in Istanbul is horrendous, and public transportation is poor. Istanbul has 15 million people, and I think they all drive, but the road system is built for about two hundred cars.

It's Friday, and we do some sightseeing—a full-day guided tour of Istanbul. It's an incredible full-scale assault on our senses. We first visit Saint Sophia, a Byzantine basilica built by Emperor Justinian in AD 537; it's "new," having been built on the same site as the first church, which was completed in 360. Today it's a museum. Then we head to the Sultanahmet (or Blue Mosque) renowned for the millions of blue tiles used in the interior decoration. Then it's on to the Hippodrome where the Romans held their chariot races, and then we head to the Grand Bazaar—a labyrinth of streets and alleys containing over four thousand shops—which reminds me a lot of the *souks* in Dubai.

It's been an amazing day, taking in all these places. So it's with some additional amazement that I discover its only lunchtime.

After a nice Turkish lunch that I can't describe (but it was tasty), we continue to the Suleymaniye Mosque and the Topkapi Palace. The palace is the former residence of the Ottoman sultans from the fifteenth to the nineteenth centuries and has been converted into a museum. It contains the famous emerald dagger, star of the film *Topkapi*, and the eighty-six-carat Spoonmaker's diamond. Finally, we have the compulsory stop at a carpet factory. It's actually quite interesting, as they explain how to distinguish carpets from the various regions of Turkey based on their designs and color of the dyes. I can buy a silk carpet here for a paltry $40,000. I think not, however, unless it's a plush, magic one with unlimited mileage and a good stereo. Windows would be nice, too.

Back at the hotel we discuss our race-day plan with the concierge, who quickly points out a serious glitch. For starters, the Bosphorus Bridge will be closed to traffic Sunday morning until after the race has started. No problem we say, we'll have a taxi drop us at the entrance to the bridge on the European side and walk across to Asia.

Apparently not. Both ways have been permanently closed to pedestrian traffic because too many Turks are jumping into the Bosphorus to kill themselves. Not what we have planned, of course, but it's a showstopper for sure. So our final plan is to have a taxi take us across a second bridge, farther down, and drive for god knows how long through the suburbs in Asia and drop us off at the entrance to the Bosphorus Bridge on the Asian side. It sounds tiring, so we head to bed. At least we have a plan. In these moments it's easy to forget you've got to run 26.2 miles as well.

Sunday arrives much quicker than I'd hoped. We're up early to get the concierge to explain to a taxi driver exactly where to take us. There is lots of nodding, so we think it's all good. The driver then proceeds to scare the crap out of both of us as he carries on a one-sided conversation in Turkish while driving like Michael Shumacher in the Indy 500! When we finally arrive, I fall out of the car and kiss the ground. I almost kiss the driver when I discover we are actually where we want to be, and it's forty-five minutes before the start.

Since we have no idea where to find the baggage bus, we'd decided not to take any baggage or warm-up clothes with us. But I did bring the customary black garbage bag. As we approach the start area, I put on my trusty garbage bag.

All hell breaks loose.

Two TV stations including CNN-TURK and a few newspaper teams descend upon me like vultures. Have I offended local culture or ancient morals? Is there an embargo on black plastic bags?

They want to interview me. Good grief. Me?! Clearly I'm being confused with someone important. At home, large sunglasses are a sign that the wearer is important. Here, it seems, it's the wearing of a garbage bag. The interview goes something like this:

Q: Where are you from?

A: The USA.

Q: Did you come here just to run the marathon?

A: Yes, and to visit your beautiful country.

Q: Are you going to win the Eurasia Marathon?

A: No (laugh), I'll be happy just to finish healthy.

Q: (As they touch the garbage bag) Why are you wearing this disguise or costume?

A: In the USA and Northern Europe, many runners wear these bags to keep warm and dry until the race starts, and then we throw them away.

Q: Are you a top runner? Are you going to win the race?

Q: Can we take your picture for our newspaper?

By now, more photographers and a big crowd are converging on me. I'm feeling a mass frenzy coming on. Any minute I could be picked up and passed around the crowds. I decide to rip the damn bag off and quickly blend back into obscurity among the other runners.

It's time for the race to start. I'm relieved; this is the easy part of the day. The gun shoots, and we're off. We soon cross the bridge with some fantastic views of Istanbul, the Bosphorus, and the Sea of Marmara. I quickly realize I have another problem. In the preceding drama I never had a chance for my last-minute pee. And looking out at the vast expanse of water is not helping things. I'm certainly not going to stop by the side of the road and relieve myself, as most runners do in a marathon, until I see some locals pull over. I've had enough attention for one day.

Fortunately, a few miles after we cross the bridge, I see some locals finally pulling over to do their deed, and I join them. Now I am ready to run; I find it difficult to run with my legs crossed.

It's a great run, steeped in history. The marathon crosses a bridge over the Golden Horn into the old city, where it passes many of the tourist sites and makes it way to the shores of the Sea of Marmara. It then heads west along the sea until the fifteen-mile point, where we turn and loop back to finish in the football stadium. Later in the race, we're sucking in wonderful gas fumes as roads are reopened. Edson catches up to me at mile 15 and we run together until mile 23, when he lowers the hammer and leaves me behind so quickly that I need to look down to see if my feet are still moving. I just don't have the energy today to respond, so I follow him across the finish line in 3:47.

After a quick shower and a massage, we head over to a small fishing village on the shores of the Bosphorus and find a great seafood restaurant and some wine. We enjoy a great meal, but it's not cheap—about the same as big-city prices in the United States. Then it's time to go back to the hotel and get ready to leave: Edson is going back to work in New York, and Nicole and I are on to the Aegean coast of Turkey. Yes…work sucks, all right.

You pick up some wonderful stories when touring, and the Aegean coast has plenty to share. If the word "littered" is acceptable, it is safe to say that the Aegean coast is littered with important historical and biblical sites. We can't visit them all, as that would make this book too long.

Our first stop after arriving in Izmir (Homer's birthplace, but not Bart's dad) is the ancient ruins of Ephesus. There have been four cities built on the same site/area dating back to 3000 BC. We were visiting the ruins of the second city, built and inhabited by the Greeks and Romans from 300 BC through AD 800.

Only 10 percent of the ruins have been excavated so far. A few buildings, such as the Library of Celsus—the fourth largest library in the world at that time—have been partially restored and are quite impressive. Across the street from the library is a brothel. In its day, it had its own indoor hot pools and bathrooms (with running water, no less), but the most ingenious feature was a secret tunnel that ran under the street to the library. When an angry wife came banging on the door of the brothel demanding that her husband come home, she was informed that her husband was at the library. Meanwhile hubby would race through the tunnel and magically appear coming out of the library with the book of the day. I don't think things have changed much in two thousand years.

The next day we pass through Smyrna (another Church of Revelation) on our way to the ancient Roman city of Pergamum. Pergamum was the Roman capital of the Aegean region even though it was smaller than Ephesus. It was built on the top of a mountain for defensive purposes. Initially the Romans were able to supply the city with water from wells and catch basins that they built into the side of the mountain. But as the city grew, so did its water problem.

The emperor declared a contest. The winner who could provide the best solution would marry his daughter. Quite the incentive. The solution was to build an aqueduct to another mountain range thirty-five miles to the west that had snow and much more rain. Since that range was two thousand feet higher, gravity and water pressure would force the water to the top of the city. However, there was a major problem. The water pressure on the route up the mountain was too high for the clay pipes to handle. So they wrapped the clay pipes in a lead sheath and encased those pipes in solid rock. Examples of those pipes still remain at the ruins. The winning engineer didn't marry the emperor's daughter. He got so excited when the system worked that he fell off the defense walls and was killed.

Marathon #172—Country #45,

Sahara Marathon, Algeria

February 2001

In the fall of 2000, a few of my running buddies from the BBR called me with a request. We'd been together to run the Paris and London marathons and had a great time. We decided to meet up again somewhere. I was given the task of finding an exotic marathon destination in 2001. I soon discovered a first-ever marathon in February to be run in the Sahara Desert. Everyone agreed that this would be a real adventure. We would share a tent in the desert and sleep with Clyde the camel.

Then the fun starts! Buddy #1 says, "Great, but it's too close to the Boston Marathon in April." Buddy #2 suddenly decides he has to go on a motorcycle ride in Mexico. Buddy #3 says sure—until just after I, the self-proclaimed village idiot, go ahead and buy nonrefundable air tickets and a nonrefundable marathon package! The village idiot realizes he is going to have Clyde the camel all to himself. And not just for two days as originally planned by the Sahara Desert Marathon race director, but now for four days.

As Nicole wisely figured, it didn't make sense tagging along with the four marathon amigos on their most excellent adventure; it was left to me to go by myself. But I manage to coerce Nicole into coming partway—to Spain—with me, since the race is being staged from Madrid. Fortunately, I find out just before we leave that at least three members of the 50+DC Club are also running the marathon, so I'll at least know some people there in the sands.

I've already spent a lot of time in Spain and Madrid on previous trips, so I know what the main attractions are. We visit the Royal Monastery of San Lorenzo in El Escorial, about twenty-eight miles out of Madrid. It's considered to be the eighth wonder of the world. It was commissioned by King Felipe II as an act of thanks for the victory of San Quintin in 1557, when the Spanish army conquered the French on August 10, the feast day of Saint Laurence. All of the Spanish monarchy of the past five centuries are buried in the tombs. It's amazing what vast amounts of New World gold can do for a construction industry. The complex is made of granite, and I counted 15 cloisters, 13 oratories, 86 staircases, 88 fountains, at least 1,600 paintings, 9 towers, and more than 70 sculptures. It was completed in 1584, twenty-one years after it was started. The library is incredible, with about 45,000 documents from the fifteenth and sixteenth centuries alone. It was made a World Heritage Site by UNESCO in 1984.

Then it was on to the Valle de los Caìdos (Valley of the Fallen) where General Franco built a huge cross (150 meters high) and carved a church inside a solid-granite mountain to honor and bury those killed in the Spanish Civil War. It also serves as his mausoleum.

The marathon package/tour requires that all runners be in Madrid for the departure of the charter flights on Friday, February 23. On Thursday night the race organizers host an informal dinner where they give us last-minute details. Since the charter flights leave at 6:00 p.m., Nicole decides to stay over in Madrid one more day to tour the city and then go to Barcelona, where she stays until I return on the twenty-eighth.

As we all leave the hotel for the airport, we start to get an idea of how disorganized the race organization is and will be—a precursor to four days of relentless frustration.

We're left on our own to get to the airport. Some of us who have already reserved an airport shuttle bus are asked to carry at least one box of race supplies with us (e.g., paper cups/plates, bottled water, camel, etc). Upon arriving at the Air Algiers counter at the Madrid airport, we're advised that the flight is two hours late. But they make up for it by giving us a dinner on the flight as well as wine. Not bad for an airline owned by a Muslim country going to a Muslim country.

We fly directly to an Algerian military base at Tindouf. Tindouf is just past the middle of nowhere. It has been deliberately built up, (about 35,000 people live here), partly because of its importance and location close to the Moroccan, Sahrawi, and Mauritanian borders. It is also the closest airport to the refugee camps—and the most secure—since Algeria is experiencing many problems with Muslim terrorists/fundamentalists trying to overthrow the government.

Since the Algerian government supports the refugees and also supports the marathon, we have no problem with immigration or customs. In fact, the normally difficult procedure of getting a visa beforehand has been rubber-stamped for all runners, and they even waived the fifty-dollar visa fee. We're passed through quickly and find ourselves unloading our own baggage and supplies, loading them onto trucks, and loading ourselves onto buses. We're then provided an armed military escort to the refugee camps that apparently we will call home for a few days.

Refugee camps? Twenty-five years ago, Spain pulled out of Western Sahara and left the country and people to rule themselves. Morocco immediately invaded the country, claiming that it had been their territory before Spain took it away. To make a long story short, Morocco kicked the shit out of the Western Saharan people, the Sahrawis. They bombed, burned, looted, etc. About one-third of the one million Sahrawis fled into the desert in the eastern part of the country. Morocco then built a ten-foot sand berm down the middle of the country from north to south (Morocco to Mauritania) and continued to bomb the Sahrawis in the eastern section, causing them to flee farther east into the Sahara inside Algeria's borders. Morocco cannot touch them there without creating a war with Algeria. Algeria, Russia, Spain, and Cuba are some of the countries that backed (and still support) the Sahrawis; the United States and Europe support Morocco; and most of the rest of the world doesn't care! We marathoners find ourselves in some interesting places sometimes.

The Sahrawis have settled into four camps in the Sahara in Algeria, named after the hometowns that they fled in Western Sahara. They have no money, no resources, and few belongings. They depend solely upon the

United Nations and their supporting nations to exist. The UN provides them with shelter, food, and water. Their allies/supporters provide education, training, and arms for their military. It sounds extremely bleak, but the Sahrawis claim they would rather live this way than live under Moroccan rule.

Knowing that they can't beat Morocco in a military war, they have wisely decided to try the political path and are trying to be recognized by as many countries and world organizations as possible. This Sahara Marathon is a subtle attempt to get recognition by world sports organizations and to be accepted as an Olympic country for the 2004 Olympics. In other words, we're part of the game.

At 1:00 a.m., we arrive at the Sahrawi refugee camp in L'Ayoun. The camps have limited electricity and other facilities. There are no streetlights, and it is very, very dark! We're to be housed in tents and hosted by a Sahrawi family. As it turns out, Sahrawi families have given up their homes or tents and have moved in with family or friends, so that six runners can be housed in each home. Each refugee camp is comprised of communities called *dirrahs*, made up of about six families or homes. Three to six runners are assigned to a dirrah with a host who speaks the language of the runners. I'm to be in tent 1 with five other male runners from the United States. After finding our baggage, we're introduced to our Sahrawi host. He leads us through the pitch-black desert to our tent. I'm so tired I just accept my sheet and blanket, lay them out on the desert floor, and go to sleep. I could be sleeping on camel for all I know, or a moving bed of angry scorpions, but I'll deal with that in the morning.

8:00 a.m. Time to get up. Where's the bathroom?

I'm directed to a small adobe hut about two hundred feet from the tent. It looks like the outhouse at my grandparent's farm but I don't recall flying back to Canada last night. I see, though, that there is no bench, just a hole in the desert floor, and my grandparents never had a desert at their place. I'm still trying to wake up, but fortunately, I'm on my game enough to have remembered to bring some toilet paper with me. I'll leave the rest of these moments to your imagination if you want to go there, but quickly afterward I'm thinking I need to wash.

The UN has to bring in water from wells located at Tindouf and distribute it to metal drums located throughout the camp. The refugees go to the drums with a bucket to collect the water needed for their home. Washing seems like a waste of precious water. We quickly discover that the refugees don't wash or bathe—instead they just spray themselves and their clothes with perfume two or three times a day to mask body odor. We're offered the same amenities. Fortunately, I've also brought a box of wipes to at least clean my hands and face.

Breakfast. Truly, it is scrumptious. Some fresh homemade bread that is very tasty if you can forget about the gritty sand that has blown into the dough. The bread is served with honey, maybe some goat cheese, and a cup of coffee. We're assuming the host family has been paid or given extra money from our entry fees to cover the cost of feeding us; otherwise, they would never have had enough food.

With a decent sleep, ablutions taken care of, and a full tummy, I'm now keen to explore the place. My host stops me before I leave the tent. It's dangerous to go outside without glasses and a turban—glasses to protect my eyes and a turban to protect the rest of my head. From sand! There is always a wind blowing, and the sand is so fine that it gets into every pore and opening in your body. We're all given a black turban and he teaches us how to put them on. Now it's safe to venture outside. I soon find myself on the edge of the camp where they house the animals—camels, goats, and a few chickens. The chickens provide eggs, goats provide milk, and the camels carry people and supplies. And, as I was soon to discover, all three provide the only meat and protein available to the refugees. As I walk around, several children approach me and ask a barrage of questions in Spanish. It turns out that the three basic Spanish lessons that I took before the trip were very helpful, as I'm able to carry on a very simple conversation with the kids. We'd been advised to bring presents for the kids, and I hand out a lot of pencils and crayons. It makes them very happy, and I feel pretty good, too. It doesn't seem much, and I wish I could do more. But if nothing else, these kinds of moments make you appreciate what you have at home.

It's time to go back to the tent and find out what the plans are for the day. And time to learn the next most important lesson of the trip! Time has no meaning in the desert and especially for the Sahrawis! They have been existing in the desert for twenty-five years with absolutely nothing to do but try to survive. If an event or activity—say a meal or festivity—is scheduled for one o'clock, it's best to plan on it being at least two or three hours late. But "late" is a Western concept. If your main concern is staying alive, you don't really care if you eat at one or at four, as long as you eat. Nonetheless, we have an itinerary for our four-day visit that includes exact times for eating. I guess they had to as we'd no doubt be suspicious if the itinerary read, "Food sometime."

We learn that the only useful information on the itinerary is that a specific event might happen on a given day! The first lunch for us four hundred runners, for example, is a community buffet for lunch *and dinner*. Our first lunch was scheduled for one o'clock. We wait at the designated site, a community administration center, for three hours. At four they open the doors for lunch. Fortunately, I'm near the front of the line and rush to a buffet table where I quickly grab whatever food is available—I'm not sure what, exactly, it's all a blur—and eat standing up. By the time the end of the line comes in, there is no food left.

I think the food included bread, some salads with mostly onion and tomatoes, a stew and some roasted camel or goat meat. Goat and camel are tough and stringy, no matter how they are prepared. I have great difficulty cutting off a chunk of camel or goat from the roast, and I'm almost too exhausted from that effort to actually attempt to chew it. I decline to eat the salads because I'm fearful of dodgy local water supplies and all it could do for my stomach, among other things. Fortunately every meal has bottles of water or Cokes.

It's been an amazing first day. Apart from lining up forever for food, we've been treated to several cultural events by the local Sahrawis, including camel races and dances. I've worked out that you simply show up about two or three hours late to enjoy them. Apparently, there is a marathon coming up, but that seems to be the last thing on my mind right now.

I decide to explore some more of the refugee camp. I watch a Sahrawi man building a new adobe hut for his family. I wish building new homes were this easy back in the United States. After deciding where he wants his home, he digs up the sandy clay loam of the desert, mixes the earth with water and makes mud blocks (I'm sure there's more to it, but it looks like the way I made mud pies when I was younger). He then sets them down in the sun to dry. The finished bricks are dry and brittle, so they'd dissolve quickly with water. But since it last rained a couple of years ago, he's probably figuring rain is not a problem. Certainly not compared to all the other problems these people face daily.

After the bricks harden, he mixes more earth with water to use as a mortar and builds his hut. When he's done with this, he constructs a tin roof and places it on top (for that seems a good place to put it), and weighs it down with bricks and stones.

At 11:00 p.m., we eat our eight o'clock dinner. It's marvelous. Around midnight, I retire to my five-star desert floor bed for another night's rest. Nothing compares to going to bed on a good bowl of hot camel stew. Who knows what the night will bring? It's winter here in the desert, remember, so the temperature will drop to the freezing level tonight and every night, although the days warm up to the low sixties. Pleasant, some might say. Our host told us this morning that the summer highs would normally reach 50°C (about 120°F)!

I'm lying on the desert floor full of camel stew and wearing a warm-up/jogging suit. I've got the single heavy blanket our host gave me, and I'm quite comfortable. It's a good feeling. Except for my head, which is currently resting on the same material as the carpet and is filled with what may be the hardest substance known to mankind. It's called a pillow, of course, but if I lower my head too quickly I'll end up with a concussion for sure. The home builder could use some of these pillows. Fortunately, I've brought along several old running T-shirts to give to the refugees, and I use them to fashion a pillow. Nobody will get any T-shirts until the final day, but I'll get some sleep.

The next day, we'll call it Sunday, we're told the marathon is being moved up one day—from Tuesday to Monday. We're also asked to repack our bags because we'll be moving to a new camp at Smara, where the race will finish. And I'd worked so hard to make a pillow. Oh well. Apart from that news, the rest of the day is spent enjoying more Sahrawi events, lots of napping and waiting for meals. The Kenyans sleep a lot when they're training, and I can't complain. We'll be running 26.2 miles, and in the desert, so I think some rest the day before the race makes a lot of sense. At eight, I decide to give up waiting for dinner. I dine, instead, on that other well-known desert running delicacy, a Power Bar, two in fact, as I'm letting it all go tonight, and wash these down with a carbo drink. I head to bed, redesign my pillow du jour, and fall into a deep slumber that includes *Lawrence of Arabia*. I'm sleeping, though, which means at least my body is resting even though my mind is racing with thoughts of camels, sand, and a monkey wearing Asics called Jibar.

It's Monday! M-day! We load our bags onto some trucks that will take them to the next camp and head for the start line. It's a big day here. Lots of Sahrawi dignitaries, including the president and other politicians, all of whom seem to have a military career. There are dozens of camels and riders dressed in their tribal colors, and about two hundred marathoners—110 foreigners and ninety Sahrawis. There is also a half-marathon and 10K race that start at a later time. A total of about four hundred runners, half of whom are foreigners.

Incredibly, the marathon starts on time at 9:00 a.m. The weather is near perfect for the race, it's sunny, and the temperature is about 40°F. More important, the wind is not strong enough to stir up the sand. I'm wearing a fanny pack with two water bottles and a pouch that carries an emergency medical kit, compass, etc. It also carries my turban in case a sand storm comes up during the race. Imagine the world's elite runners preparing for such an event. Every runner is advised to carry a water bottle to refill at the water/aid stations because there are no cups along the way—the airline apparently forgot to load these. I feel quite heavy and loaded down but the alternative—not wearing these things—is foolhardy and downright dangerous. The water bottles keep falling out, and I know that will bug the crap out of me in the race. That would infuriate Maddog in a race at home, but here it's different.

We're off. We run the first kilometer out of the camp on a soft sand road/ track that leads to a paved highway. I'm assuming it's a paved road between some Algerian military installations. We turn and run on that road for the next three kilometers, and I'm thinking this is not bad at all, apart from my damn water bottle falling out of the pack every 200 meters. My joy with the road is short-lived, however. At the four-kilometer mark the course turns north, right into the wind. We then head straight across the Sahara—no road, no tracks, no trail—for what will be, gulp, the next 38 kilometers. Oh dear!

Part of the desert is compacted sand covered with billions of small sharp rocks (I counted them). The rest of the desert is soft, deep sand. I'm glad I'm wearing worn trail shoes because the tiny rocks are very treacherous to run on. But the sand is worse. It takes two to three times the effort to run through the deep sand. Much of the course is flat but there are many, many hills or dunes that just seem to roll on forever, and then some. The course is marked about every three kilometers, which is a long way in the desert, with rock markers and/or old tires, and there are water/aid stations about every three kilometers. I always have another runner in sight, ahead of me, so I don't have any navigation problems. A few of the runners do get lost for a brief period, but no one gets seriously lost or injured. Given where we are and what could happen with sandstorms and the like, we're probably very lucky.

There are very few distance markers, so it's difficult to tell where I am in the race. At the halfway mark, though, I pass another refugee camp called Aoserd. I'm shocked to discover that my time is 1:59. I've been running as hard as I can, and already my legs feel like they've been beaten up with a two-by-four. My quads and calves are killing me, and they normally never hurt during a race. With half of the race remaining, I know it's going to be a long tough day, and my hopes of a sub-four-hour marathon are being blown away. I decide to keep on running for as long as possible and not to walk!

The second half of the course is harder than the first. By about 28 kilometers, I'm starting to go out of my way and off course to find rocks to run on because it's so much easier than running on the deep, soft, sucking sand. It becomes a tactical error—I trip on a rock and fall. At exactly that moment both of my calves cramp and lock up. I'm in excruciating pain. I drop immediately as if I've been gunned down. I'm writhing around on the desert sands and tiny fragments of rock, looking for a position to ease the cramps and pain and trying to stretch and massage both legs. Eventually, I'm able to massage the cramps and ease the pain so that I can at least walk, albeit gingerly, a few minutes later. Holy crap! Whose idea was it to run in the desert?

After what seems like an hour or so, but was really only a few minutes, I'm back running and with only minor discomfort. What a relief. The last 10 kilometers of the course follows an ancient riverbed into the camp at Smara. It's flat now, but the sand is really, really deep and soft. As I approach the camp, I see the finish line with lots of people standing by and flags all around. My time is about 4:25. I might break four and a half hours!

As I near the finish line, a volunteer approaches and tells me I need to make a ninety-degree turn and run a scenic loop through the camp *before* I reach the finish line. I'm gutted.

Actually, I've never felt so pissed off and frustrated at the end of a marathon as I am now. But I can't do anything about it. And I certainly shouldn't be feeling sorry for myself. So I pull my big-boy panties up and struggle on. I finally cross the finish line in a time of 4:33—the longest time I have ever taken to complete a marathon. At first I'm very disappointed with both my time and my performance. Until I talk to the other runners and discover most runners have taken an hour and a half to two hours longer than normal. Many of the runners complain that the course has to be at least five kilometers too long.

It's just like home. But I'm heartened somewhat by the conversations as they make me focus on the reality of what we've all accomplished here—myself, in particular. In fact, not that I would say this out loud here, but I'm feeling a bit silly right now as I wander around. Why on earth would I possibly think I'd have a great marathon time? I feel my body humbling by the second as I process all of this. Heck, my race could have been much, much worse. And I think of all the things that could have gone wrong—the weather, falling and hitting my head, getting lost, a sandstorm, bitten by scorpions. These are a few of my favorite things. So it didn't take me too long, and now I'm feeling good again. Let's face it, running an extra three minutes to finish outside 4:30 should not make my world a worse place.

Mind you, I struggled with the damn bum bag for 42.2 kilometers, and I didn't need it, except for the water bottle! But I didn't know that until right now, and how could I possibly risk running without it? I may be a Maddog when I run, but I'm not stupid.

Now, though, it's time to find my bags, my new home (tent) in Smara, and enjoy a promised shower and rest. Hmmm. I'm assuming that's still possible.

After an hour of looking, I find my bags with my soap, towel, and fresh clothes. I eventually find the showers—twelve outdoor shower stalls—which is great, because I only need one. The problem is there are eighty thousand refugees and four hundred runners who only need one as well. I strike it incredibly lucky, though, as right now there's only one person in the lineup. I strip off my clothes, and wait along with the other naked runner for the next shower to become available. Oops—a female runner from Italy rushes into the shower ahead of me, strips in the shower, and begins to bathe! Not that I can determine where naked people are from just by looking at them. She talks to me, in Italian. I ask her if I can share the shower (to conserve precious water). She doesn't understand English but must understand my look/request because she smiles and nods her head as if to say, "No, but thanks for your good intentions!" So I have to stand there buck naked and watch her finish her shower.

Now it's my turn. Damn this water is cold, but it feels sooooooo *good*! But I'm done in just a few minutes, because I'm feeling guilty about using too much water. I'm feeling clean for the first time in two days and now focus my attention on a hunger that could see me eat a camel alive.

They promise that a meal will be served at three o'clock—in twenty minutes. At four, we're still waiting. Which we continue to do until five, the new three. Holy moly. There's lots of food. I manage to get half a chicken and some baby back camel ribs, some rice, and french fries! It's the best meal I've had in a few days and the most food I've eaten in the desert.

Fully satisfied with lots of food to regenerate my body, I'm thinking of a long sleep in the new tent I must find. Turns out I have that quite wrong. The Sahrawis and the race organizers are not ready for us to rest, despite our exhaustion. We're captive now—to the awards ceremony and political speeches that take about two hours. There's no place to sit or lie down; we're standing for the whole ceremony. People around me think its sweat, but it's actually my legs and feet crying. Finally, around eight o'clock (the marathon started at 9:00 a.m., and we've been on our feet with no rest since then), we're shown to our tents by our new hosts. There's announcement that a dinner will be served at ten o'clock. There's more chance I'll build a pyramid this evening than go to a dinner where I'll stand and, no doubt, wait till midnight.

Instead, I fall into my new bed/blanket, eat a Power Bar, and go into a deep sleep.

Tuesday arrives! Too soon. But it's Sahrawi National Day. The itinerary says that there will be lots of celebration events, starting with a parade at 10:00 a.m. We're pumped.

The parade starts at noon. The Sahrawi government/military marches almost their entire army and military equipment past us for four hours. Soldiers, camels, trucks, scorpions, tanks, missile launchers, and even mobile SAM missile launchers! It all sounds good and menacing, as military stuff should be, but I'm told the army is poorly trained, and the equipment is out-of-date surplus Russian hardware. I spend most of the time talking to an American soldier from Chicago, attached to the UN delegation.

The noon lunch is served at four o'clock. There's lots of food.

There is another parade scheduled for six o'clock, where the Sahrawi civilians/refugees will do their tribal dances. To be perfectly frank, they look more menacing than the military marches we saw a few hours ago.

This parade starts at nine in the evening and goes on until three. I give up at ten, though, thinking we should get another medal for standing all day. I go to bed with another Power Bar because the eight o'clock dinner is still to be served. I wake up at midnight when I smell something good in our tent. Our hostess has prepared a camel stew for us. Damn, it smells good. I eat some very tasty stew then drift back to sleep with the celebrations still going on.

Wednesday arrives, which means it's time to head back to Madrid. We pack our bags and give everything we don't want to carry back to our host family and the Sahrawi kids. We all chip in and give our hostess about 15,000 pesetas, which is a lot of money for them. Hopefully, they will eat very well for the next year! We load the trucks with our bags at ten o'clock, get on the buses, and wait for about an hour until our armed military escort shows up to take us back to the Algerian base at Tindouf. We runners hold a raffle to guess when we may actually leave Algeria—the charter is scheduled for a 1:00 p.m. departure. I almost win with a guess of 4:12 p.m.—we finally get off the ground at 3:52 p.m. Sometimes a planeload of passengers will applaud when a plane lands safely—this time we all applaud when the wheels leave the ground.

Despite the adventure, I'm very happy to return to the luxury and comfort of Madrid. As soon as we arrived back at the hotel, I crack open possibly the best bottle of cold beer ever with many of my new friends and then we all scurry to our rooms for a long and hot shower. As a result, I'm late meeting Nicole who had spent her days in four-star hotels in Barcelona and Montserrat. Sounds brilliant, but right now I've no regrets having a few days with wonderful people, camels, sand and relentless standing. Oh, and that marathon too.

Nicole and I have five more days in Spain, so we tour the country, visiting Cordoba, Seville, and Toledo. Unfortunately, it rains for all five days, which is just a tad ironic, given my time in the desert. And, finally, it's time to return home! As usual, we're looking forward to returning to the comfort and familiarity of our own city, home, and friends. Time to reflect, rest up, scratch the sand out of my ears, not wait for meals, reflect some more, and plan and prepare for our next adventure.

Marathon #177—Country #47, LGT

Alpine Marathon, Liechtenstein

June 2001

The principality of Liechtenstein is a small country (61 square miles) divided into the Lower Country along the Rhine River and the Upper Country in the Alps, lying between Switzerland and Austria. Thirty-two thousand people live in eleven villages or hamlets that straddle the river, although there are a few villages in the Alps. Vaduz, the capital, has a population of five thousand, and Malbun, a hamlet or ski resort in the Alps, has a population of five hundred. The scenery is spectacular, with the Swiss Alps on one side and the Austrian Alps on the opposite side. The country is affluent and meticulously groomed.

We visit the whole country in one day. As we travel up one of the mountains with eight- to twelve-degree slopes, I blurt out, "This marathon is going to be a bitch."

Indeed, the local runners confirm that we will also run mostly on single-track trails and suggest I add 50 percent to my normal marathon time for this trail race. More fun times.

Sure enough, it's a tough course. It's raining and the temperature is in the midforties as the race starts in Nendeln. I decide to wear just shorts, a T-shirt, and no gloves. The first ten kilometers are run on a flat and paved bike path along the Rhine River. I run a five minute/kilometer pace for this part of the course because it will be the fastest part of the course. At Vaduz the course changes direction, runs through the town square and heads up a dirt trail past Schloss Vaduz (Vaduz Castle). And the fun begins. At 32 kilometers it's so steep that I have to scramble up on my hands and feet for two kilometers. I struggle to manage a 12.30 minutes/kilometer pace over these two kilometers. At 35 kilometers, we reach a point on Augstenberg that overlooks the village of Malbun. I can hear the cheers of the crowd at the finish line and hope we have an easy five kilometers to the end. Apparently not. The sadistic race director takes the course up to the top of the ski bowl on Augstenberg and across three snowfields in the ski bowl. The snow is wet and slippery, and the footing is extremely treacherous. I know that if I slip, my legs will not have the flexibility or capability to recover, so I just follow the trail made by the other runners and pray I don't slip. After traversing the ski bowl we hit the 40-kilometer mark on the opposite side of Malbun and start our descent to the finish line.

Within seconds of crossing the finish line—in a time of 4:46—my legs and my arms cramp due to fatigue and the cold. I struggle over to the equipment tent to get my sports bag with my warm-ups. I try to put my warm-ups on as my whole body starts a series of spasms. I have to ask a race volunteer to help dress me. As the volunteer is dressing he tells me I'm the first and only American to ever run this race. So that's something, at least.

I'm also a freezing cold American. I wonder where Nicole is.

She's back in the warm hotel watching the French Tennis Open.

Marathon #178—Country #48, Lake Myvatn Marathon, Iceland June 2001

Iceland is a volcanic island that lies about nineteen hundred kilometers northwest of London, England. That's where Nicole, my friend and fellow runner Tad, and I are heading right now after completing the marathon in Liechtenstein. On a map it looks like it's in the middle of nowhere, which is because it is. I'm assuming the pilots know where it is.

They do. We fly into the international airport at Keflavik, located on a small peninsula about fifty kilometers west of the capital city of Reykjavik. It reminds me of Hawaii with all the lava flows and volcanic ash, and of the Canadian Arctic because of the desolate and harsh terrain with very little vegetation.

The downtown area of Reykjavik is small, so it doesn't take long to see the attractions. The Perlan or Pearl, a dome structure built on a hill overlooking the city, contains six one-million-gallon tanks to store geothermal hot water to heat the city. Geothermal water averaging 185°F is pumped to all the homes and buildings for heat and hot water. Some homes then use the water to heat their pools and also run it through pipes under their driveway to keep it snow- and ice-free. The average home pays $300 per year for all the hot water and heat they need! It's the only thing in Iceland that's cheap.

We head next to the Laugardalur pool, the largest outdoor swimming pool in the country. It is, of course, heated with geothermal water and open year round, since the hot water is free. The pool is surrounded by hot tubs that Icelanders use as social meeting places to discuss politics, work, how cold it is, nosey American tourists—that sort of thing.

What do we do now? We had planned to stay two days in Reykjavik, and we have seen the city in the first morning. Off to the tourist/information center to determine what else we can see and do. They are very helpful as usual. One question we need answered is how long it takes to drive to Lake Myvatn on the southern route. The answer is two days along the south route and one day along the north. This fits our plans perfectly and still gives us two more days to explore the city and surrounding area. No problem, since one of the most famous tours in Iceland is the Golden Circle, a 250-kilometer circle around Reykjavik that takes in several famous tourist sites. We visit Hverageroi, a "flowering" town of greenhouses heated by geothermal energy, where all the vegetables and flowers are grown for the island. Other sites on the tour are: Kerio, a huge volcanic crater with a beautiful lake; Skálholt, a small historic village that was once the religious and cultural center of Iceland; Faxi Falls, a small isolated waterfall; Gullfoss, Iceland's most famous and picturesque waterfall; Geysir, a geothermal area with several active geysers (the two biggest are Strokkur and the Great Geysir); and Pingvellir National Park, which contains the site used by Iceland's parliament from 930 through 1798. The park also contains Lake Pingvellir, Iceland's largest lake, and the Great Atlantic Rift where the North American and European tectonic plates collide. There are some interesting canyons that looked just like the earth was being torn apart.

After one more night and "fish of the day" dinner in Reykjavik, we are ready to depart on our journey around the island. There is only one national highway in Iceland—Highway 1—which follows the coastline completely around the country. Since we are heading east, the Atlantic Ocean is always on our right, and volcanic mountains and glaciers are on our left. The mountains typically rise sharply, and there are hundreds of waterfalls cascading down to the ocean. After stopping and taking pictures of the first dozen or so, I become immune to them except to note, "There is another spectacular waterfall!" We pass through the tiny village of Vik, with a population of three hundred. The southernmost village in Iceland, it is noted for its beautiful black sand beach. Next we skirt for several hundred kilometers around Vatnajökull Glacier and pass many areas where the glacier almost reaches the ocean. At Jökulsárlón, the glacier is calving into a glacial stream only a few hundred meters from the ocean, and the icebergs are spectacular in color and form.

Our destination is Egilsstadir, the largest town in East Iceland. The highway becomes a dirt road as it turns inland at Höfn and climbs up and over two mountain ranges. The dirt roads up the mountains are steep, narrow, and wet, and they have no guardrails. One mistake or slip and you won't stop for two thousand feet! I drive on the wrong side of the road and hug the mountain all the way up. Fortunately, there's no traffic on the roads. Talk about desolate. We stop at Viti, a huge explosion crater with a lake near the volcano Mount Krafla and again at Námafjall, which has hot springs, boiling mud pools, and hissing steam vents.

Finally, we arrive in Lake Myvatn. Lake Myvatn is the fourth largest lake in Iceland and frequent lava flows have left the lake irregular in shape, with many islets and rock formations in it. There are only two small villages on the lake, and the marathon host hotel is located in Reykjahlio. We check into the hotel and then make our way to the tourist office, where we learn more details about the race and also that my buddy Tad, from London, has already arrived and is looking for us.

When I discover that the nearest government liquor/beer store is a hundred kilometers away, they ask a local hotel manager (a sponsor of the marathon) to sell me a few bottles of beer. He agrees to do so, even though it's illegal. Of course he charges me bar prices so it costs me twenty dollars for four beers! But I state this as an example of how friendly the Icelandic people are. We also ask the information office if there's anyplace to access the Internet. There isn't, but they offer us access to their own computer and refuse to accept any payment—nice people!

When I pick up my race package, they tell me some need-to-know facts about midges. The race loops around Lake Myvatn, which means "water of the midges." No kidding. Zillions of these things infest the area in the summer. Midges are like a small fly or mosquito. Some bite but mostly they just annoy the hell out of you by buzzing around and flying into any open orifice. They strongly suggest I buy a head net to keep them away from my face during the race. I buy one, mainly to show I've been listening, but I'm thinking, *How bad can it be? Can I seriously wear this thing for forty-two kilometers?*

They also advise that, since the loop around the lake is only thirty-six kilometers, we'll be bused back six from the finish line to the start line, which means we'll wait along the lake and make pleasant idle chitchat with the midges. There are only forty-two runners and two foreigners. Oh. Tad and I are the token outsiders. And no doubt, virginal skin for the midges to enjoy.

Friday, June 22, 8:00 p.m. Running with the late night sun is pretty cool. Tad and I drive to the finish line to catch the bus back to the start line.

The sun is still shining brightly, and the temperature is in the low fifties. There's a strong wind, luckily, which keeps the midges at bay. We decide to wear shorts and T-shirts and carry gloves and our head nets with us in case they are needed later in the race. At 9:05 p.m. a gun goes off, and so do we, running.

It's a strong head wind to begin with, so I tuck in behind a young local runner and draft off him. He's running faster than I want to run, but I feel like I'll save energy by drafting. I keep doing this for 10 kilometers then let him go. At 11:15 p.m., I approach our hotel at about the twenty-five-kilometer mark, I see Nicole run out of the hotel to clap and cheer me on. That's nice, especially at that time.

At twenty-nine kilometers, I can see three runners in front, and I'm catching them. I pass one runner, but the other two dig in—and, look at that, it's all on. We run our butts off for the next ten kilometers, with no one giving any ground. But with just over two kilometers to go, my legs want to fall off. I back off and coast the last kilometer to finish in 3:34. I'm quite pleased with my effort and time.

I wait at the finish line (in my head net) for Tad. While I'm waiting, I watch the sun set at 00:45 a.m. and then rise again twenty-six minutes later as we return to our hotel, where I treat myself to a hot bath—no problem here with hot water—for about thirty minutes and then go to bed to try to sleep. I'm not sure what it is, but I have experienced this reaction before—the sunset/sunrise trick, the bright daylight at 2:00 a.m., or my body and mind being all juiced up from the race—but I cannot sleep! I count Icelandic sheep crossing Highway 1 for about two hours, and finally at six I give up and decide that we might as well have breakfast and leave early for the trip back to Reykjavik.

We depart around eight on the infamous Highway 1 and skirt around some fjords on the north coast before turning inland to follow some glacial valleys. We stop at Godafoss (Waterfall of the Gods) for a Kodak moment before traveling on and through Akureyri, the second largest city in Iceland (population 15,000). After Akureyri, the trip is boring except for our encounters on the blind haeds (hills) with the sheep until we reach Borgarnes, a small seaside village with some spectacular views.

We arrive back at Reykjavik about four o'clock, which is much earlier than planned. We drive to Keflavik airport to see if we can catch a flight back to London that evening instead of waiting for our morning flight the next day, but no luck—no more flights that day. So we check into our hotel near the airport and enjoy our last "fish of the day" dinner. Really, the fish in Iceland is excellent.

Marathon #194—Country #53,

Thailand Temple Run, Thailand

March 2002

I decide to look into a new marathon in Thailand because it's being run out-side of Bangkok, which is polluted and has too much traffic. I also want—well, I need—a second marathon in the area to spread the travel costs over. I find a marathon in Bali, Indonesia, two weeks later. On a roll, I look for a third marathon. And I find Cambodia.

It's where it's always been, of course, just down the road from Thailand. Nicole comes along with me to make sure I don't do anything stupid. Forty-two hours after we left Florida we finally arrive in Bangkok. Not my luggage, though. That seems destined for more adventures. Somewhere.

Twelve hours later we're flying off again, this time to Chiang Mai, the capital of the northern region and the main center for hill-tribe trekking. Northern Thailand's hill tribes, about 750,000 people living in about thirty-five hundred villages, have so far preserved their way of life with little change over thousands of years.

We have a fun day of touring, capped off in the evening with a dinner and a show that features traditional Thai music and dances at the Thailand Cultural Center. The next morning, I run around the moat of the old city twice before we head north to visit an elephant camp and one hill tribe. Elephants were used as work animals for logging, etc., but now they're kept in camps to do shows and provide rides for tourists. We ride an elephant for one hour across rivers and up a mountain trail.

The next day, we head back to Bangok for the Thailand Temple Run—organized by a runner who wanted to offer an alternative to the Bangkok Marathon. The runner, a Swede, is the manager of the Amari Watergate Hotel, a five-star hotel that is the flagship of a chain of hotels throughout Asia.

The marathon route starts and finishes at the Phumrinkudeethong Temple in Samut Songkram, a rural community about sixty kilometers west of Bangkok. It rolls off your tongue once you say it a few times. It's a narrow country road winding past plantations (bananas, lychees), rice fields, and eighteen temples in the half-marathon loop before returning on the same path.

On marathon day, we're up at the crazy time of 2:00 a.m. to catch the bus at 2:45 a.m. Needless to say, Nicole can find a million excuses not to be on the bus with me.

It's 4:00 a.m. now at the start line. It's also 80°F—at 4:00 a.m. There are about 150 runners in the Full and 250 in the Half. I and one other runner, also from Sarasota, are running this gig topless. What a sight. The race starts at five o'clock, after monks from the temple spray all the runners with holy water for good luck and close their eyes near two keen Americans.

Apart from a few streetlights over the first kilometer, we're in total darkness in the country. I can't even see my feet, although I know they're with me. I can't see or read my watch, and I can't find any distance markers until the 16-kilometer mark. Thank goodness, there are race volunteers and police stationed at many of the turns; otherwise, I'd be sailing off the edge for sure. They also prevent me from getting lost, and out here is one of the last places you'd want to get lost.

At about 5:30 a.m., the locals start going to work. There are very few cars but lots of bikes and motorbikes, none of which have lights. This is fun.

The motorbikes make it interesting, but the emergence of many dogs along the route moved the OMG meter from interesting to holy crap! It seems that there are two dogs for every house in Thailand, and most of them are out running the marathon today. Most of them seem too tired and hot or afraid of the topless Americans to really bother us, but there are still some mangy, snarly dogs that cause me to slow down and challenge them to back off.

With the emergence of the daylight come even more motorbikes. And they're faster. I cross the Half in 1:43—way too fast, but I'm keen now to get off this course as soon as I can. At about 34 kilometers, a Japanese runner in my age group catches up with me and we begin playing a cat and mouse game. Neither of us wants to take the lead at this point—just hang on to the runner in front and make a final kick at the end. So at the 38-kilometer marker, I go for it. I quickly leave him behind, but now I'm hurting. Ten minutes later, when I should be reaching the 40-kilometer mark, another marker says 38 kilometers. Again? This kills me. I don't have enough left to push for another four kilometers. Sure enough, the Japanese runner passes me, makes his final kick, and disappears.

Even with only two or three kilometers to go, I'm in serious trouble. I'm extremely overheated, my fingers and arms have started to go tingly and numb, and I'm dizzy and nauseated. My blood sugar level has dropped to zero, and there are no more water/aid stations before the finish line. I can only struggle on and cross the finish line in 3:35. I throw a bucket of ice over me and keep it, applying ice until my body temperature goes below 100°. I'm looking for a Coke or something sugary, but after a few minutes, I'm so dizzy I collapse on the temple grounds and wait for a race volunteer to come to my aid.

A few minutes later, after I explain my problem, a wonderful guy, my fairy godfather perhaps, brings me a cold Coke. Within two minutes of guzzling the Coke, the tingling and numbness go away, and I can get up and walk around.

Back to the hotel for a quick shower and a nap. Now it's time to pack and move on to Cambodia.

Marathon #200, Silver State Marathon, Reno, Nevada

August 2002

It's been twenty years since I first stood on this start line. My hair is still blond but not as thick and plentiful. I'm still in fairly good shape and, at 144 pounds, weigh fourteen pounds less than I did for my very first marathon. I have a lot more wrinkles, scars, and nagging aches and pains due to running injuries I've inflicted on myself in training and running two hundred marathons.

No regrets.

The biggest changes are not visible or apparent. They are the psychological changes I've experienced. I'm no longer that nervous and frightened novice runner. I'm still Maddog, though; can't shake that puppy off.

I've now hit the magical two-hundred-marathon mark. On my way I've run a marathon in all fifty states and all thirteen Canadian provinces. I've run marathons on all seven continents and in fifty-five countries. And so to come back to where it all started simply feels right. Am I pleased? Am I proud? You bet I am!

I believe also that these past twenty years and two hundred marathons have brought me to a stage in my life where the effects of age and associated physiological changes on the human body cause such a rapid degradation in physical and athletic limits and capabilities, I want to test where I am on that scale of life. One way of testing it is to run the same marathon on the same course, and under the same conditions, I hope.

I'm not very confident that I can match or beat my time in that first marathon. I've not even announced this dream to anyone, for fear it will put too much stress and pressure on me. But I've trained seriously for this challenge. I'm lucky to live in the mountains in the summer, because that has provided me with altitude training every day. But I've also been running "fourteeners" during the week just for extra hill work and altitude training. Oh yeah, I do want to beat my time of twenty years ago.

Fortunately, the weather gods are kind to me and the temperature is a chilly 37° at the 6:00 a.m. start, and there's no wind. The only potential problem is the course. There is now a six- to seven-mile stretch of off-road trails instead of paved road, but I'm assuming it's okay to run on.

My good friend Edson has flown out from New York just to run the race and help me celebrate my two hundredth. As I stand at the start line with Edson, I reconfirm in my mind that if I want to achieve my secret goal, I will have to go out as hard as I can and run right on the edge of my physical limits until I either cross the finish line or crash and burn in flames. Rather dramatic, I know, but it's my story. I need a time of 3:28 or less. I'm driven today, even for Maddog.

The race starts. So do I. I go out right behind the lead pack, and they drag me through the first three miles—uphill—in 23.04. (7:41 pace). Miles four and five are flat and fast, but then we hit the first off-road section— OH DAMN! I'm greeted by two miles of sand trails running along the lake. Anyone who has run along a beach knows how difficult it is to run on sand. My feet sink into the sand, and I can't get good traction. I continue to expend the same amount of energy, but my pace now slows to eight minutes/mile. Not happy. It'll hit me later in the race, I know.

At seven miles, the course gets back to the paved road. My pace drops back to the 7:40s until mile 11, when the course turns off-road again. If I keep shaking my head like this, I'll burn up too many valuable calories. We're faced now with four torturous miles of sand, and my pace slows to 8:05s and 8:10s. I'm pushing as hard as I can. This really sucks!

I pass the Half in 1:41. In spite of the sucking sand, my overall pace is okay, but I know I can't run this same time in the second Half.

At mile 15, we finally emerge back on to wonderful pavement. I could kiss it. Because I know that the toughest hill on the course is located at mile 20, and that will certainly cost me time, I feel I need to push my pace through the next five miles to bank some more minutes. It's risky, but I push the pace back down to 7:40s and 7:50s over the next five miles. I pass mile 20 in 2:37. I close in on another runner who looks like he might be in my age group, and we use each other to push ourselves up the hill, a two-hundred-foot vertical climb over the next mile to the highest point of the course (5,250 feet). It feels like Mount Everest.

We crest the hill at mile 21 in 8:31—my slowest mile split; still five miles to go. There's an aid station at the top of the hill, thank goodness. It gives me an opportunity (well, okay, excuse) to slow down while I swallow another carbo gel and wash it down with some water. I'm really hoping my body starts recovering as we enjoy a short downhill before attacking the last hill, a small one, at mile 22. I calculate that if I can run an 8-minute pace to the finish line, I'll just beat my time of twenty twenty years ago. "But can I do that?" I ask myself. My body is crying now; I'm in pain and feeling fatigued.

I've come so far, though! I decide to take a huge risk that I rarely take at this point in a marathon. I decide to make an all-out push over the last four miles to the finish line!

My heart rate soars to 93 percent max as I increase my pace to a 7:36 minutes/mile over the next mile—my fastest mile split so far. My body is screaming in pain, but I've got to ignore it for three more miles. I continue to push, and it feels like it's going to work until suddenly, we hit a sandy trail!

I am so pissed at the race director right now. Why would he do this crap at this point in a marathon?

I suck it up and carry on; what else can I do? I emerge from that soft, sucking sand from hell, excuse me, at mile 24, onto a paved road that runs straight and flat to the finish line. I ignore the screams and pleas coming from pretty much most quasi-functional parts of my body. I'm exhausted and really hurting now, but I'm clocking a 7:50 mile pace. I can smell the finish line.

I reach mile 25 in 3:16—just one more mile to go! But my body tells me it's used up all readily available energy. There's nothing left. It's now breaking down fat and muscle tissue for energy, but it's a slow process, and it can't support a fast pace. I've got to slow down.

No! No! No! Not acceptable. I have come so far and endured too much pain, and I'm too close to success. I can't be denied. I refuse to slow down. I call my Lifeline. Maddog.

He appears seemingly from nowhere. "Pain is only temporary—memories are forever," I hear. I love that mantra. "Now get your lazy, tired ass moving."

I will never truly understand the power of Maddog, but he has fused willpower, adrenaline, and energy into my heart. My heart rate is up to 97 percent max, and I'm pushing hard. I'm giving it everything I have.

I reach mile 26 in 3:24, and I know now it's going to happen. I can see the finish line and the finish clock. The excitement and exhilaration of sweet success completely overwhelm my pain and fatigue. I slip into another zone, a dream dimension, and float through the final 285 yards. The finish clock says 3:25:57. I've done it!

Three feet across the finish line, and I'm stranded. I can't move. Not one single step more. I have no energy. If it wasn't for the pain shooting everywhere in my body I'd be wondering if I've died. It sure would be less painful. I check my pulse.

Apparently, I'm alive. Good.

Life, or fate, has presented me with a golden opportunity to come full circle in my running life and test the capabilities and experience of my older body and mind. I've responded with one of the best running performances of my life. I will cherish this sweet memory forever.

But now it's time to get some recovery fluids into me and wait for Edson. I expect him to finish under four hours, but he's run into problems and wisely decides to take it easy and finishes in a time of 4:13.

It seems I've placed third in my age group (50–59). The age-group awards are solid silver medallions minted at the Nevada City Mint. I plan to put together a special memento of the race and I'll include the medallion.

There is a another important event happening during this trip. It's our thirty-fifth wedding anniversary. Nicole and I travel to Lake Tahoe for a few days after the marathon to relax and celebrate our anniversary. It's been an amazing few days!

Marathon #213—Country #62,

Belgrade Marathon, Serbia

October 2003

When Nicole and I arrive at the airport in Belgrade, we are met by our host and race director, who introduces us to his daughter—a junior in high school who speaks very good English. She and her classmate will be our guides/escorts during our stay in Belgrade. As they help us check into our hotel, they inform me that they will pick us up at 8:00 a.m. tomorrow to escort us to the press conference. Press conference?

Sure enough, the next morning they're waiting in the lobby to take me to the press conference at city hall. We arrive there along with several of the elite runners. I try to take a seat in the back,—but no, they insist I sit at the table on the podium with the elite runners and dignitaries from the race committee and city hall.

I'm sitting beside Ramzi Mehovachi, an elite runner from Tunisia. A translator assigned to us for the press conference makes sense of the speeches. Then, oh no…it's my turn to say something.

I have to think fast. I'm not prepared for this. I thank the race committee and the city for their great hospitality, etc. and then admit to all that I have no chance of winning tomorrow, but I'm making great progress toward my goal to become the first to complete a marathon in every country in Europe. This BS seems to please everyone.

I sit down. The grief, I think is over. No, wrong. They go along the table asking all the runners for their PR. Most of the men are around 2:10 to 2:15; the women around 2:35. And finally Maddog, 2:58.

Thank goodness. Race day. I get up early and eat a light breakfast. I end up eating with the Kenyans and notice very clearly that this is all business and money to them. There's no conversation, no humor, no smiles at the breakfast table.

My escorts show up to take me to the start line. Probably a good thing. There are only two hundred runners in the marathon and another four hundred in the Half. Both races start together. But the real problem is the five-kilometer fun run; there are more than twenty-one thousand runners in that race.

Fortunately, it starts fifteen minutes after we take off. The marathon starts in the center of Old Town, with the first eight kilometers run through hilly streets before we cross over the Sava River into New Belgrade. Then we run two 16-kilometer loops through New Belgrade before returning to Old Town to finish in front of our hotel. The last two kilometers are uphill from New Belgrade back into Old Town.

At this point, the race organization is starting to fall apart. There are few race volunteers left on the course, and the course is not marked very well. At several intersections, I have to ask a cop or a spectator which way to go. And I'm not sure they understand me. Eventually, I cross the finish line in 3:28. I'm pleased. It's good enough for second place in my age group, though admittedly the grouping is only five years (55–59).

After a nice long hot soak, it's time for my last official function—an awards ceremony for the elite runners. The mood is much different from breakfast. The Kenyans are all smiles, as they've taken the top three places and prize money. One of the Kenyans gives us his resume and school marks and asks if we can help him find an athletic director at some college who might be interested in offering him a scholarship. A young runner from Soweto, South Africa, meanwhile, proposes to one of our escorts—begs her to marry him so he can move to Belgrade.

Marathon #214—Country #63,

Podgorica Marathon, Montenegro

October 2003

An early departure on Monday morning from Belgrade to Podgorica, Montenegro. Our first lesson of many to come is that there is very little infrastructure in Montenegro. There's only 650,000 people living in there, and almost half of them live in Podgorica, the capital.

After all the wars and turmoil in the region, the economy is in a shambles. It, and the country in general, needs to be rebuilt from the ground up. Nicole and I arrive at the airport in Podgorica at 7:30 a.m.; there's no tourist information center, no ATM, and no currency exchange at the airport.

As I've only made hotel bookings for the marathon at the end of the week (Saturday), this is not a good start.

Our fly-by-the-seat-of-the-pants plan has been to go directly to the Adriatic coast for some rest and some more rest and return to Podgorica on Saturday. We move to plan B; I find a taxi driver who accepts dollars. He nonchalantly doubles our fee and takes us to the bus station in town, which also is lacking an ATM machine, tourist center, or currency exchange. And to make matters worse, the ticket agent refuses to accept any payment—except cash in euros—for a bus ticket.

I find another taxi driver who speaks a little English and convince him to drive us to the only working ATM in the city to get some much-needed euros and bring us back to the bus station. So we buy bus tickets to Budva.

Our hotel in Budva is on the edge of the old walled town overlooking the Adriatic Sea. The old walled town is over twenty-five hundred years old. The first written record of Budva dates back to Sophocles in the fifth century BC, who referred to the Illyric town of Butua. We spend the rest of the day exploring the resort town and decide to use Budva as a base for exploring the whole coast of Montenegro (by bus). Budva even has an ATM machine, and it works.

We have a few days of being tourists along the coast. Great scenery, amazing food. Everything is cheap. Later in the week, we take a bus back to Podgorica, arriving at our hotel two days early.

The oldest building still remaining is the clock tower, which for Europe is a comparative baby at two hundred years old. It's the only building more than fifty years old in the city. The rest of the city is a blend of those ugly, large, and decaying concrete buildings made famous by the Soviets. The city has no beauty except for the mountains that surround it. And there is nothing to do in Podgorica.

In a purely coincidental moment, the race director arrives at the hotel at the same time we arrive. He insists that the race committee will pay for our complete stay including all our meals. He introduces me to a very cute red-head who will be my escort/translator during the official events of the race. She tells me that I and another runner, Emmanuel Kosgei—a Kenyan whom I had met in Belgrade—will be going to a press conference tomorrow morning. Uh-oh.

Our translator picks us up at eight o'clock and drives us to the TV station. Once seated for the interview, the race director asks me to take my jacket off to show my 50+DC T-shirt. I stand up, take off my jacket, and walk away to leave my jacket somewhere—they're calling out for me to get back, though, because in ten seconds we're going live on something like "Good Morning, Montenegro." I get seated just in time and the show rolls.

Emmanuel begins by saying he's going to try to win the race and beat the course record of 2:12. I say a whole lot of flowery words that sort of sound important, but on reflection, they mean very little. But I put on a great smile all the same. The other elite runners arrive later in the day, and I quickly become a nobody again.

Sunday is marathon day. I join a few runners from Moldova for breakfast, and we talk about races in Moldova. The runners invite me to stay with them if I visit Moldova. Nice guys—like all runners.

The rain stops at nine, and the sun starts to shine. There's also a light dusting of snow on the mountains surrounding the city. The race is supposed to start at ten o'clock. Unbeknown to Nicole and me until we panic and ask around—but known by everyone else in Montenegro—they put the clocks back one hour last night. It explains why it's like a ghost town here at the start line.

I find a park bench and lie down to rest. Granted, it's a small race with only 150 runners in the marathon and another two hundred in the Half, but it would have been good form to have at least one portable toilet at the start/finish line. I've no option but to find an alley and take care of some last-minute duties.

It's now ten o'clock, the real ten o'clock, and it's warmed up significantly. The course is a 42-kilometer loop south out of the city almost to the Albanian border and back to the city center. I'm running a sub-five-minute/kilometer pace for the first few kilometers. I start drafting a group of runners to minimize the effects of a strong wind but damn, it's a 4:38/kilometer (7:20/mile) pace they're running, and I can't sustain this pace. We reach the Half in 1:39—much too fast for my usual marathon pace.

I still feel strong but don't believe I can hold this pace. Do I run faster than I should and continue to draft off the group, or slow down and waste energy by battling the head wind on my own? Maddog leaps in front of me and shouts, "What the hell! Do it!" It could get very ugly. And very painful over the last ten kilometers.

Around 28 kilometers, I get a burst of energy and surge to the front of the group. We're passing through a small village called Tuzi, near the Albanian border, and it looks like all two thousand inhabitants are lined up along both sides of the narrow road. The crowds start cheering and applauding loudly.

One of the Serbs in the group runs up beside me and says, "All that noise and cheering is for you."

"Why?" I ask.

"They are cheering for the American."

"How do they know I am an American?"

"You were on the local TV, and there was a big article in the papers about you and your feats."

"But how do they know I am *the* American?"

"The papers published your race number."

So I'm running around the country with a huge number/bull's eye pinned to my chest designating me as an American! I better speed up and finish quickly. Everyone is friendly, though, and this scenario is repeated as we pass through a few more villages. It's pumping me up, actually, and I want to pick up the pace some more. But I decide to drop back and draft off the group until the 35-kilometer mark. If I still feel good there, I'll push as hard as I can for the last seven kilometers, because I know I'm running my fastest race in many years.

We reach the 35-kilometer point in 2:48. The group starts to slow, but I surge ahead. Fortunately, one young Serb comes with me. We urge each other on.

At 40 kilometers, I'm running out of energy. But it's only two kilometers from one of my best finishes/races in years, and I'm not going to let exhaustion and pain stop me. My young Serb friend wants to slow the pace, but I beg him to help me, especially since I'm in some significant pain. He holds the pace, and we cross the finish line together in 3:20. I almost shake his hand off, but truth be known, the grip is helping me stand up right now, as I'm exhausted.

And thrilled. And extremely grateful. I'd never have finished in this time without his help. It's my fastest marathon since White Rock (Dallas, Texas) in December 1996. I'm also pleased to hear that my friend Emmanuel has won the race, although not in a course record.

Marathon #218—Country #65,

Mumbai Marathon, India

January 2004

When our younger son Jason and his fiancée, Ami, ask if it was okay if they get married in India, we are excited and overjoyed! Although Ami was born and raised in Houston, her parents emigrated from Ahmadabad, India, and still have most of their family there. They want the kids to get married in India so they can share the wedding with their family. We agree after the kids agree that we'll have another (second) wedding in Houston for their friends and family who cannot go to India.

The wedding is planned for early January.

We figure if we are going to go that far for the wedding and we have never been to India, that we should spend at least a few weeks exploring India before and after the wedding. And of course Maddog immediately starts scouting for the possibility of running a marathon while there. What luck! An inaugural marathon is scheduled in Mumbai the weekend before the wedding.

Our older son Chris is to be best man at his brother's wedding. Since Jason and Ami have to travel on a different schedule to be there for the final wedding plans, we invite Chris to join us for a one-week tour of the Golden Triangle the week before the wedding. The Golden Triangle is a tourist circuit that includes Delhi, Agra, and Jaipur. We are concerned about travel and illness, so we book a tour with a private guide and driver and luxury hotels.

We cash in all our combined Delta air miles to book first-class seats. When we arrive in Delhi, our guide and driver pick us up and take us to our hotel to rest and recover from jet lag. The tour will start the next day. That evening, as we walk around Delhi near our hotel, we are shocked to find people—lots of people—conducting their private duties in the street. That is disgusting! When I wake early the next day to get a short run in before the tour starts, I encounter the same problem. There are so many people defecating in the street that it is difficult to avoid them and the "landmines," or mess they leave behind. They squat in the street and pull their clothes around them and when they stand up and walk away they leave a steaming landmine behind. I give up on trying to do a short run and return to the hotel.

Our tour starts after breakfast. The first thing our guide explains is that we will be harassed by beggars constantly. We should not talk to them or give them anything, and we must avoid any eye contact. Many of the beggars are pros who were purposely maimed or disfigured to solicit more pity—and money. This tour and visit is off to such a good start.

We start with a tour of Delhi, one city with two distinct features, the combination of the traditional and the contemporary. The Old Delhi tour includes a visit to the Red Fort (Lal Quila). The fort is a massive construction and an architecture marvel. Started in 1638 by Shah Jahan and completed in the year 1648, it has been part of the Indian history since then. Next stop is Jama Masjid—a typical Mughal architecture, built by Muhammad Ali Shah on the western side of the Hussainabad Imambara. The tour of Old Delhi includes a visit to Mahatma Gandhi's memorial site, the Raj Ghat. The tour continues with New Delhi and a visit to Humayun's Tomb, one of the earliest examples of Mughal architecture in Delhi. Qutub Minar is one of the focuses in the Delhi tour, as it the world's tallest brick minaret with 72.5 meters in height. Then we drive along the Rajpath past India Gate, Parliament House, the president's residence, and the diplomatic enclave to finish with a visit to the Lotus Temple before returning to the hotel for the night. The third day starts with an early breakfast (I skip any attempt to run around steaming landmines), and then we depart by car for Agra to visit the Taj Mahal. It is difficult to find words to describe this beautiful structure! The white marble tomb, which has found its place in the Seven Wonders of the World was built by Shah Jahan in 1631–1648 for his wife, Mamtaz Mahal. The mausoleum is an architectural marvel and the Turkish and Persian influences are eminent in the building. Next we move on to the Agra Fort, which is situated on the northwestern side of the Taj Mahal. The pristine white marble building can be seen from one part of the fort, where Shah Jahan spent his old age. In the evening we attempt to go for a pleasant walk near the hotel but they have landmines in Agra, too.

The next morning we continue on to Jaipur. But before going to the Pink City we stop at Keoladeo National Park, a UNESCO World Heritage Site, and a former duck-hunting reserve of the maharajas that is one of the major wintering areas for large numbers of aquatic birds. I think about doing a short run in the park, since the only landmines here were left by birds. However, we go to Jaipur for an overnight stay at a hotel in the Pink City. Up to now the meals have been good. Our guide took us to high-end restaurants mainly in luxury hotels, so the food was good and safe. But it was mostly Indian food—and vegetarian. I need a steak, but that is hard to find except in a Western hotel, so I have to make do with chicken. We enjoy one more night in Jaipur. By now we have learned not to venture outside the hotel without our guide and driver.

The next day we return to Delhi and fly to Mumbai to begin the next leg of our adventure.

Did I mention that one week before we left for India I received an e-mail from the race director of the Mumbai Marathon informing me that the race had been postponed two weeks? I responded that I had a wedding to attend—I would be there on the original scheduled date, and I expected to run a marathon! I could not delay my trip—and the wedding—by two weeks!

We plan to stay in Mumbai for a few days to run the marathon and then go to Ahmadabad. We also plan to meet up with Jason and Ami and Ami's family in Mumbai to shop for a sari and other items needed for the wedding. We have booked a hotel south of downtown and on the Arabian Sea. I assumed that I would be able to run along the beach or coast. Wrong! When I go out for a morning run—my first, since I have not yet found any place safe from landmines—I try to run along the beach. The beach is totally occupied by locals doing their morning duties—and leaving behind landmines! Others walk into the Sea to deposit their landmines. It is still disgusting, and I return to the hotel. I guess the actual marathon will be my only run in India. If there is a marathon.

Nicole joins Ami and her family to shop for a sari, and I visit the race director. I am fortunate to meet with him and Hugh Jones, whom they hired as a consultant and to certify the course. I explain that I am there now and cannot not come back in two weeks. I am going to run the marathon, and hopefully, the official course, with or without their support. Fortunately, Hugh is on my side and recommends that they support me. And we compromise on a solution. That evening they are holding an official press conference for the marathon. They request that I attend the conference; after the conference finishes they will provide a team of volunteers and a vehicle to guide and support me to run the official marathon course solo starting at 3:00 a.m.

It actually turns out to be a strange and fun(ny) affair. I am invited to the podium along with the governor of the province, the mayor of Mumbai and other dignitaries. I am asked to give a short speech where I thank the race director and the city for allowing and supporting me to run the official marathon course later that night. After the conference ends, there is pandemonium as TV and newspaper reporters descend on me for a story. I spend over two hours giving interviews to the press and TV. The race director provides a room for me at the hotel where the press conference is held. We plan to start the marathon at three. I get to bed at 11:00 p.m., and a TV station wakes me up at 11:30 p.m. and requests that I come downstairs and run sprints up and down the street in front of the hotel for their camera crew.

I finally get back to bed at midnight and wake up at 2:30 a.m. to get ready.

At three I appear at the front of the hotel. I am besieged again by reporters and a TV film crew. They are going to accompany me on my marathon adventure—the entire adventure. A taxi takes the RD and me to the start line, where I am joined by two young race volunteers on a moped. They are to guide me through the course and provide any support needed, such as water and carbo gels. It is a circus. I am followed for the entire marathon by a taxi full of newspaper reporters and photographers who jump ahead and wait to ask questions and take photos. At the same time, a pickup truck with a TV film crew follows me and films most of the marathon. I am afraid to stop for a potty break, because I am sure they will film it.

My two friends/support team and I develop a friendship and pattern as I run the entire marathon—on the official course—without a potty break to finish in 3:50:55! Once again there are interviews, and then, finally, I am left alone! I return to the hotel room provided by the race for a short nap. I wake to find my face and the story of Maddog plastered all over the morning TV shows and on the front page of the Mumbai newspaper. You have to admit—Maddog sure knows how to make an entrance!

Now that I've completed marathon #219 and country #65, I can relax and play tourist and get ready for the wedding. I convince Nicole to give up shopping for a day to join Chris and me on a tour of the city. The tour starts at the Gate to India, one of Mumbai's most unique landmarks. The colossal structure, constructed in 1924 at the tip of Apollo Bunder, overlooks the harbor. It was constructed to commemorate the visit of King George V and Queen Mary to Bombay (Mumbai).

We take a ferry from the Gate of India to Elephanta Island to visit the Elephanta Caves where there are mythical stories of Lord Shiva carved out in the rocks of the caves. The caves are a collection of mythical figures, shrines, ancient Indian architecture, statues of many Hindu gods and goddesses carved out of the rocks.

We return to the Gate of India to tour downtown Mumbai and then drive past the movie studios of Bollywood and along Marine Drive to Kamala Nehru Park that is located at the top of Mumbai's Malabar Hill. It is named after Kamala Nehru, the wife of India's first prime minister, Jawaharlal Nehru. From this garden, one can enjoy the spectacular sight of the Chowpatty Beach and also Marine Drive (Queen's Necklace). Kamala Nehru Park is a shoe-shaped structure, with widespread lush greenery and is famous for a unique structure, called the Old Woman's Shoe, or Boot House, that famously attracts kids.

Our last stop, the Haji Ali Dargah, is a mosque and dargah (tomb) located on an islet off the coast of Worli in the southern part of Mumbai. Near the heart of the city proper, the dargah is one of the most recognizable landmarks of Mumbai. An exquisite example of Indo-Islamic architecture, associated with legends about doomed lovers, the dargah contains the tomb of Sayed Peer Haji Ali Shah Bukhari.

It's time for the main event—the wedding! We fly to Ahmadabad where we are met by Ami's family. We are provided accommodations at a wedding compound with members of Ami's family. No other Wallace family attended because of the distance and cost. And remember, we are planning a second wedding in Texas.

An Indian wedding is quite an experience. It is very interesting and colorful, with lots of music and dancing that goes on for days and days! There are traditional ceremonies that have to be completed in a specific order. A member of Ami's family is assigned to babysit us, to explain the ceremonies and culture, to make sure we are in the right place at the right time, and to tell us what to do and expect.

Our hosts and all their family and guests treat us very kindly. The wedding is a fantastic experience. One downside to the wedding is there is no booze, and most of the meals are vegetarian. However, there is always a way. Our babysitter takes us to a "special" store where we can buy beer (that we only drink in our room). The area is dry—no booze in hotels or restaurants, yet many of the locals seem to have beer in their homes. He also sneaks us out to a Western hotel a few time for a carnivore fix!

When the newly married couple have left for a honeymoon in the Maldives, we thank our gracious hosts and return home with a two-day layover in Singapore. I won't bore you with details of Singapore. I will be going back—I need to run a marathon there.

Marathon #226—Country #66,

Minsk Marathon, Belarus

July 2004

I met some good contacts last year while running the Belgrade Marathon in Serbia and this spring decided to follow up to see if they could help me. A runner in Moldova who works for the Moldova Sports Federation got back to me. He promised to help me find marathons in Belarus and Ukraine and confirms there is no "official" marathon in Moldova. But, he says, he will help me run a solo marathon in Moldova. Meantime, two other marathons fit into place after this one, and before you can say "Belarus," I'm there in part 1 of a three-part running odyssey.

It's tough trying to get travel sorted out in these countries. I find a travel agency in Atlanta that specializes in travel to Russia and the former Soviet countries. I hand the whole trip over to this agency, including the visas. It costs me a lot more money because the agency charges a fee to process the visas. The three visas end up costing me about $550, which would have killed the trip if it weren't for the fact that I need these countries to complete my goal.

After twenty-four hours of airplanes and airports, I arrive in Minsk. Since the airport is located about forty-five kilometers outside the city, I've arranged for a private car to pick me up. The driver doesn't speak English, so it's a long boring ride to what turns out to be a one-star hotel that is used by local businessmen on the north east side of Minsk. Nobody in the hotel speaks English.

But good news, the hotel is located right next to the last metro station of one line so I have easy access to the city. Now, I only have to figure out how to use it and where to go.

Since all the signs and directions are in Cyrillic, I just count the number of stations to my destination(s) and make sure I don't fall asleep or get distracted.

There is no tourist infrastructure in the city or the country and no "canned" city tours, so I book a private guide and car for the day. Minsk and most of the towns in Belarus were completely destroyed during World War II, and 25 percent of the population of Belarus was killed by the Germans. Thus there are very few old buildings in Minsk, and the Belarusians have very little love for Germans. After the war Minsk, was rebuilt by the Soviets in the "grand" Stalinist style with ubiquitous gray high-rises. The apartment buildings are called "Khrushchev apartments"—four- to five-story concrete buildings with no imagination and very small apartments.

My guide also shows me an old farmhouse near the city center where all the charter members of the USSR met in 1922 to form the USSR. Right next to that museum is an apartment building where Lee Harvey Oswald lived. Like most people, I assumed he lived in Moscow.

At the end of the day, I go to the Olympic Sports Center for race registration. For the ten-thousand-ruble ($4.50) entry fee I get my race number, a T-shirt, a finisher's medal, and a diploma. What a deal! And I haven't even run the race yet.

Saturday is race day. The race doesn't start until 4:00 p.m, so I can join Minskers, or rather the people of Minsk, and enjoy the Independence Day celebrations. There has to be a least a half-million people making their way to the hill where the Minsk Hero-City Monument is located. It looks like the entire Belarus military is marching by, with all the dignitaries and military brass followed by military equipment—jeeps, tanks, missile launchers, etc.—while MiGs, attack helicopters, Superman, etc. fly overhead. It's impressive enough that I decide not to invade Belarus any time soon. I also decide I need to eat pizza before the race starts.

We start the race at Victory Square, where there are about a hundred thousand people gathered around waiting to see us off. Well, closer to the truth is the fact that there's a concert in the square. And two, count them, two port-o-potties for the runners (and partygoers). But there's a very good-looking tree looking lonely, so I go and use it instead.

One hundred thousand fans cheer us on as we start the race. The road is closed for the first five kilometers, but around eight kilometers, it becomes a four-lane divided highway going east to Moscow. We're required to move to the shoulder of the highway, and the traffic resumes driving past at more than 100 kph. There's little or no traffic control from now on.

The course is much hillier than I expected. Nonetheless, I reach thirty kilometers at 2:28, and I'm feeling good. Around thirty-seven kilometers in, we turn off the Moscow Highway and head into the suburbs toward the finish at the sports center. I'm hurting badly, and I almost get run over by a car as I cross the road in a curve to shorten the course. It's a tough slog from here. I know a sub-3:30 time is in the bag if I just keep running. I use every last ounce of willpower to overcome the pain in my body and the deadness in my legs. The old bod gives me a final jolt of adrenaline as I see the sports center and enter the stadium. I sprint the final lap around the track to cross the finish line in 3:27. I win my age group by more than twenty minutes, which is surprising.

On Sunday I catch a train at 12:40 p.m. that takes twenty-five hours to travel from Minsk through the Ukraine to Chisinau, Moldova.

Marathon #227—Country #67,

Moldova Marathon, Moldova

July 2004

I've found my train, coach, and seat in Minsk, the capital of Belarus. I'm on my way to Chisinau, the capital and largest city in Moldova. Moldova is a landlocked country of about three million people between Romania and Ukraine.

I had booked a first-class sleeper cabin (two beds) for the twenty-five-hour train ride from Minsk via Ukraine to Chisinau. As the train pulls out of Minsk, I'm pleased to see I have the cabin all to myself. My fun starts soon after, when the conductor enters my cabin and begins asking me a lot of questions in Russian. Fortunately, a man in the next cabin comes to my rescue. He speaks some English and explains that if I want sheets and a blanket for my bed, it will cost two dollars. I pay the conductor, and she's smiling now.

Since the journey is twenty-five hours long, I assume that there is a place to get food on the train. Wrong. In fact, there is no food on the train. I can buy tea, coffee, beer, or pop from the conductor, but not food. But being a runner, I've packed six Power Bars. Looks like I'll be having those for lunch, dinner, and breakfast.

My new neighbor comes to my rescue again. He invites me to his cabin to share a lunch that his wife had packed for him—bread, cold meats, and some kind of pancake stuffed with fruit. It's delicious, much better than a Power Bar. In return, I go to my cabin and bring us both a treat—a bottle of

Crown Royal whiskey. My neighbor, now elevated to friend status, can drink! I mix my whiskey with pop, but I still can't keep up with him. He downs his whiskey straight. As the train travels, we drink more whiskey; he speaks more Russian and less English now, but the more he does, the more I seem to understand him.

As we approach Chernobyl in the Ukraine I notice there are very few farm animals. I shouldn't be surprised, of course. In 1986, Chernobyl was the scene of the worst nuclear disaster ever. Thirty-one people were killed at the time, when an explosion and fires released large quantities of radioactive particles into the atmosphere. The winds spread the fallout through Europe. The long-term effects have been incalculable in terms of cancers, disorders and deformities, environmental damage, and so on.

My Crown Royal buddy says there is a hundred-kilometer restricted zone around Chernobyl that nobody is allowed to enter. The zone will not be habitable for another two hundred years. We pass very close to the zone border and see that many people still live and farm just outside the zone. I see a guy with two heads riding a bike.

No I don't, but it makes you wonder—at least it makes me wonder. Or maybe it's the whiskey. Surely these people still living here are crazy, but maybe they have no other option.

As we approach the border, the typical customs process begins. The train stops on the Belarus side and the Belarus border/custom police check our passport and baggage. Then it proceeds across the border to the nearest town/station and stops again for the Ukrainian customs police to do the same thing. I'm lucky my new friend is here, because neither police officer speaks English, and he either translates for me or answers all the questions.

The rest of the day is uneventful—boring, actually, as the countryside in Ukraine is like Iowa and Nebraska, no offense, but I resort to a Power Bar for dinner and go to bed early, thankful for my nonradiated Power Bar and the reminder of why I never took that job offer in Nebraska years ago.

The next day, I wake up early to my Belarusian friend inviting me to his cabin for breakfast—more of the same bread, meat, and pancakes. Not much, but light years ahead of another Power Bar. By midmorning we reach the border of Ukraine and Moldova. This time I encounter some tough questioning from the Ukrainian customs police, and my buddy is not with me.

They want to know how much money I'm taking out of the country. I jokingly tell them I'm taking fifteen Power Bars, but it doesn't raise even a smirk. I pull the "I only speak English" card, and that bombs as well. They radio in for an English-speaking officer to interview me. He's actually very nice and polite, so I tell him I have no Ukrainian money and $1,000 in US funds. That's okay, apparently, and I'm cleared.

The Moldavian customs police, on the other hand, don't even ask me for my passport. It's not long afterward that we arrive in Chisinau, and I say goodbye to my Belarusian friend and thank him for all his help and hospitality.

I step off the train in Chisinau, and I'm greeted by another friend, Dmitry. Dmitry is a 2:20 marathoner whom I met last year in Belgrade and Podgorica. He's one of the best runners in Moldova and works for the Moldova Sports Federation.

He's been instrumental in helping me get information and organizing this trip. Because the other race directors didn't speak English, Dmitry would e-mail or telephone them to get the necessary information and pass it along to me. It would have been impossible to put the trip together without his help. Dmitry spent two years in San Diego, so he speaks good English.

He takes me to my hotel and helps me check in. I invite him to lunch, and we discuss our plans for the marathon. Since there is no official marathon in Moldova, Dmitry has agreed to support me to run a solo marathon. We plan to use the same course that is used for an ultra/twenty-four-hour race in Chisinau—a 1.6-mile loop around a lake in a city park. Dmitry has measured the course and tells me I need to run just over sixteen loops to complete a "certified" marathon. He offers to run part of the marathon with me, but I figure I'll be too slow, which would be painful for him, so I suggest he just show me the course. I can do the rest. But he insists on providing me with support during the run. He says he can bike along with me or just stay at one point and pass me water. We decide to run a few loops the next morning so I can check out the course.

After my meeting with Dmitry, I become a tourist. I explore the city while he catches up on some work in his office. Chisinau is a small city (700,000 people) with one main street that's about a mile long. Chisinau was totally destroyed in World War II but rebuilt by the Soviets in the "grand Stalinist" style. Apart from the odd statue and one church older than sixty years, everything else is in that ugly, gray, dull, ugly, dull, and ugly again concrete style. Moldova is the poorest country in Europe, but there is no shortage of gray and dull.

I was expecting it to be a lot dirtier and poorer than some of the Balkan countries that I've labeled affectionately as the "shit holes" of Europe, but I'm pleasantly surprised to find the city clean and with few signs of poverty. There is the odd beggar around, but they don't bother you. Using my acute observational skills, I see there is no tourist infrastructure, and in fact, no tourists. Except me.

As I explore the shops for my mandatory souvenirs and postcards, I quickly realize there is no need for such things if there are no tourists. And there are few people with money, so there is very little to buy. Prices are low for essentials, however, and I enjoy a great dinner in a fancy restaurant for about ten dollars (including beer and wine). I'm feeling a bit guilty about my own lifestyle and feeling very lucky.

I meet up with Dmitry the next morning. He tells me people frown and curse at him when he runs through the streets because they think it's frivolous—he should be digging ditches or picking vegetables in order to survive like everyone else instead of wasting time and energy on sports. Great context.

So in any case we run two laps around a paved path that loops around a lake in the park. I spend some of the time looking for veggies to dig up. There are very few other runners, or even walkers, but lots of stray dogs with vegetables in their mouths and a few dogs that owners don't have on a leash.

In the afternoon, we go on a tour with a private guide in his car, an old Russian limousine left over from the Soviet days that used to chauffeur Soviet diplomats around town. The seats, floors, and doors are upholstered with multicolored Turkish carpets. It's not a long tour, because there's not much to see. And after a while, all the gray and drab just simply looks like gray and drab.

I try to liven things up by asking about politics and the government, but Dmitry and the driver clam up instead. The government is corrupt, and there is nothing that can be done about it. End of story. But they add the same thing I heard in Belarus; that the majority of people feel very strongly that things would be better if they could rejoin Russia and go back to the good old days.

After the tour I tell Dmitry about my problems finding souvenirs. He insists on helping me find some. As we wander through town, I ask why there are so many currency exchanges on the main street when there are no tourists. It's because of the poor economy in Moldova. About a quarter of the population works outside the country, and they send money home, so the family has to exchange the currency to buy food, etc.

Several hours later, I finally find a silver charm of a buffalo, which is apparently the symbol of Moldova. There are no silver teaspoons! Nicole will be gutted, although I think the buffalo is cute. And I buy a plain silver teaspoon and have a jeweler engrave "Moldova" on it. The final thing I need is a T-shirt with "Moldova" or "Chisinau" on it, since I won't be getting a marathon T-shirt. In spite of several hours of effort, to our amazement there are no such T-shirts in Chisinau. Dmitry promises he'll have a solution tomorrow. I head back to the hotel slightly dejected but refocusing on my marathon the next day.

Dmitry meets me at the hotel at 5:45 a.m., and we take a taxi to the park. I bring with me two two-liter bottles of water and a smaller bottle to drink from. I start my solo marathon at six o'clock.

There's no point in running fast, as I've no one to compete against except myself. Dmitry sits at the start/finish line and hands me a carbo gel and water after every second loop (I run fourteen minutes per loop, it seems. He also records each loop and the time, and does this for four hours. Wonderful man. I'm having a good run with no problems until the last loop. A stray dog decides to challenge me. I turn and snarl back at him with a full set of Maddog teeth—and flossed and American white at that—and he takes off.

I finish the marathon feeling good, in a time of 3:50. I get a taxi back to the hotel, and Dmitry goes to his office. We're both pleased and decide to meet later for a celebration beer.

At 3:00 p.m., Dmitry shows up at the hotel with a friend. He has with him an "official" diploma certifying that I've completed a solo marathon in Moldova in 3:50. It's signed by both Dmitry and his boss—the president of the Moldova Sports Federation. I'm honored!

Dmitry introduces me to his friend Sergei. Sergei is the coach of the Moldova National Olympic running team. I'm honored again. Sergei congratulates me on my marathon and presents me with a T-shirt that had been given to the Moldova running team. It's got the Moldova crown and Olympic rings on it—I'm feeling like I'm an honorary member of the Moldova Olympic team. I'm totally overwhelmed with the hospitality and friendship I receive. People wonder why I run marathons around the world. It's moments like these that reaffirm the immense pleasure of all the experiences I have. No amount of money can replace these moments in life.

Unfortunately, Dmitry and Sergei have other commitments tonight, so I enjoy my celebration dinner and last night in Moldova by myself. Probably a good thing, since I've got to catch a train to Ukraine at 6:40 a.m. It's a quiet night but fills quickly with a very deep sense of happiness, satisfaction, pride, and faith.

I'm at the station by six to make sure I find my train. The train is a milk run that only has wooden bench seats and no reserved seating. It's a six-hour train ride. There's no problem getting a seat in Chisinau but, as the train stops at every little town, it soon fills up with farmers carrying boxes and baskets of vegetables and fruit on their journey to the markets in Odessa, where they'll get better prices than in Moldova.

I, on the other hand, have some Power Bars. And a very cool T-shirt.

A few hours later, we stop across the border in Ukraine. I have to go through the same customs ritual about money, but luckily, they call the same customs officer I had a few days earlier, and he recognizes me. I clear without a hassle.

The evidence is mounting, though. I don't have any veggies, I'm eating a Power Bar, and I'm speaking English. It seems most of my fellow passengers have never met an American before. Unfortunately, no one speaks English, but a few kids poke me with a stick and ask my name. I ask them their names in return, but that's the extent of our conversation. Still, smiles go a very long way, and I give the kids a bunch of American change I have with me. Grateful for the excitement and happiness I've produced, the parents give me a bunch of their fruit and vegetables as a gift. Finally, some produce of my own. I'm starting to blend in.

I'm feeling good yet again, thanks to the Moldavian generosity, but upon arriving in Odessa, I give the veggies to a beggar.

Marathon #228—Country #68,

Rivne Marathon, Ukraine

July 2004

I arranged for a private car (and its driver) to meet me at the train station, because I booked an apartment in Odessa and figured I'd need help finding it. It was a good plan. The apartment I booked had water problems so the agency upgraded me to a bigger apartment at a different address. The driver drove me to the new apartment and showed me how to work some of the appliances.

I booked the apartment because hotels are very expensive in Odessa. I also figured it would be a chance to live a little bit like a local. The "Khrushchev apartments" built after the Second World War were based on the central command/control principle. All the utilities were supplied and controlled by the government.

For example, the buildings are heated by a central hot-water system that is turned on (and off) by the government on specific dates. So the apartments are heated in the winter but not in the summer. It also means there is no hot water in the summer months for washing, etc. I ask how they take showers and baths. Cold showers, apparently, and if you want any warmth in a bath, heat some water on a stove. The owner of this apartment has added an instant-type water heater and, a bonus, a satellite TV system. I'm living in luxury compared to my neighbors.

Later that day I find out the city turns off all water between midnight and 6:00 a.m. I can live with that. On my first morning, the water in my section of the city is not turned back on until 2:00 p.m. I'm experiencing life just like the locals.

My apartment is located in the old city and only half a block from the main street, which has been been converted into a pedestrian mall. It's lined with shops and sidewalk cafés and bars; a great place to stroll or sit and drink a beer and people watch. After exchanging some money at an ATM, I shop for water and some food. I'm looking forward to a regular American-type breakfast (orange juice and cereal) in my apartment.

Odessa does not have much of a tourist infrastructure, even though there are lots of tourists. I see busloads of Japanese tourists—a bit bizarre—but there's a cruise ship berthed in the harbor, which is a good place for a ship to be. There is no tourist office, but I do find a travel agency offering several tours of the city. I book a city tour and a tour of the catacombs for the next day. I drop into a nearby luxury four-star hotel and talk to the concierge staff. They speak excellent English and are very courteous and helpful. They give me an English map of the city and tell me I can run on a road along the Black Sea called the "Road to Health" where, apparently, all the locals run and walk. Must be crowded.

I'm a little teary-eyed because the hotel looks so good, and they speak English, but it's three times the price, which makes my apartment more appealing. The rest of that day I explore the old city.

There seems to be a good chunk of wealth. A number of BMWs and Mercedes-Benzes are parked on the streets, and the main street has several high-priced jewelry stores. There must also be a high level of crime, because every jewelry store and upscale restaurant has an armed security guard on the premises.

Most of the buildings in Odessa are old but in good condition, and there is lots of interesting architecture to see, like in other parts of Europe. My mind is constantly taken off the buildings, though, as there seems to be a never-ending stream of people wandering around with beer in their hands. I'm getting thirsty. And I'm not sure if it's the thought of the beer or not, but I'm also noticing, just like in Belarus and Moldova, that the younger women (18–25) are all slim with long slender legs, unbelievably slim waists, and big boobs! I can't comment on their looks—my eyes never seemed to get above the breast line. Thank god this is only a thought bubble.

Eating meals here is easy, because most restaurants have an English menu and at least one server who speaks English. I'm able to enjoy some fresh seafood and, although prices are much higher here than in Moldova, it's still a bargain compared to the United States.

The next morning, I'm up early and find myself running from my apartment, which is about one mile from the Black Sea, to the Road of Health. I'm getting some strange, curious, and dirty looks from some people as I run through the city streets to get to Shevchenko Park. I ignore the looks, but I can't ignore the packs of stray dogs in the park.

Without my snarling, though, I discover these strays are scared of people, and they leave me alone. I'm feeling more relaxed when suddenly a pack of about twenty dogs attacks a pet dog that foolishly wanders in. Pet death is averted when the owner leaps into the pack and saves the dog.

The Road to Health not only sounds better, it looks and feels better. It runs along the Black Sea for six kilometers to the sea resort of Arkadiya. It's lined with shade trees and is marked every hundred meters in case you want to do speed work. There are hundreds of locals running and walking along the Road to Health. It feels good. I continue running on into the sea resort.

Arkadiya is known as the "play" area for Odessa. Great beaches, several restaurants, bars, and discos. The locals and tourists play on the beaches during the day and at the discos at night. They're still drinking and partying at 6:30 a.m. as I run by.

I get back to my apartment to discover I have no water. I realize this is not uncommon, because there are several large jugs of water spread about the apartment. I use one of the jugs to wash myself in the sink.

Breakfast time. Uh-oh. The milk I pour on to my cereal—Snow Flakes, the Russian version of Frosted Flakes—isn't actually milk. I don't know what it is, but it's thick and yucky! Not as thick as yogurt, but close. I throw it in the sink and walk across to a store to buy milk. Everything is labeled in Cyrillic, so I can't read a damn thing. I decide to buy a plastic bag of white stuff that looks like milk and looks very liquidy. I take it home, and it's the same shit!

Now I'm frustrated, but I'm on a mission. I really want milk on these damn Snow Flakes. I go back to the store and stop a young person hoping he can speak English and plead "milk"? He can't speak English but he takes me over to the dairy cooler and points to a bottle and says, "Moloko." I trust him, pay for it, and rush back to the apartment. Hallelujah—it is milk—and it tastes wonderful on my Snow Flakes. It's great living like a local.

Having eaten most of the box, I'm now ready to tour the catacombs. When Catherine the Great founded Odessa in 1794, she granted the citizens free land, the right to mine the limestone under their land to build their homes, and the right to eat Snow Flakes with milk. As the city and surrounding region is built on a solid outcrop of limestone, the residents would mine and cut the limestone down to twelve feet for a basement and use the blocks to build their house. Then they would continue to mine down two or three more levels and outward from their property to get more limestone blocks for their house. It was free building material. Every building was built with limestone blocks mined from the ground below it. The result is an amazing labyrinth of catacombs stretching over two thousand kilometers under the city and surrounding area.

Most of the entries and exits have been closed, because there are only maps for less than half the catacombs and people (mostly children) were getting lost in them—never to be found again. The city has left only two openings to the catacombs on the outskirts of the city. These were used by the Resistance fighters in World War II. They lived in the catacombs for four years. My tour is taking us through a section of the catacomb where the Resistance fighters had set up camp. It's very cold and very dark. I couldn't stay down here longer than a few hours, let alone fight a war as well.

In the afternoon, I take a tram to Arkadiya to check out the beaches and cafés once more without my running gear on. Not that I'm looking for the advertised nude beaches, but I never do find them. But the beaches are sandy and nice despite the lack of nudity. I mucked around the resort and had an early seafood dinner. I decided not to stick around until midnight when the action really starts, as I wanted to run ten miles at 6:00 a.m.

The next day I'm running like a local along the Road to Health. I take a hot shower like a spoiled local, and eat a hearty breakfast of Snow Flakes like an American. I'm now ready for the city tour. I'm eager to learn the history of the city.

Odessa is a relatively young city compared to those in Europe, founded in 1794. Catherine the Great wanted a seaport on the Black Sea and so opened the development of the city to all nations and nationalities in Europe. So we have an interesting mix of architecture, and almost all of the original buildings survived the Second World War.

Apparently, Romania had asked Hitler to give it Odessa as a present for joining his alliance, so Odessa was spared from bombing—except for the train station and seaport, but they were rebuilt after the war. After the tour, I explore the old city on my own and enjoy some time in the city's central park. The local artists set up booths in the park every day and sell arts and crafts such as matryushka dolls—the Russian nesting dolls first made in the 1890s in Russia.

But as interesting as all this is, I'm getting a bit bored, and I still have one more day to go. So on the last morning, I do a thirteen-mile run along the Road to Health, because I'm not sure how easy it will be to run at my next destination, Kiev. Later in the day, after checking out of my apartment, I eat some more seafood and head back to the train station to catch the overnight train to Kiev.

The train leaves at eight, and I find myself in a first-class cabin, but with a roommate—a businessman going to Kiev. It doesn't matter—after drinking beer all afternoon in the park and then a bottle of wine with dinner, I immediately pay the conductor two dollars for sheets and a blanket, make my bed, and pass out.

The conductor wakes me up early for our five o'clock arrival into Kiev. I step off the train to begin the next part of my adventure in Ukraine.

Armed with some local knowledge from my roommate, I proceed into the train station in Kiev to negotiate/hassle with a taxi driver for a ride to the hotel. As soon as I open my mouth and speak English, dollar signs register to all the drivers and they demand twenty dollars. After arguing with three of them, I finally find a sane and honest driver who will charge me six dollars.

Off we go to Hotel Rus. I selected this hotel because of its price: seventy-nine dollars a night for a three-star hotel. It turns out to be a good choice. It's located next to the Olympic sports stadium, close to the metro, and only a few blocks from the main street (Khreschatyk). It's been renovated recently and is modern and luxurious. The front desk staff speak English. But I discover the hotel only has me booked for one night, not the four I had paid the agency for.

The hotel lets me check in at six o'clock, so I nap for a few more hours and shower before venturing off to explore the city. It doesn't take me long to figure out I like Odessa much better. Kiev is the capital of Ukraine, and it's big, spread out, and more difficult to explore.

There are lots of Hummers, more beggars (mostly old people) in the streets, and just as many alcoholics walking around at all hours with a bottle of beer in their hand. Beautiful women must be prohibited in Kiev; I can barely see any (the same observation I made on my trip to Moscow four years ago).

To top off my opinion of Kiev, I am the target of a scam within the first hour of my walk. What's the scam? As I walked along the main street, a guy passes me quickly, bends over, and picks up a big roll of bills. He shows me the roll, which includes some fifty-dollar bills, and then exclaims, "We were so lucky to find this money. We should share it!" Well, I wasn't born on a Russian fishing trawler, but it takes about ten seconds for the light bulb to light, and I realize I'm being scammed. This is how the dropped-money scam goes. Guy pretends to find some money on the street and offers to split it with you. You take half, and off you go, wondering how you got so lucky. Next thing you know, another guy is running up to you, saying, "You found my money," and he is now requesting the full amount back. The first guy is nowhere to be seen, so you are left to pay all the cash back.

So I tell him to keep it all and go away. He persists for a few minutes until I shout, "Get lost, or I will call the police!" He disappears quickly. I just love big cities. But it's my fault. I've become lackadaisical in my dress in Odessa. I am wearing jeans and running shoes instead of my European/Russian disguise—black pants, black shirt and black shoes! Nobody in Kiev wears running shoes—I am obviously a tourist!

On the metro, my first destination is the Dnipro station on the Dniper River. My friend in Moldova told me that this is the best place to do a long run, and I want to check it out. I find the station and decide that the sidewalk along the river and a park will work for a run. My next stop is the Podil district—the oldest section of the city. The cobblestone Andriyivskyy path is Kiev's most touristy area with cafés, bars, galleries, and souvenir vendors lining both sides of the street. At the top of the hill is Saint Andrew's Church, a restored eighteenth-century Baroque church.

But I've had enough for one day and decide to return and regroup back at the hotel. The travel agency has sorted out my accommodation with the hotel, so all is good. Early to bed for Maddog.

The next day I'm awake very early and head to the Dniper River for my run. I stay on the path near the river and park, but it's only five kilometers. It starts raining, and people are giving me strange looks, maybe because I'm the only runner on the path. So I run two loops and call it a day. After a hot shower and a great hotel breakfast of eggs, bacon, hash browns, and toast, I'm energized for another day as a tourist.

As there is no tourist infrastructure in Kiev and no tourist office, the hotel offers to arrange a private tour for thirty dollars an hour. But it's raining heavily, and I don't want to spend (waste) that much money for a tour in the rain. So I end up spending the rest of the day and night in my room watching television, including the Tour de France in Russian. Unique for sure.

It's still raining the following morning, so at seven I go to the track in the Olympic stadium next door and run laps in the rain. I don't know if I'm allowed on the track, but the guard just looks at me and shakes his head. Most likely it's raining too hard for him to come outside to tell me to stop. I'm the only one on the track. I run three miles and retreat to the hotel looking like a crazed, wet puppy. But I feel ready for the next marathon.

And then it occurs to me that perhaps there isn't actually a marathon. Paranoia setting in?

I've not communicated directly with the race director in Rovno, because he doesn't speak English and doesn't have e-mail. My friend Dmitry would telephone him and pass the information to me via e-mail. What happens if I get to Rovno and the race has been cancelled or postponed? The rain is clearly affecting my confidence and faith, so I decide that later I will balance it off with a few drinks in the hotel. It will all work out, I tell myself.

After another wonderful breakfast, I decide to explore the city, rain or no rain. The front desk staff gives me an English map of the city that includes a suggested one-day walking tour, so I set off.

Most of the touristy sites are within a one-square-mile radius of the city center, so it was actually quite easy to tour the city on my own. Kiev, like Minsk and Chisinau, had been almost totally destroyed during World War II. Only a few monuments and churches survived. But many of the palaces, churches, and monasteries were restored or rebuilt since independence in 1991. The oldest structure in the city is the Golden Gate, an impressive, actually remarkable, wood-and-stone gate that has been the entrance to the city since 1037.

I figure that I probably won't get a marathon T-shirt from the race, so I buy a souvenir T-shirt from Kiev. I then visit Kiev's oldest and holiest religious site, the Kyiv-Pechery Monastery, which sits on a hill overlooking the Dniper River and dates back to the twelfth century. It provides some spectacular views of Kiev from the Bell Tower.

There are three smiling and happy faces to greet me when I step off the train the next day after an eight-hour train ride from Kiev to Rovno, the marathon destination. The race director, Yuri, has brought along a friend, Alex, and an English teacher from the university, Tanya, to translate for us. They take me to my hotel, the Hotel Mir, which means peace in Russian. It's a one-star hotel but the best hotel in the city (and only eighteen dollars a night). I feel like I've walked into an old Soviet movie as I walk past a security guard to get to the elevator. When I get off on my floor, there's a matron at a desk to monitor the floor. I recall the James Bond movie *From Russia with Love* and think about the scene with the Russian bad girl/matron with the knives in her shoes. Fortunately, Tanya's there to help me check in and help me through these moments, because nobody in the hotel speaks English.

My hosts and I sit down and discuss the agenda for the race. I have lots of questions and want to see the course. Tanya and Yuri agree to pick me up at the hotel at six to go to the stadium and the course, which is close to the hotel. Tanya insists on helping me shop at the supermarket for water and some snack foods.

After I get my supplies, I tell Tanya I can survive on my own and I'll see her at six o'clock. At six, my hosts meet me at the hotel and take me to the stadium. Yuri gives me a race number and explains that after the race, he'll give me a book about the city of Rivne (Tanya explained that the city is called Rovno in Russian but Rivne in Ukrainian) and a ceramic statue of the club symbol.

His running club is called the Flame, and the symbol is a runner with an Olympic torch. I thank him and ask how much for the entry fee. He says there's no entry fee but that I can make a donation if I want. I donate twenty dollars, and he seems thrilled.

Yuri shows me some bottles of tea and local water that I can use on the course. He also has some bottled sparkling water. I explain I'm concerned about intestinal problems from local water, so I would buy some bottled still water and place it at the water station for my own use. Tanya, my dear, sweet translator/angel says she'll come to the race and hand me my water and watch my belongings. I'm feeling pretty special.

Yuri and Tanya walk me over to a park near the stadium and show me the course, a figure-eight loop with a water station placed in the middle of the two circular loops.

Sunday arrives, and it's all on. I'm pumped, in part because this huge trip has worked out as planned. Yuri picks me up at 6:00 a.m., and we walk over to the stadium. There are twelve runners in the marathon and another twelve runners in the half marathon. The race starts at 7:00 a.m.

I decide to stop every second loop for water and gel. By the time I finish the second lap, Tanya is standing there with a cup of water (what an angel). Because of the strange distance of the loop, it's impossible to determine my pace. All I know is that I'm averaging about twelve minutes per loop.

It gets a bit warm and toasty by the end of the race, but I finish comfortably in a time of 3:38—good enough for first place in my age group and fifth place overall. More important, I've accomplished my goal of three marathons and three countries in three weeks!

After the race, Yuri pulls me aside for interviews and photos with the local press. They're writing an article for both the Rivne and Kiev papers. Tanya says she will translate the article and send me a copy.

Yuri then presents me with the book and ceramic statue. He invites Tanya and me to a dinner party at his place. The party starts at three o'clock, so I have lots of time to go back to the hotel for a hot shower and rest. After my shower, I decide to eat some pizza because Yuri has warned me that there will be lots of vodka at the party.

Tanya picks me up, and we walk over to Yuri's apartment. He's invited some runners, friends, and local musicians. He's also prepared a special traditional Ukrainian meal—a type of meat pie. It's like a meat dumpling with minced pork; it's very good.

I've brought along what was left of my bottle of Crown Royal. All the locals drink my whiskey while I drink vodka for the many toasts. Everyone is very interested and curious about life in North America, and they ask many questions about salaries, pensions, health care, and all sorts of stuff. The conversation is flowing, and the alcohol is flowing, and I'm in a room full of wonderful friends.

After dinner the musicians play Ukrainian/Russian music. One musician, a National Opera singer, has written a song to commemorate my visit to Rivne that she sings to me (in Russian). According to Tanya's translation, the song is about "John, the American runner who traveled all the way to our city of Rivne to visit us and run our marathon when he could have gone anywhere in the world."

I'm truly overwhelmed. Incredible kindness, warmth, and friendship. These people, these new friends, are poorer than church mice, but they all have big hearts of pure gold.

After the party, Yuri and Tanya escort me to the train station, as I have to leave this evening. I now wish I didn't. They make sure I get on the right car, and only then do they wish me good-bye.

My second-class cabin is full, but I don't care. After a marathon and plenty of vodka, I simply make my bed and pass out. Again.

The conductor wakes me up at 4:00 a.m. for our 5:00 a.m. arrival in Kiev. I hear some voices speaking English. Turns out it's a church group of twelve people in my coach from New York State. They've been operating a church camp in Lutsk for two weeks for Ukrainian children. We chat for a bit, and I find they have the same observation as I do: the Ukrainian people are poor but so very warm and friendly.

As soon as I arrive in Kiev, I head back to the Hotel Rus. I'd wisely negotiated a room for half price for eight hours. That allowed me to leave my larger bag in the hotel luggage room while I was in Rivne, and now I have a place to sleep for a few more hours, shower, and have another great breakfast before leaving for the airport.

I'm at the airport by noon to catch my 2:15 flight to London. I'm ready to head home!

I feel immensely relieved and satisfied when I pass the final customs hurdle and go straight to the business-class lounge for BA for a nice English beer and a chance to read my first English newspaper in three weeks. I feel even better when the wheels lift off the runway; I know I'm on my way to London Heathrow.

Four hours later, I'm in the London Tube heading to my friend's place in the Vauxhall district. After a quick beer, we head out to a pub near Victoria Station to meet up with another running mate—and a surprise. A new English ale has just been introduced. It's called Mad Dog Pale Ale! My buddies have called the brewery to find out which pubs are serving it.

It's quite good. At nine o'clock, after testing it several times to see how good it really is, we head off to another pub to meet up with two more friends. We drink at that pub until they kick us out.

I blame the hangover the next morning on that damn ale and call it a wee Mad Dog hangover. To get the poison out of my body, I coax Tad to take me on a five-mile run through the heart of London.

I have one last wish before I leave England—I must have a good feed of fish and chips. Tad comes through, and I get my fill of fish and chips. It's been an incredible, unforgettable three weeks!

Time to go home, rest up, and train for the next adventure.

Marathon #241—Country #72, Belfast

Marathon, Northern Ireland

May 2005

The planning for this trip started last year when my buddies from the United Kingdom told me that I'd have to run a marathon in Northern Ireland to complete my goal of running every country in Europe.

Since the race is on Monday, a bank holiday, Nicole and I decide to take a day tour north to Antrim County and the Giant's Causeway.

The Giant's Causeway is a most extraordinary natural phenomenon—a rock formation of volcanic origin consisting of forty thousand vertical basalt columns of varying sizes and heights. According to legend, the Causeway was the work of the giant Finn McCool who fell in love with a giantess from the Island of Staffa (in the Hebrides) and began to build a causeway as a means to bring her to Ireland. It's interesting for sure, but it's so damn cold and rainy when we get there that we don't spend much time out of the bus.

After some dubious pizza, we head back to the hotel where I realize I'm in BIG trouble! I'm really sick all night and suffer a very high fever and chills—sometimes together. I put an extra blanket on the bed in the hope that I might burn the bug out if I keep my temperature high. It partially works. By eight o'clock my fever is down to about 100°F, and the chills are gone. Should I run? No choice, really. I'm not waiting another year to come back here. And it's too expensive to make another trip.

The good news is the start of the race is only a few blocks from the hotel. The bad news is that it's very cold and raining again. I'm standing on the start line in the freezing rain with a temperature of at least 100°F, thinking what a stupid #^*&$#$% idiot I am. Nicole has disowned me. I will be lucky just to finish this race alive; there will be no heroics from me today.

There are about five thousand runners at the start—two thousand marathoners and three thousand relay runners. The race starts at 9:00 a.m.—in the rain—at city hall. It goes through Ormeau Park and then along Falls and Shankill Roads past many of the political murals. There have been no mile markers until finally at mile 10, so I've been having trouble working out my pace. I reach the first marker at mile 10 in 1:22—an 8:15 pace. That's not good. I try to slow down, expecting to find another marker at least at the half, but the marker or timing mats are not where they should be.

I don't understand why until the next day. The IRA, a terrorist group, had planted a bomb on the course around twelve miles. Luckily, they called it in to a newspaper, and the police found the bomb—yes, a real bomb with a remote control. Only the twenty lead runners had run past the bomb before the police diverted the course. They added 1106 meters to the length of the course, and bypassed the original half-marathon mark, I suspect.

I finally reach another marker at fifteen miles—in a time of 2:06. Still too fast. I know I'm in trouble. I start to slow drastically. By the time I reach sixteen miles (another ten minutes), I feel my race is over. I start walking. The rain has stopped, and the sun is shining, so now I start to overheat. The water stops are located about every five kilometers, but by now they're starting to run out of water. It's a very long and painful struggle just to walk and run the last ten miles. But I finally cross the finish line in 4:17. The official website states that 1106 meters were added to the course because of the bomb and runners should adjust their own time. My time is adjusted to 4:09, and given my sickness, I'm pretty damned pleased.

The bomb not going off was good, too.

Marathon #246—Country #73, Torshavn

Marathon, Faroe Islands

July 2005

The Faroe Islands. I'd heard of them but wasn't even sure exactly where they were until one of my buddies in the United Kingdom told me they were considered a country because they have a soccer team that competes in the World Cup. Fair enough. So I added the Faroe Islands to my list of European countries.

Off the top of my head, I think the Faroe Islands are located in the heart of the Gulf Stream in the North Atlantic at 62 degrees north-northwest of Scotland and halfway between Iceland and Norway. The archipelago is composed of eighteen islands stretching seventy miles long and forty-seven miles wide. There are 687 miles of coastline, and at no time is one more than three miles from the ocean. The highest mountain is 2,883 feet, and the average height above sea level for the country is 982 feet. But I could be wrong.

Since I have to route through London and Stansted airport, I arrange a layover in London to visit my former colleagues at the Bishop's Stortford Running Club and join them for a club race. Then I continue on.

The first thing I notice when I arrive in the Faroe Islands is the sheer ruggedness and desolation of the terrain—and it's so green! Everything everywhere is green—everything being grass, though, because there are no trees on the islands. The islands have the highest annual rainfall in Europe, and there are thousands of waterfalls cascading down the mountains into the ocean. The forty-eight thousand people who live here have majestic beauty all around. Of course, they see it more like isolation and desolation. Two of the islands, Streymoy, where Torshavn is located, and Vagar, where the airport is located, are connected by a very long tunnel under Vestmannasund. Steymoy and Fysturoy are connected by a bridge—yes, there is a bridge across the Atlantic Ocean. The other islands have to be reached by boat/ferry. How cool is that?

Boats are the livelihood here; the top industry and export is fishing, and other boats bring in tourists—by the boatload. There are usually two cruise ships in the harbor at Torshavn each day of the summer.

The airport on Vagar is fifty kilometers north and west of Torshavn. It's a very scenic drive into the capital. Most of the marathon course is along this two-lane highway. At this time of the year the Faroes enjoy nineteen hours of daylight, with it getting dark about midnight and then light again at five o'clock.

At breakfast the following morning, I meet a friend I've been looking for—Jaap—a runner from the Netherlands who is also trying to run all the countries in Europe. We've e-mailed but have never met each other until now. Jaap is also a "birder," and he plans to stay for a week to do some birding. Since I've only got one day to explore, we decide to take a bird tour to the cliffs of Vestmanna. These cliffs are famous for their huge colonies of puffins.

We take a bus to the village of Vestmanna and then a boat out into Vestmannasund and the Atlantic Ocean. It's all very scenic, since the cliffs soar as high as twenty-eight hundred feet straight out of the Atlantic Ocean. The boat takes us into many coves and grottos to view the various species of birds nesting in the cliffs. There are thousands and thousands of puffins. I take lots of photos. It's a terrific tour and, as it turns out, a wise decision, since it's the only nice weather I'll see in my five days on the islands.

It's an afternoon marathon. I hate afternoon marathons! It's difficult to prepare for them, and they waste the whole day. And the weather is really miserable: cold, foggy, windy, and rainy.

There are about three hundred of us runners lined up in the town center for the start of three races at two o'clock—marathon, half and a 5.8 kilometer fun run. The first 5.8 kilometers is a loop around—and up and down—the town streets. Since Torshavn is built on the side of a mountain, there are no flat streets in the town.

I start with Jaap and another American. We finish the first loop at a sub-five-minutes/kilometer pace, and I warn the young Yank that we've gone out too fast. He ignores me and continues on while I slow my pace. At eight kilometers, we leave town and head north along the coast directly into a north wind.

The marathon route has several rolling hills and two badass hills that climbed from sea level to about 250 meters in elevation. I'm now running with, and mostly behind, a female who I figured was leading the Half, but when we reach the turn-around point for the Half at the 16-kilometer mark, she keeps going.

She's running the marathon. I decide to pass her. Good idea but much harder to implement. At the 20-kilometer point we'd already climbed and descended both badass hills and now approach the first tunnel to the airport. We also turned away from the wind so the gusts (20–30 mph) are now at our backs for the first time. I pass the lead female at the Half-marathon mark in 1:48. I'm pleasantly surprised.

At 28 kilometers, the lead female passes me, so I decide I will have to catch her back. I decide to charge up every damn hill to the finish line and relax on the downhills. I start my push. At 30 kilometers, I pass the young Yank, who is struggling. At 32 kilometers, as I push up a badass hill (BAH), I pass a ROF (real old fart) who appears to be in my age group and close to within a hundred meters of the lead female. However when I crest the BAH and glance over my shoulder, my ROF competitor was right on my ass and charging! Shit! This is going to be an ugly, painful pissing match all the way to the finish line.

I try to relax and let gravity help me on the backside of that BAH, but "Mr. Won't Give Up" stays right on my butt and even closes the lead some. And so it continues for the final 10 kilometers. I charge up the hills to increase my lead, but he charges down the hills to reduce the lead. As I approached the last BAH at 38 kilometers, I decide I needed to bury this guy once and for all, so I give everything I have to charge up that last BAH! Maddog's "Suicidal High-Altitude Training Camp" at our summer home in the Rocky Mountains had prepared me well for this race. The Faroe hills are easy compared to the thirteeners and fourteeners I've been training on, and the really big difference is that there's lots of oxygen to keep the legs churning all the way up the hills! When I crest the hill at 39 kilometers and look back, I've increased the lead to about three hundred meters. But the last three kilometers are slightly down-hill, so I can't back off. At 40 kilometers, I glance over my shoulder again only to discover that Mr. Wouldn't Give Up has closed the lead again.

Damn—I'm hoping he'll give up so we can both relax and cruise to the finish line. This SOB just won't quit! But there's no way I was going to lose a race this close to the finish line. I decide to suck it up—dig deep—ignore all pain—and drop the pace to sub-five minutes/kilometer for the last two kilo-meters. I draw on every last ounce of willpower to focus on that goal and keep my legs moving as fast as I can. At 41 kilometers I steal a glance back over my shoulder. The lead has increased to three hundred meters again. I have him! There's no way he can make up that distance and pass me in the final kilometers unless I stop! But the SOB still won't give up.

However, the sweet smell of success/victory is enough to get the old bod to produce one final shot of adrenaline—even some endorphins—and I float through the final kilometer in a "zone"—no pain, just a wonderful feeling as I cross the finish line in 3:38:52! I wait at the finish line to congratulate my opponent on a fine race. He finished one minute behind me. I'm not sure whether I should thank him for pushing me or give him shit for hurting me. But I remember one of Maddog's famous quotes: "Pain is only temporary—memories are forever." And the pain has already vanished, so I thank him for pushing me. But he's not a happy camper. He's upset because he won our age group the past two years of the race and has lost his senior title—to an American, no less. Holy crap! He's the guy I didn't think I could beat on paper.

After a quick shower, I return to the finish area for my usual finish line photo and to collect a gold medal for winning the senior division (fifty-plus). Obviously I'm quite pleased with both my time and performance. The only disappointment is that I had not caught the winning female—she beat me by one minute. I have got to find a way to change this frustrating trend. This is the third straight race where I have chased the winning female only to be beaten by one minute.

There's an official postrace party and dinner being held on Saturday evening, but it's very expensive, so two Dutch friends and I decide to eat at a local restaurant. I order breast of puffin, but unfortunately it's not available that day. After dinner and a few well-deserved Faroese beers, my friends returned to the guesthouse, but I decide to go to a popular bar to meet some locals. I join a group of young Faroese lads, and over many Faroese beers (at ten dollars a pint) I learn much about Faroese history and culture that you won't find in *Lonely Planet* or other guidebooks. For example the Faroese language has its roots in the Old Norse language from the Viking Age. After the Reformation, Danish became the official language and the Faroese language almost became extinct. It was revived in the nineteenth century by a famous local scholar and poet.

How did he do it? There were no written records of the language or vocabulary. The answer is the renowned Faroese dance, for which it is necessary to learn and remember a long story. The dance is a continuation of the medieval ring dance that was forbidden in many parts of Europe. Since there is no instrumental accompaniment to the dance, only the voices and feet are heard. The scholar collected many of these stories, which had been handed down for many generations, and from these ballads was able to re-create and reinvent the Faroese language. It is now the official language of the country—and you won't learn that interesting story in any guidebook! I love learning about the local people and culture, even if it can be hazardous to my health (and head) the following morning.

After an eighteen-hour delay at the airport the next day due to fog, the plane finally departs for England, and I am heading back home.

Marathon #251—Country #75 Jesenji Marathon, Bosnia-Herzegovina October 2005

After completing a marathon in Sofia, Bulgaria, I have an eight-hour bus ride to Sarajevo, so I've got time to reflect on how events can change so much, and so quickly, trying this multiple country marathon gig of mine. Originally Sofia was supposed to be the official marathon and Bosnia had just been an idea for a Maddog "special" marathon. It's been turned around so that now, in part because of my quest, I'm off to what will be the first official marathon in Bosnia since the war.

As Bosnia didn't have an official marathon, I've been working for the past year with a runner in Germany, Wolfgang, to organize a marathon in Bosnia to complete my goal of running a marathon in every country in Europe. Bosnia was to be the final marathon/country. One month before the race date, we struck pay dirt. Wolfgang made contact with the Bihac Athletic Club and the president, Nedzad Hadzic (Dzipsi). Dzipsi wrote back that the club is considering a half marathon on October 15, and furthermore, he will add a marathon for us! (two loops of the Half-marathon course).

Since I've never been to Sarajevo, I decide to visit it on my way to Bihac and also to meet and thank my contact in Sarajevo for his efforts.

So now I'm looking out the window on my eight-hour bus trip and immediately notice the change in terrain as one goes from Serbia to Bosnia. Serbia is flat and boring while Bosnia is very mountainous with lots of forests and lakes. Really pretty, in fact.

After hours of driving on mountain roads, the bus approaches Sarajevo and drops down into the city. The city is located in a narrow valley with steep mountains on all sides. I'm lucky to find a hotel on the east side of the city overlooking the Old Town and the Miljacka River, which runs through the city. I call my contact, Vladimir, and arrange to meet him for dinner. I then go shopping for my souvenirs and postcards in Sarajevo, as I'm not sure if I'll find such things in Bihac.

Later that evening, Vladimir and his wife, Nidzara, meet me at the hotel, and we walk over to the old town for dinner. They're much younger than I expected; students in their early twenties. Vladimir is studying computer science, and Nidzara is in her third year of medical school. They both have part-time jobs and have run a marathon!

They give me a guided tour of old town, and we eat some traditional food—a cevabdzince serves cevabd—a flat, leavened bread filled with meat. Nidzara calls them meat fingers. They're not spicy but have a strong taste and are delicious. A buregdzince serves buregd—a kind of pastry or pie filled with cheese, meat, or vegetables. A typical dinner costs about two dollars. We talk about the history and culture of Bosnia. Everyone starts out every sentence with either "before the war" or "after the war." Vladimir was a young boy in Sarajevo during the war (1992–1995) and was not allowed to go outside for four years. Four years! He's bitter that the war robbed him of his youth, but he's also determined to get on with his life and be successful. They're friendly and gracious hosts.

The next day, I explore the old town and the city. There are lots of old churches and mosques. Sadly, there are still many signs of the war. The old city hall, which had been converted to the National Library, was badly damaged and burned, along with all the books and artifacts. There is no money to restore it. Across from the Holiday Inn (the only international hotel in the country) stands a row of military and government buildings that were also bombed. The exterior shells of the damaged buildings are covered with pockmarks from bullets, as are many houses in the city (and indeed in the country).

The next day, I catch an early bus to Bihac so I can meet up with Wolfgang, as we plan to meet with Dzipsi and another club member—Branislav Versic— to offer them any advice and assistance we can provide. They have more good news. The city has provided some financial support, and they have enough medals, certificates, and T-shirts for a hundred runners. They've printed up posters and invited runners from neighboring countries. And to alleviate traffic problems, the marathon now has its own course. They've pulled this race together in less than one month. We're very excited.

On Friday, my friends Tad and Chris arrive from the United Kingdom. We go on a guided tour of Bihac. It's a small city of seventy thousand people in the northwest of Bosnia near the border with Croatia. The region around Bihac is probably the flattest area in the country.

Saturday comes. It's race day! We walk over to the start/finish line, talk to the local runners, and watch registration. The weather is chilly, and it's foggy as we start. I'm not feeling well—a cold that's gotten worse over the past three days. It's like Belfast all over again.

At 11:00 a.m., Dzipsi is ready to start the races. There are twenty-one runners in the Half and thirteen in the marathon. Strangely, there are no women entered in either race. I look over the competition in the marathon, and I figure there are two runners who will be hard to beat.

We're off! We run two short loops around the city center before heading south out of the city. I'm running with a small group of half-marathon runners and can see three marathoners in front of me. At eight kilometers, I find I'm running all by myself, but, fortunately, they've assigned a young boy on a bike to accompany me so that I don't get lost.

At 20 kilometers, I'm into a tough climb to a castle, and at this point my guide leaves me. It's a bit of a concern until I realize there are no turnoffs on this road, so it'll be hard to get lost.

At 25 kilometers, I pass one of the lead runners, a twenty-year-old, who by now is walking. At 26 kilometers, I pass a second runner, and at 27 kilometers, I pass a third runner. As I approach an intersection for the small loop across the river, I meet the leader (and eventual winner) finishing the loop. That means he is about two to three kilometers ahead of me. I know I can't catch him unless he crashes. And since nobody can catch me, I decide that there's no sense in pushing the old bod too hard, so I ease off my pace. I'm running slower now and have more time to take in the beautiful scenery around me.

As I approach the road to the castle and the 30-kilometer marker, I'm shocked to see something I hadn't noticed on the first loop. On both sides of the road there are large red signs and areas marked off with bright yellow tape warning of land mines.

Land mines?

Some of these areas are less than two feet from the sides of the road. Thank god I didn't need to make a pit stop or even pass out earlier. Kaboom! What a mess. And likely a DNF (Did Not Finish). I later confirm with Dzipsi, who works with the military to clear mines, that these areas along the course are indeed active minefields that haven't been cleared yet. He also says that there are more than one million mines and another one million unexploded ordnances that need to be located and cleared from Bosnia. We are very lucky in the United States. We just don't know how lucky we really are, and it's worth it to pause and reflect, which we also seldom do.

Soon I'm climbing up the road past the castle again and then a two-kilometer downhill section, which helps my legs to recover. I reach the main road again at 40 kilometers in a time of 3:38. I coast the last two kilometers back into town and cross the finish line in 3:51.

I've done it! I've finished my final country in Europe, and I've become the first person in the world to run a marathon in every country in Europe. And as a nice reward and surprise, I've finished in second place overall.

That evening, we invite Dzipsi and his colleague, Bran, to dinner to celebrate and thank them for all their work. Dzipsi says they'll hold the marathon again next year, and it will be bigger and better. We promise to help in any way we can. It's a great night to round off a great trip.

Marathon #252—Country #76,

Everest Marathon, Nepal

October 2005

Mount Everest is the world's highest mountain at 8,848 meters (29,029 feet) above sea level. The international border between China and Nepal runs across the precise summit point. It was given its official English name by the Royal Geographical Society, named after Sir George Everest who had been the British surveyor general of India. New Zealander Edmund Hillary and the Nepalese Sherpa Tenzing Norgay made the first official ascent of Everest in 1953.

I'm not going to climb it, of course. Where's the fun in that? Besides, it's been done before. No, instead I plan to run the Everest Marathon—not to the top, but pretty damn high all the same. The Everest Marathon is billed as "the highest and toughest marathon in the world." It is! It is also the hardest marathon in the world for getting to the start line.

The marathon first got my attention a few years ago. It's only held every two years in the fall, and you have to qualify for the race. You must have experience in endurance events at high altitudes and the cutoff age is sixty-five. It's also very expensive, because the packaged trip/tour to do the race lasts twenty-six days, which includes three weeks of trekking in the Himalayas. I did try to get corporate sponsors but in the end decided that this was a once-in-a- lifetime experience so I'd suck it up and pay the cash. Life is about experience and memories, after all.

I thought I was in good shape for Everest. I'd trained all summer in the Colorado Rockies to get used to mountain trails and high altitudes. By the end of the summer, I'd climbed eight fourteen-thousand-foot-high peaks and raced three mountain-trail marathons.

To save money, I've booked my own air travel with free miles and will meet the group in Kathmandu. The downside, of course, is that my free flight routing has meant forty-one hours of quality airplane and airport time from Florida to Katmandu.

It's Friday. All the runners have assembled in Katmandu to discuss the trip. There are seventy runners, race volunteers, and medical staff, so we split into three groups of about twenty-four people: the Early Birds, the Late Birds, and the Cuckoos. I'm with the Cuckoos and my roommate (or tentmate) for the trip is a very nice gentleman, Francisco, an economist from Argentina. Our group seems to be the most laid-back. We have a few fell runners from the United Kingdom, but most of the team members are running their first marathon. Wow! The other groups have fell teams from different regions of the United Kingdom, and most are very intent on competing and winning the race. I quickly realize I'm totally out of my league here, and any sense of being competitive has gone the way of the Yeti.

Yet here I am. Pinching myself. Experience of a lifetime. In the afternoon, our tour operator takes us on a tour of Kathmandu, starting with a visit to the two-thousand-year-old Buddhist shrine of Swayambhunath, or the Monkey Temple, which sits on a hill overlooking the city.

Next, we visit Durbar Square with its multitude of palaces and temples. It was started in the fifteen hundreds by the Malla kings and enlarged in the seventeenth century. We stop at the Kumari Bahal, the home of Nepal's living goddess—a young girl selected from a Newari Buddhist family at the age of four. She can only leave her palace seven times a year; she is carried through the streets to assure Kathmandu of her protection. When she reaches puberty, she is no longer considered pure and is replaced. Tough crowd.

Kathmandu is a madhouse of pedestrians, rickshaws, motorcycles, and cars fighting for room on the narrow streets as hawkers try to sell you their junk souvenirs, and centuries-old temples.

We're limited to a total weight of twelve kilos for our kit bags. Not that we carry them, that's the job of the Sherpas (porters). Our bags are weighed before they're taken to the airport on Saturday morning. My oversized, heavy sleeping bag is already a problem. I've had to stuff more equipment into my daypack, which I'll have to carry myself. Crap. I've also got to leave a lot of clothes and gear in Kathmandu.

On Saturday morning, we head to the airport for a flight to Lukla, which is the gateway to the Everest region to the east of Nepal. There are no roads into Lukla, only an airport and trails. The airport in Lukla is built into the side of a mountain at 2,860 meters/9,438 feet. It's only five hundred meters long, and if I didn't know I was about to fly in, I'd be thinking we'd arrived at Lukla's only ski jump.

Planes land up the ski jump and take off down the ski jump. All landings and takeoffs are visual, and there is only one chance. The odds must be good, though, because they've been doing this for years, using old Canadian Beaver aircraft equipped to carry sixteen passengers and land on ski lifts.

It is an exciting flight. We are at the top of the world and realize just how insignificant we are as we rock and roll our way to Lukla, surrounded by majestic beauty. But now is not the time to talk about the air hostesses; there is great scenery to be seen out the window. We arrive in Lukla safely, collect our kit bags, meet our Sherpas, and depart for Phakding, where we will camp for the first night.

Francisco and I trek together, and we all arrive in Phakding after about three hours. The terrain is similar to Colorado—lots of forests, but the mountains are higher. The trails are much wider than in Colorado, and much busier. There are hundreds and hundreds of trekkers, Sherpas, and yaks going in both directions. It's almost as if I'm trekking on Forty-Fifth Street in New York City. And since the trail is the main route into the Everest region, there are teahouses or lodges located every kilometer along the trail. These teahouses serve tea, beer, pop, and food to the trekkers and offer a dormitory room or double room for as little as fifty cents a night.

Francisco and I eat lunch while we wait for our Sherpas to arrive with our tents and kit bags. The Sherpas set up our tents in an area adjacent to a lodge.

There is a charge for using the campground and an outdoor cookhouse. If we eat in the dining room of the lodge, which is warmer and more comfortable than eating in a mess tent, there is also a fee for that (paid by the event organizer).

For the whole trip, the Sherpas typically arrive at our campsite after us (they are carrying more than eighty pounds of gear up and down mountains, after all) but hopefully before the sun goes down and it starts to get cold. After they put up our tents, we empty our kit bags and get our sleeping bags, etc. prepared for the night.

When the sun drops behind the mountains, the temperature drops very quickly to about 20–30°F. So cold, in fact, that it's necessary to change into our sleeping clothes before the sun goes down. ! At four o'clock each day, the Sherpas serve hot tea and biscuits in the mess tent or lodge dining room. I usually go to afternoon tea in my PJs and stay in the warm lodge until dinner is served at six, as did most of the team. We'd read, play cards, or write our daily logs until dinner. By five o'clock it's dark and very cold in the tents. Read: DAMN MISERABLE!

Dinner always starts with a bowl of hot soup (usually quite good) with some kind of bread or popcorn—they put popcorn in the soup because it's easy to carry and prepare. Then we have two or three portions of veggies—usually potatoes or rice served with lentil soup (the Nepal traditional dish of dal bhat)—and another veggie such as steamed cabbage. I admit to getting very frustrated because there is very little meat served. After our delicious veggie dinner we get a dessert. All of the food is prepared in an outdoor cookhouse and carried to the mess tent or dining room. After dinner, hot tea and/ or hot chocolate is served. I get tired of tea very quickly so start drinking a lot of hot chocolate.

While the Sherpas are setting up our tents in Phakding, I decide to do a short hike along the trail to explore the next day's route. About one mile from the camp, I come upon a young Nepali woman lying on the side of the trail. Another woman is trying to coax her to get up. I ask if she is sick and if she has sent for help. We have a communication problem because I initially understand that help is coming, but thirty minutes later on my return back to our tent site, the woman is still lying on the trail.

So I run back to our camp, explain this to our team doctors, and ask them to go and look at the woman. I escort them back to the young woman, and she's unconscious. They can't revive her so we carry her back to the camp on a stretcher. They revive her and give her some IV and antibiotics to treat a serious chest infection. The doctors arrange to put her up in the lodge for the night so they can continue to treat her.

The next morning we check on her but she's gone. She's yanked out the IV and left during the night. Bit of a headbanger, but I feel good that at least I tried to help.

We enjoy our first breakfast in the (cold) mess tent and get to learn the morning pattern. A Sherpa wakes us at about six o'clock with a cup of hot tea. Then we have about thirty to forty-five minutes to pack up our kit bag and leave it outside the tent for the Sherpas to pick it up to carry it to the next campsite. I change from my PJs into my trekking clothes. Holy crap, it's cold on my butt at six o'clock in minus zero temperature. "Bracing," I could charitably say.

Breakfast starts with a bowl of cereal served with hot milk made from powder. They can't use cold water because it won't be safe to drink. I try it, but I can't stomach the idea of cereal with hot milk so I skip it after this first day. Sometimes we get porridge just to mix things up a bit—a kind of a sloppy, liquidy mixture of oatmeal. I'm pleased I've brought along my own pound of brown sugar, as it makes the porridge edible. At least we get eggs after this, usually an omelet on dry toast or some kind of local bread. This is actually quite good, although after eighteen days, I swear I will never eat another egg or drink another cup of hot tea!

Then, after breakfast, it is serious trekking—or climbing, really. Nepal doesn't seem to use switchbacks; the trails go straight up the mountain—if it gets too steep, they add steps. Climbing steps for half a mile at 11,000 feet is not easy.

At the end of the day, we arrive in Namche Bazaar, the administrative center of the Khumbu or Everest region. We have two nights here for altitude acclimation. And we stay in lodges, so we get to live in relative comfort for two days. Francisco and I share a room above the kitchen, so our room actually has some heat until about 9:00 p.m. Each room has two cots, where we spread our sleeping bags out. The walls are paper-thin, probably because they're made of paper, so we can hear people picking the lint out of their belly buttons three rooms away. We don't hear toilets or showers because they're located outside. This doesn't bother Francisco and me since we both have come equipped with pee bottles. That's right, we pee in the bottle during the night and empty it in the morning, a far more civilized way of being civilized than getting out of a warm sleeping bag to go outside—in Nepal for Pete's sake—at three in the morning! I don't know what the women do, and I don't ask.

Many of the runners use the time to buy additional gear that they now realize they need. I buy a fleece sweater for another layer of sleeping clothes and some trekking poles for the steep trails.

The marathon will finish in Namche (elevation 3,440m/11,286 feet) and the twenty-mile mark is located on a trail above the village, so it's good to wander around for the two days. Francisco and I run an easy five miles out and back, and it takes eighty minutes. The following day, the whole group runs a ten-kilometer loop to become familiar with the route; ninety minutes to run ten-kilometers, and that's on lodge-rested, fresh legs. I'm thinking my prerace finishing time goal of six hours may be significantly unrealistic.

Most of us also trek about three miles up above Namche to the Everest View hotel for our first view of Everest, which is about thirty miles away. It looks huge even at this distance. Tomorrow we head off on a one-week trek up the Dudh Kosi Valley to Gokyo, which is at 4,750meters/ 15,675 feet. This will be our first real attempt to acclimate to the high altitudes and strengthen our legs for the race.

We're advised to leave a clean change of clothes in Namche to change into after the race. I take the opportunity to leave some more clothes behind to lighten the weight of my kit bag and day pack.

Our first day sees us up and down trails in the Khumbu region. The region is dominated by Ama Dablam (6,856 meters/22,624 feet). Although the mountain is not that high, really, it stands alone and looks quite spectacular. For dinner we are treated to yak curry to fortify us and get us ready for the cold night. The temperatures drop to −5°C, and my water bottle freezes. Thank god I'm wearing thermal underwear.

As we climb higher the next day, the trails are rocky and covered in ice. It's very dangerous. At the end of a tough day, we finally take a very steep climb to Dole (4,048 meters/13,358 feet) where we camp for the night. Taboche (6,501 meters/21,453 feet) towers over the village.

The next day is the same as we head to Machermo (4,460 meters/14,718 feet) where we will camp for two days to acclimate to the higher altitudes. Machermo sits in a large valley that is dominated by three mountains: Machermo (6,186 meters/20,413 feet), Taboche and Cholotse (6,410 meters/21,153 feet). The trails are very dusty and are covered in yakshit. The combination of dust and shit is ingested by trekkers. By the time we reach Machermo, everyone is suffering from the "Himalayan cough," a dry, irritating cough caused by the dry air/dust/yakshit. Wonderful. I try not to think about it too much.

For many runners in the group, the cough turns into a chest cold or infection. Some of the group are also having intestinal problems (vomiting and diarrhea) in spite of our constant attention to hygiene. But we can only take care of our own hygiene. I watched a Sherpa in a lodge add yakshit to a fire and then prepare and serve food to trekkers without washing her hands. Were we eating yakshit? Another thought that is not good to have linger in my mind.

Fortunately, we have team doctors with us. They're able to keep all of the runners going in spite of the problems and illnesses. But at 15,000 feet some of the runners start suffering from AMS (acute mountain sickness or altitude sickness). One of our teammates, Justin, gets so seriously ill with AMS that he can't walk and has to be carried by Sherpas down the mountain in the dark accompanied by a team doctor. The only cure for AMS is to get to a lower elevation to acclimate so they carry him back down to Dole where he stays for three days, acclimating and waiting for us to pick him up on the way back down. Even some of the team doctors suffer from AMS and have to retreat to lower elevations for additional acclimation.

The doctors and race organizers strongly advise us to rest and acclimate during our two days in Machermo, and not to do anything too strenuous. I follow the advice for the first day. Francisco and I do our laundry in a mountain stream. The water coming off the Machermo Glacier is so cold that my hands turn blue within a few minutes of scrubbing. But I then enjoy a hot shower at the lodge where we camp. I don't really want to get out of it, but I suppose other people might want a shower. I could always share.

The shower is an outdoor stall with a forty-liter bucket on the roof that is filled with hot water heated on the kitchen stove. I stand on an inch of ice covering the concrete floor of the shower stall while the hot water scalds my head and body. It's truly wonderful as it's not only hot, I get to rinse all the dust and yakshit off my body and wash my hair.

And it only costs two dollars. Then, yes, I must be close to heaven; I enjoy yak steak and chips at the lodge. It's a great rest day.

The next day, I'm out doing a hard training run—a fast ten kilometers back toward Dole. I'm probably running with an "I'm stupid" sign on my forehead, because I start getting a headache—a sign of AMS. After the run, Francisco and I climb up a ridge overlooking Machermo. We climb to 16,000 feet, and the headache gets worse, and the font size of the "stupid" sign gets larger. From out of nowhere, common sense arrives, and I decide to rest and take it easy in the hope that the headache will disappear by morning.

It does. I'm very lucky, I think. We pack everything in the morning and continue the trek to Gokyo. It's only a short journey and we only climb three hundred meters (a thousand feet), but my headache comes back by the time we arrive in Gokyo.

We find out that the lodge area where we are to camp cannot accommodate all of our tents. Eight of us must volunteer to sleep in the lodge. Being the oldest members of the team, Francisco and I do the honorable thing and volunteer to sleep inside the lodge. That night turns out to be the coldest night of the trek so we're happy, almost giggling with joy, with our decision.

I wake up not only warm but without a headache. So I join some teammates to climb to the summit of Gokyo Ri (5,483 meters/18,003 feet). I've climbed many 14,000-foot peaks but, believe me, there is no comparison when you start climbing at 16,000 feet and have to climb another two thousand vertical feet on a very steep ascent.

I'm sucking air all the way up and have to make lots of rest stops. But the climb is worth it.

Gokyo Ri stands all alone and thus offers a spectacular and panoramic view of the "Top of the World." We can see twenty peaks over 20,000 feet tall—from Cho Oyu (8,153 meters/26,910 feet) in the north, to Everest (8,850 meters/29,205 feet), Lhotse (8,501 meters/28,053 feet), Makalu (8,475 meters/27,968 feet) to Thamserku (6,608 meters/21,806 feet) near Namche. It's incredible! This moment with this view, alone, is well worth the cost of the trip. It's a memory I'll never forget!

After a couple of days of more trekking and amazing views, dust, and yakshit, we rejoin the actual marathon route. Francisco and I have skipped the usual egg breakfast and stop instead at a bakery in Khumjung, the highest bakery in the world, for a good old-fashioned cinnamon bun and hot chocolate. It's wonderful! We then descend to Sarnassas and continue on down to the river at Phunki Tenga (3,250 meters/10,725 feet).

This is the lowest point of the Everest Marathon course—at about seventeen miles. Then we climb 617 meters/2,036 feet to Tengboche (3,867 meters/12,761 feet) over three miles. We're warned that this is the steepest and most dangerous section of the marathon course and will be a descent on the actual marathon. The trail is very steep and dangerous, and it's at this point that I decide that my primary goal is not a specific finish time but, in fact, simply to finish the race safely and to be healthy.

As we arrive in Tengboche, we discover that we're walking into a five-day religious festival. The monks are blowing their horns and performing very colorful ceremonies that we watch. I manage to order a chicken burger at one of the lodges—well, pressed, canned chicken, but at least it tastes like chicken. I also discover a satellite Internet café—the highest Internet café in the world—and e-mail an update to my friends.

As we arrive in Dingboche the next day, it's very evident that many members of our group are falling like flies. Nine days of trekking now, the ingestion of dust and yakshit, bad food, and dodgy water are taking their toll. Many runners are very sick and opt to stay in a lodge room instead of suffering the cold and misery of the tents. I decide to tough it out and stay in the tent, which I now have all to myself as Francisco heads to the lodge as well.

I rest for long periods in this two-day acclimatization stay and do not run at all. Instead of freezing my hands doing my own laundry, a local Sherpa woman says she will do it for me. I send her many customers from our team, and she's very happy with the extra income. I enjoy another shower, more so since I know it will be my last until I finish the race.

I'm lying here tonight, alone in the cold tent, and wondering if my cough is turning into a chest cold. And race day is almost upon us.

We arrive at the end of the next day at Lobuche (4,910 meters/16,203 feet) for another two-day camp and more high-altitude acclimation. We've been told that Lobuche is a dump.

It sure is! The lodges and campsites are filthy; the outhouses are so despicable that everyone refuses to use them, choosing instead to find places on the side of the mountain to do their job. The lodge where we camp is also a dump. On this first night they don't even start a fire in the stove until we chip in and bribe them to start a fire, which they let go out after a few hours. On our second night, they have a full house of guests and kick us out of the dining room.

We discover there's a new lodge that has just been built on the edge of the village. We rent every spare room in the lodge, mainly because many members are sick, and the others are sick of staying in cold tents.

I opt, however, to stay in my tent (by myself again) and stick with the program.

By this time, most of the Cuckoo team members are sick to some extent, nerves are frayed, and many people are edgy. The other teams (including their group leaders) get angry and upset with the Cuckoos, letting us know that we are wimps and would have an unfair advantage in the race because we are staying in lodges. I feel like I'm eight years old in a new school with bullies. *Lord of the Flies* sort of stuff.

Another group leader forbids his group from staying in a lodge. "It would not be in the true spirit of the game," he says. It gets very ugly and personal. One of our team members, a young British army officer, invites the belligerent group leader to step outside to settle the affair. It's a good thing he declines, because Matt is a champion kickboxer. Finally, the group leaders get together to diffuse the situation. It ends well. It's amazing how quickly a group of total strangers can bond and become a close-knit team when they face hardship and adversity together.

The next morning, a few of us Cuckoos trek three miles to Gorak Shep, and climb Kala Patthar (5,623 meters/18,555 feet) for a different view of the Top of the World. It's worth the effort because Everest and Nuptse are only a few miles away and tower over Kala Patthar. It's hard to believe I'm standing at 18,000 feet, and these mountains still tower 10,000–11,000 feet above me. Other than this view, the last two days are the most miserable days of the whole trek. As we head back to camp, all I can do is count the days and hours till we run the marathon and put an end to this misery.

The next day we move on to Gorak Shep where the marathon will start. But we first have to pass a medical check and collect our numbers in Lobuche before we can begin the trek to Gorak Shep. Almost everyone is sick with chest colds, infections, intestinal problems, and AMS.

The medical test relies mainly on honesty. Although nobody wants to be pulled from the race, it's simply idiotic to lie and risk serious illness or death. We also have to perform a toe-to-heel walk forward and backward, much like a sobriety test. Apparently, this is difficult to do if you have serious problems with AMS. We all breathe a collective sigh of relief when we find out every one of the fifty-six runners is deemed fit to be at the start line!

It's a treacherous three-mile trek to Gorak Shep across a moraine field deposited by the Khumbu Glacier. It takes us more than two hours to trek these three miles. But at least we arrive in Gorak Shep (5,200 meters/17,160 feet), our final camp, by noon. The marathon is just hours away now.

Some runners climb Kala Patthar for the magnificent view of Everest, but most of us just rest and wait for a practice run of the race that starts at 4:00 p.m. All the runners (including twenty Nepali runners) gather at the start line in the sand bowl to listen to instructions about the race and the start. Attila the Hun (our belligerent group leader) gives the instructions.

1) At 6:50 a.m., all runners will line up at the start line. Attila will shout, "Number one." Runner #1 would confirm their presence and then all subsequent race numbers will shout their numbers in numerical sequence. We practice this difficult procedure.

    But the Nepalese have difficulty with this process because they are shy and don't like to be loud or flagrant in public. Attila gets very angry. I'm feeling embarrassed for both him and the race organization, because he makes an ass, perhaps a yak, of himself.

2) All runners must carry a minimum survival kit (three layers of clothes, a whistle, headlamp, first-aid kit, anti-Yeti spray, etc.) at all times during the race. Failure to do so will result in disqualification from the race.

3) Every runner must wear a race number on the front and back, shout out their number at each checkpoint, and then verify that the number was heard. This will simplify any search for a missing runner. Fair enough.

4) If a runner comes across a colleague who is injured or ill they must stay with that runner and provide assistance until another runner comes by who can go to the nearest aid station for medical help. Failure to do so will result in disqualification from the race and possible throwing off the side of a tall mountain. And because there are many anal runners here, any time spent assisting another runner will be deducted from the final finish time of that runner.

It seems everyone understands and agrees with these rules and acknowledges that they're necessary for the safety and security of all runners!

After the lecture, I visit the team doctor because I feel like my Himalayan cough is indeed turning into a chest cold, and I don't want to wake up tomorrow, on race morning, with a terrible cold. He offers me some antibiotics but warns that they will probably cause diarrhea.

Fantastic! I decide to decline the drugs and risk the cold. I go back to our tent and change into my race clothes, because the last thing I want to do in the pitch black and cold of an early race morning is fumble my way to race readiness and dress myself with cold—perhaps blue—digits.

I ordered my traditional pasta dinner from the lodge—spaghetti Bolognese (in which I believe the meat is minced yak; so perhaps it's spaghetti Nepalese). Then we're served a light veggie dinner by the Sherpas that I pass on.

After dinner, our group leader, Bruce, a very nice gentleman from Troon, Scotland, reads us a poem. Bruce is running Everest for the fifth time, and I have to wonder why. The poem is about terminally ill patients, with the main thrust being nobody knows how long they are on this planet, so if there is something you want to do—or somebody you want to love—then seize the moment.

I seize the moment and go back to the tent to check on last-minute race preparations, and then I head to bed. I want my running shoes to be warm in the morning, so I stuff them in my sleeping bag, as well as my water bottle, because I need to mix an energy drink in it in the morning. I have two layers of running clothes on and decide to also put my down jacket on and sleep in it, too. My god, it's getting crowded in my sleeping bag! I scribble some notes in my book throughout the night as I lie there wide awake praying for daylight to come so the race can start and I can put an end to this ordeal. I'm thinking there are about fifty-five others in the same state of mind. Except for Bruce from Troon perhaps, who may be planning his sixth visit.

Mercifully, I doze off for a few hours and almost hit my head on the tent roof as I wake up and leap out of my sleeping bag to get the day going. It's freezing cold, though, so I leap straight back into my sleeping bag. A 5:30 a.m. wake-up call is followed instantly with a cup of hot tea thrust into our tent. Francisco and I decline the hot porridge because it's porridge, for one thing, and we want to stay in our warm sleeping bags as long as possible.

We think briefly about running the marathon in our sleeping bags, but we don't have time to cut holes in the bottom for our feet. Reluctantly, we get out of the bags and pack them, so the Sherpas can carry them down to Namche. The kit bags would probably not arrive in Namche until the following day. By the time we finish packing, we're freezing. I can't feel my toes, which shouldn't be a surprise when we hear it is –20°C. At 6:45 a.m., we walk as if we're off to the gallows to the start line, and the race starts ingloriously a few minutes later.

The big dogs—the fell runners—race across the desert sand and charge up the hill of glacial moraine (at 17,000 feet) as they ignore the burning in their lungs. The mortal runners, including a sad-looking, jaded Maddog, jog across the desert sand, struggle to walk up the glacial moraine, and suck desperately for oxygen while trying to get frozen feet to navigate around and over the dangerous rocks.

Unfortunately, I find myself in front of a pack of about ten runners, so I feel obligated to push myself faster than I want. It's about eight minutes into the race now, and I'm hurting already. Fortunately, we soon reach a short downhill section. I pretend my shoelace has come undone and let everyone in this pack run by me.

My feet are frozen solid as I stump myself across, up, and down two miles of glacial moraine. I discover the water in my CamelBak is frozen when I try to get a drink. We reach a flat and smooth section of the trail, and I start to run. I use the term "run" loosely, given that I'm hurtling along with twenty pounds of survival gear strapped to my back and sucking in any thin air at 17,000 feet I can find. I check a couple of times, and I'm pleased to say I'm at least not running backward.

I run a bit with Bruce from Troon. We reach the first-aid station/checkpoint in Lobuche (three miles) in fifty-seven minutes. This is going to be a long day.

Oh wow. The sun is rising. I stop at the aid station and remove one layer of clothes, drink some water, and continue on. The next three miles of trail descend 290 meters to Dughla (4,620 meters/15,246 feet). The trail is in good shape, and I can run most of the flat and downhill sections. I reach Dughla in 1:35; it's a blazing thirteen minutes/mile pace now. Look out. Here comes Maddog.

I stop and remove another layer of clothes. At this rate, I'll soon be naked. The next checkpoint is in Periche (4,240 meters/13,992 feet) in three miles. There are more rocks on this section, and it's much more difficult than the flat sections. We reach the third checkpoint in 2:16.

I stop and remove my last layer of removable clothes; I'm now running in polypro tights and a thin long-sleeve T-shirt. But now my daypack is getting heavy with all the clothes I'm carrying. The CamelBak has finally thawed out, so at least I have some water available between aid stations.

Trekkers on the trails step aside and cheer us on when we meet or overtake them. Only the yaks are discourteous and a pain in the ass. Several times I get caught behind a yak team and have to walk for a few minutes before I can find an opening to scamper past them on the uphill side of the mountain. We're warned, "Always the uphill side" in case a yak charges to knock us off the mountain.

I reach Pangboche, our next station, in 3:19. I'm not even halfway. I push on to the next checkpoint at Tengboche at fourteen miles. We have to climb a very steep hill between Deboche and Tengboche; it's a bitch! I struggle just to simply walk up the hill, which makes my badass hills from home seem like a gentle slope for a wheelchair.

I want to reach Tengboche (3,867 meters/12,761 feet) in under four hours but can't do it. I reach the halfway checkpoint in 4:02. I push on, running down the very steep and dangerous descent to Phunki Tenga (3,250 meters/10,725 feet). I catch up with Justin, and we run the descent together, which really helps. We are able to push each other (mentally, that is) and watch out for each other. When we reach a nasty uphill section to Sarnassa (3,597 m/11,870 feet), I push on, and Jason wishes me good luck and drops back. I try desperately to reach the checkpoint above Namche at twenty miles in under six hours but arrive in 6:01.

The last six miles of the course is the Thamo loop. I'm feeling pretty confident that I can run the loop in under two hours, which will mean a sub-eight-hour race could be in the bag. I pass many of my teammates and other runners on the loop. I keep pushing myself now, as I'm getting a strong whiff of finish line. I push the pace as hard as I can at the end and cross the finish line in Namche in 7:43. Not fast. Not pretty. But I've finished! And as far as I can tell, I'm alive.

I wait around at the finish line to watch a few of my new friends cross the line. Then it's off for a hot shower. We get to enjoy a beer and some snacks while we wait for everyone to finish. All but four runners finish the race.

Some of the young runners still have enough energy to celebrate and party. Most of us just want to go to bed and sleep. Most of us are also broke. The trip information we were given advised us to take about 100 GBP ($200) on the trek and leave the rest of our money and credit cards in Kathmandu. But that information is severely outdated, and the amount is not enough. As a result, most of us are either broke or only have enough money to get back to Kathmandu. I have to borrow twenty dollars to pay for food and a room in Lukla. And I also have no money with which to celebrate right now.

Miraculously, over the next day or so, many of the illnesses and ailments that people had been suffering seemed to disappear now that the marathon is finished and we're back at lower altitudes.

There is a curfew in Lukla on our arrival. Nobody is allowed in or out of the village after 5:00 p.m., and nobody is allowed outdoors in the village after 6:00 p.m. Because of the airport and the strategic location of the village, the Nepal government is very worried about Maoist rebels capturing the village. There are hundreds of soldiers and machine gun placements all around the airport and village. We are warned that the soldiers will first shoot anyone violating the curfew and then ask questions.

We arrive in Kathmandu the next day—wonderful, noisy, polluted, congested, *warm* Kathmandu! As soon as I get to the hotel, I go straight to the bathroom and stand under scalding hot water for about three days. I get the last remaining Himalayan dust and yakshit off my body and then walk over to Thamel to order a hamburger. It's a real hamburger with real beef. I wash it down with a beer, and I am in heaven!

That night, our team goes to a popular restaurant, Mike's Place, owned by a British expat—Mike, I'm guessing—for dinner. I'm pleasantly surprised to discover that Mike has a special buffet—a Thanksgiving turkey dinner. I spend a long time at the trough and eat about five pounds of turkey and mashed potatoes.

After dinner, I make the mistake of accompanying a group of young runners (my friends now) to some bars to celebrate, and then I make a bigger mistake of trying to drink with them. Around three o'clock, I stagger to a rickshaw, which takes me back to the hotel.

The resulting hangover is so massive that I miss a nine o'clock tour of Kathmandu. I think it's about three in the afternoon when I fall out of bed and begin the process of recovery to get ready for the awards banquet and ceremony.

The winner is a runner from the United Kingdom, who finishes the race in a sickening time of 4:57. My friend from New Zealand, Robert, finishes second.

The following morning, the main group is preparing to depart, and I'm getting ready to transfer to another hotel. The owner of the tour agency/race organization approaches me and gives me a trophy for the super vet category. A competitor who beat me across the finish line has been disqualified for not carrying a survival kit during the race! I accept the trophy, of course, but add that I'm accepting it also on behalf of my twenty-plus-pound survival kit, which can't be here with me right now in Kathmandu. I think it's pretty funny, but I guess humor is in the eyes of the beholder. In any case, the trophy will be proudly displayed in my trophy case at home.

I go to a popular steakhouse and enjoy a real beefsteak. It's great, but my enjoyment of it lasts for about an hour, after which I decide to be very sick. I'm not sure if it's food poisoning or just all the germs and illnesses finally catching up with me. But it all happens at once. Every possible body fluid I have is now making an exit from the nearest orifice. It's an ugly scene, one that lasts all night. By nine the next morning, I'm starting to feel okay, which is good, since I have a tour booked.

I'm keen to visit the neighboring cities of Pattan and Bhaktapur. These cities were separate kingdoms in the fifteenth century, and each has its own Durbar Square with royal palaces and temples.

The tour is good, but to be honest, I'm flagging, and I think I've had my fill of giant mountains and Nepal. By early afternoon, I'm suffering a relapse and return to the hotel. I'm facing a forty-hour journey home tomorrow, and I'm a tad worried at the prospect of gutting this one out.

I start to overdose on Imodium to plug up one end and decide not to eat anything (only sips of water to stay hydrated) until I get back home. I crawl out of bed and drag my sorry, plugged-up ass onto the first flight in Kathmandu. I'm able to buy some medicine at a pharmacy in the Bangkok airport to settle my stomach. I sleep for six hours on the twelve-hour flight from Hong Kong to Los Angeles. By this point I feel good enough to eat some greasy fries at a Burger King while waiting for the red-eye flight to Dallas. Better still, the fries stay down—and don't leave too quickly, either.

Nicole meets me at six in the morning in the Dallas airport, since she's taken a red-eye flight from Seattle where she was visiting our kids for Thanksgiving. It's cute. We fly the final leg together to Tampa, and she drives me straight to our family doctor in Sarasota. I want a medical checkup and tests to see if I've picked up some strange parasite or bug in Nepal.

My doctor won't give me any drugs until he gets the results of the tests. I have no option but to go home and lie in bed for five days, coughing and hacking and suffering from a high fever with chills and sweats and constant hallucinations that I'm back in the Himalayas with all the yakshit. For five days, I'm never more than a few feet from a bathroom.

I force myself to eat simply for nourishment. It stays down, but I'm amazed at how quickly the body can change solid food into liquid waste. Or is that too much information?

On reflection, as I lie here in bed, I have to say these were the most miserable few weeks of my life.

If I focus on the memories of how cold and miserable it was camping in the tents or the week of post-Everest illness, the answer seems obvious. But I can still remember the spectacular scenery along the trek, my immense pride when I climbed two eighteen-thousand-foot peaks, and the mother of all magnificent views of the "Top of the World." I remember the warm, friendly smiles of the Nepalese people, especially the children, and I remember the camaraderie and friendship of the many new friends I made during the trek. And I became a member of a special group—fewer than five hundred people have finished the Everest Marathon—the highest and toughest marathon in the world!

When I put it all together, the Everest experience was incredible. Would I go back again, to read a poem perhaps? Not likely, mate. I don't have to go there physically in any case, because I have my memories and souvenirs that will keep me going back any time I want.

And sometimes when I don't even plan to think about it, too.

Marathon # 275—Country #78, Maraton Tres Cuidades Patagonicas, Argentina October 2006

Once again I use an author's liberty to count this marathon for Argentina since it was more interesting and memorable than the first "underground BA marathon" that I ran in Buenos Aires one week earlier.

The Maraton Tres Cuidades Patagonicas in Patagonia is an amazing experience. The race goes between three Welsh cities in Patagonia. Yes! Welsh cities.

Francisco (my former tentmate at the Everest Marathon who invited us to visit him in Argentina) explains how settlers had emigrated from Wales in the eighteenth century and settled in a valley along the Rio Chubut. Because that area of Patagonia is so desolate and isolated, the Welsh settlers maintained their Welsh heritage and language up to today. In the eighties, Wales decided to reintroduce the Welsh language into its schools but couldn't find any teachers who spoke the old, traditional Welsh language. So they traveled to Patagonia and hired teachers in these Welsh cities to go to Wales to teach their teachers how to speak and teach the old language.

We arrive a few days early to enjoy some sightseeing in Patagonia. We start in Peurto Madryn that is a gateway for a huge national park located on Valdes Peninsula, surrounded by the Atlantic Ocean and the Golfo Nuevo and Golfo San Jose. We see lots of whales—mostly northern right whales (ballena franca austral)—and also a rare baby white whale that plays with the boat and spectators. After the whale tour we drive another hundred kilometers through the park to the Atlantic Coast to check out a colony of Magellan penguins. A few miles down the road, we find several colonies of sea lions and sea elephants.

On Saturday we depart for Gaiman. The marathon starts in Gaiman and runs through Trelew to Rawson. All three cities were founded by Welsh immigrants, but Gaiman is the city with the strongest Welsh heritage remaining.

Sunday is M-day! The race starts in the city center of Gaiman. On Saturday we had driven the course from Trelew to Gaiman and learned that there are two nasty/steep BAHs—one at five kilometers and another at nine kilometers. The rest of the course is flat. The course runs west to east and normally the prevailing winds blow in that direction.

The weather gods are smiling down on us. The temps are in the high forties at the 7:00 a.m. start, and the winds are blowing 20–30 mph—west to east—so we would have a strong tailwind for most of the race! My strategy is to run the first ten kilometers at an easy 5:20/kilometer (8:30/mile) pace until I get through the BAHs and then push the pace.

I reach five kilometers and the main two-lane highway to Trelew in 25:21. And become totally shocked and then amused with the bedlam I encounter. The marathon course follows a major two-lane highway that runs from the Atlantic Ocean to the Andes Mountains. One lane is reserved for the runners. However, every runner has an entourage of family and friends accompanying them on every type of vehicle—bike, motorcycle, car, truck, ATV, etc. Typically there would be one or more vehicles on each side of a runner so that any vehicles trying to use the highway are forced to drive in the ditches beside the highway! There are all types of vehicles going in every direction—all at the same time! This craziness lasts throughout the whole race with no concern or control by the police. Francisco later told me that this is the only race in Argentina with such bedlam. I quickly learn how to cope. As long as you stay on course and run straight ahead, the vehicles adjust to you. But if you foolishly make a sudden sideways move, your life could be in danger!

I soon catch up with a group of local runners that includes a female runner and a huge entourage. She has four male runners pacing her, and a bike, motorcycle, and car on each side of the group. I figure I will be safer staying with that group. We approach Trelew around 18 kilometers, run about six kilometers through the city, and pass the Half in 1:44:49.

When we pass the 35-Kilometer mark in 2:53:59, only she and I are left in the group, but we still have numerous support vehicles. I am starting to tire but am determined to stay with her, since we are on pace to finish the race in sub-3:30! She can't speak English, so there isn't any communication, but we have developed a silent bond to support and push each other to the finish line. Or so I thought. However, when I slow down at a water station at 37 kilometers to swallow my last carbo gel with water, she continues to push ahead, and I am soon a hundred meters behind her. I try desperately to catch up and lower my pace to 4:50/kilometer over the next three, but I cannot catch her.

When I pass the 40-kilometer point in 3:18, I figure a sub-3:30 is in the bag. But then disaster hits suddenly. My right calf starts to cramp. It then cramps severely and locks up. The pain is so excruciating I have to slow down and stop once to stretch it in the hope of getting it to release. It won't release, but the pain decreases enough so that I am able to jog and limp the final mile to cross the finish line in 3:30.

Soon after, my name is called to go to the podium to collect the first-place trophy for my age group. The trophy is huge—so huge that I figure that there is no way the airlines will let me take it on a plane. A few minutes later, Francisco collects a similar trophy for second place in his age group. We throw them into the car and rush to the airport. We make the flight, and even more surprising, they let us carry the trophies on to the plane. When we arrive in Buenos Aires, his partner, Mercedes, is waiting at the airport. I give her my trophy and ask her to keep it or donate it to a charity for kids.

It was an incredible trip! Three marathons and two countries in eight days. We met many new friends and saw some amazing places.

Unfortunately, my leg doesn't heal. After two massages and a week of rest, I attempt to run the Breakers Marathon in Rhode Island but am forced to drop out of the race after two miles because of the pain in my leg. Then the nightmare truly begins. I visit my orthopedist, believing that I might have a torn calf muscle or stress fracture in the tibia. An X-ray doesn't show any problems with the leg as expected. So we schedule an MRI, because we both feel that there is a strong possibility of a stress fracture in the tibia.

After I leave his office, he calls to ask me to play along with a hunch and go for a venous ultrasound scan of the leg. I am totally shocked (as was the technician) to discover a DVT (deep vein thrombosis) or blood clot in my lower right leg. I am ordered to proceed directly to the emergency room of a local hospital to begin treatments with anticoagulants and blood thinners! Nobody can tell me what caused this problem. I was aware of the risk of DVT and flying and was supercautious in my efforts to stretch and exercise on long flights to reduce the risk. I can only guess that the combination of three marathons in one week and the long flight home from Buenos Aires was the cause.

Marathon #276—Country #80,

Marabana Marathon, Cuba

November 2006

The hardest part of this marathon was planning the logistics to get to Cuba!

The first obstacle is the regulation that prevents Americans from traveling to Cuba. Fortunately, Nicole and I have been able to renew our Canadian passports, so we can officially travel as Canadians. They love Canadians in Cuba. We've also had to plan our route via a country other than the United States, so we've chosen the Bahamas. Finally, to pay for it all, we have to go through Marie, Nicole's sister in Canada, who wires funds from her Canadian account.

The flights on this trip cost more than $1,000—just to fly from Florida to Havana. If you don't mind the odd shark, you could probably swim there for a lot less.

As I was diagnosed with DVT (blood clot) in the right leg not so long ago, I carry a certain amount of guilt and trepidation with me to Cuba, which fortunately doesn't cost us extra on the flight. The leg is so painful that I can't run very well. The doctors tell me to take at least three months off from running.

Well, no way! I've gone through too many hoops setting up this trip, and since it's paid for, we're going. I'll complete the marathon even if I have to crawl.

I spend three weeks before the trip cross-training in a pool at the YMCA. In the last week before the trip, I attempt a few training runs where I'm able to run and walk without too much pain. I'm confident, I think, that I can run and walk the marathon.

We stay in the Hotel Plaza, a magnificent old Colonial hotel on the edge of the City Square and Old Havana. We explore the old city near the hotel, but it's very sad and depressing. The beautiful old Colonial buildings are decaying and crumbling due to lack of upkeep. But people still live in these buildings. Most of the stores are abandoned and boarded up due to lack of merchandise. The few stores that are open have people lined up for hours to buy the few pieces of merchandise (shoes, clothing, etc) that they still have in stock. And we are amazed with all the old vintage American cars that are still used for transportation in Havana.

The race package includes registration for both of us and they refuse to give us a discount for a nonrunner. Nicole thus registers for the half marathon and picks up a race T-shirt. We decline to go to the prerace pasta dinner (served at noon). But I do accept the course tour that's part of the package. The only people interested are foreign runners. And there are enough to fill one bus. We're given a military police escort through the city and are whisked through all intersections and red lights as we tour the half-marathon loop. Got to admit it, the Communists can be efficient when the military is involved.

The course starts in front of the Capitol (a model of the US Capitol), runs down to the Ocean and along the Malecon, a wide road that runs alongside the ocean, through the Vedada, past the Plaza de la Revolucion and back to the Capitol. The first nine kilometers are flat, but the next eight have several hills. Because of the DVT and lack of training, I plan to run ten minutes and walk one minute for the entire race.

It's Sunday, race day. I join about a thousand runners at the start line for the 7:00 a.m. start. It's dark, and it's warm and humid already.

There are about three hundred runners in the marathon—mostly from Europe, with large contingents from Norway, Denmark, and Germany. Many local runners have already approached me asking—well, begging—for my shoes after the race. Some even ask for them so they can run in them during the race. Most of the local runners in fact, are running barefoot. I wish I had known about the scarcity of shoes; I could have brought several other pairs with me.

There are lots of police and military along the course, and the roads are closed, so there are no problems with traffic. There are distance markers every kilometer and water stations every two kilometers. I drink lots of water at every station to reduce the risk of further complications with the DVT.

I stick religiously to my prerace plan of running ten minutes and walking one minute. I'm pleasantly surprised when I complete the first half in 2:00. I can't help myself, of course, and I start planning to break four hours. Why do I do this? But I'm too concerned about increasing the risk of complications or reoccurrence of the DVT, so instead all I do is stretch the run interval to twenty minutes during the second half.

Now I start to pass a lot of other old farts, mostly Europeans who have succumbed to the heat and humidity. When I pass the 32-kilometer mark in 3:03, I realize I still have a chance at breaking four hours. But my legs are tiring, and my quads are starting to hurt due to my lack of training. I pass 37 kilometers in 3:30 and I realize I'll have to push the pace and accept pain to finish under four hours, but I wisely decide not to risk it and instead slow down and cruise to the finish line in 4:02. This is still much faster and better than expected or planned, so I'm quite pleased. I'm also still alive!

And proud. Proud that I didn't push my luck. I'm also surprised Maddog didn't rear his ugly head, as I'm sure he would've got ahold of me and forced me to run myself into the ground.

Not surprisingly, there are no results posted at the finish line, so Nicole and I go back to the hotel and return to the finish line later to find that there are still no results. A few weeks later, I learn that I won my age group.

Marathon #287—Country #83, Fiji

International Marathon, Fiji

May 2007

The idea for this trip was incubated during the Everest adventure in 2005. I met two brothers from Christchurch, New Zealand, and they invited me to visit and run a marathon in New Zealand. Since it is such a long trip, I searched the web and running calendars to find another marathon in the South Pacific to spread the cost over two races. I came up with marathons in Fiji in mid-May and New Zealand in early June. That would work—we could spend one week in each country.

We wanted to use air miles for free tickets to Fiji, which required booking almost a year in advance, because it is a popular destination. We booked our free tickets and bought tickets from Fiji to New Zealand in the summer of 2006.

When I booked the hotels in Fiji, availability was scarce and rates not cheap. Little did we know that there would be a military coup in Fiji in December 2006. The coup killed the tourist industry in Fiji, and many tourists canceled their reservations. That event helped us, because the hotels reduced their rates to entice tourists back, and we were granted the lower rates for our reservations. The race director informed us that the coup would not result in cancelation of the marathon and that events and turmoil had cooled down, so we did not change our plans.

The Fiji Marathon is held on the Coral Coast, which is on the west coast of the main island of Viti Levu, so we book a hotel close to the start/finish line. After a long flight to Nadi, the first thing we notice upon arriving at 5:30 a.m. (two days after leaving Florida) is that the Fijians are very friendly and hospitable—and it is sincere. We arrive at our hotel after a bumpy and slow drive along the Queen's Highway, about 120 kilometers south of Nadi. The hotel is a small boutique hotel, and it is almost empty. Only four of nineteen rooms are rented. The coup is still affecting the tourist industry severely. But it is good for us during our whole stay, because the Fijians are eager to please the tourists who are there! We quickly learn that Fijians are serious about guests relaxing—there are no TVs and no telephones in the rooms, and Internet access is hard to find. To be honest, I don't like it!

We arrive early Thursday morning so we spend the rest of the day reconnoitering the area where our hotel is located. We are within walking distance of the small village of Korotogo, which has one small grocery store, and a short taxi ride to the fishing village of Sigatoka, which has shops and restaurants. We go into Sigatoka in the afternoon for lunch and finish all our shopping for souvenirs the first day. We also arrange to hire a taxi driver—an

Indian who speaks good English—to be a private driver and tour guide for Friday. It costs $100 FJ to rent a car, not including insurance and gas. It costs $120 FJ to hire Babu for a day. That is a no-brainer and a wise decision! We are fortunate that our hotel is known as the gourmet restaurant in that area, so we eat most of our meals there.

On Friday, Babu drives us south along the Queen's Highway to Suva, the capital of Fiji. We stop at a few ritzy resorts that seem to have more tourists than the hotels in our area. We visit Pacific Harbor—an exclusive resort area with hotels, private homes, golf courses, etc., but it is very isolated. Babu takes us to a small native village where a guide escorts us through his village. He shows us one of only three native temples left on the island and explains how the Fijians in the village are self-sufficient. They live off the land, using plants for food and medicines, and to build their homes, as they have for several hundred years. Babu later explains that native Fijians own about 90 percent of the land in Fiji, although the population is 51 percent Fijian and 49 percent Indian. The Indians were brought over by the British in the eighteen hundreds as indentured servants and stayed. There is a lot of animosity between the Fijians and the Indians. The Fijians don't like to work, and most live off the land. The Indians run the economy, but have to lease most of the land and buildings from the Fijians! We arrive in Suva in time for lunch. Suva is big, congested, dirty, and not nice. I would not recommend staying there. Babu drives us past most of the tourist spots—the Parliament buildings (closed because of the coup), the president's palace (now occupied by a military commander), old churches, and the harbor. A few hours to visit are all we need.

We plan to hire Babu to take us into the interior and mountains on Saturday, but when we return to the Coral Coast and pick up my race packet, I discover that the marathon is on Saturday. I thought it was Sunday. I can't find pasta on any dinner menus—even at the host hotel—but the chef agrees to cook pasta for us.

Saturday is M-Day! The marathon is supposed to start at 6:00 a.m., but we have already learned that nothing happens on time in Fiji. The start/finish is about half a mile from our hotel. I line up with eleven other runners for the marathon—all foreigners—no runners from Fiji. It is still dark, but the temps are already in the eighties, with humidity to match. The course includes a four-kilometer loop along a private road where our hotel is located, before climbing a BAH up to the Queen's Highway, and along the two-lane highway to the Naviti Resort, where it turns around and returns to the finish line. When I pass five kilometers in 24:35, I know I have started too fast and slow down. It is early Saturday, so there is not much traffic on the narrow road. Water stops are located every five kilometers. As I reach the Half in 1:50:30, the lead male runner flies by me. I know I won't see him again. Then the two lead female runners fly by. They are only a hundred feet apart, and I figure that is going to be a tough race (turns out they finished one minute apart). I pass one more male runner when I enter the Naviti Resort, before the turn-around at the 24-kilometer marker. I pass the 25-kilometer point in 2:11:33 and am starting to hurt, but I can see two more male runners in front, so I continue to push. I pass the second runner just before I reach 30 kilometers in 2:38:21. By then I am hurting, and I know I am becoming dehydrated, be-cause I can't think clearly. I am confused and can't remember how many male runners are still ahead of me. I ask the runner as I pass, and he confirms that there are still three male runners (and two females) ahead of us. I know I can't catch the lead male or the two females, but if I want to take home some sil-verware, I need to catch one more male, because the awards only go to the top three runners in each sex! So I let Maddog talk me into continuing to push the pace for another five kilometers. But I grab two bottles of water at the water station—one bottle inside and one bottle outside to cool down, hoping that will ease the dehydration. It doesn't. By the time I approach 35 kilometers in 3:06:01, I am in serious trouble. I am overheated, dizzy, and nauseated—all symptoms of serious dehydration and heat stroke.

I have promised myself that, if I don't see any runners ahead when I reach the 35-kilometer marker, I'll slow down. It isn't difficult to keep that prom-ise. The second I pass 35 kilometers, my body and mind shut down. I start to walk and grab three bottles of water in a desperate attempt to rehydrate. I am in *bad* shape! The water seems to help ease the nausea, and after a few minutes, I try to jog. That lasts about one minute before my body shuts down again, and the nausea returns. There is not going to be a quick recovery or cure. The next five kilometers are pure hell. I keep looking over my shoulder expecting one of the runners I have passed to catch me. And each time I try to jog, I last a minute or two before my body just shuts down again.

I reach the BAH in 3:47:02—forty-one minutes to walk and crawl five kilometers. And there isn't a damn thing I can do about it! I walk up the BAH with still some hope that I can finish the race under four hours. At the top, I valiantly try to run the final kilometer to the finish line. Doesn't last long! My body shuts down again after one minute, and I reluctantly accept that sub-four hours is not going to happen. I will be happy to cross the finish line alive! Finally, as I approach the final corner about five hundred meters before the finish line, I suck it up and manage to jog to the finish line and cross it in 4:02:26. I am so nauseated that I want to throw up but start drinking tons of water instead, hoping that I can replenish the much-needed fluids.

Finally, I feel well enough to walk back to our hotel where I drink a liter of high-carb sports drink to replenish electrolytes. That turns out to be a *big* mistake. It doesn't stay down more than a few minutes. Everything comes back up, but I feel much better! This has happened twice before—both times at Boston—when I pushed my body beyond its limits.

Now that I feel much better, I am able to have a nice hot shower, and we return to the awards ceremony. I am even able to enjoy a beer! I am very shocked when the race director announces that I finished fourth overall, second place male. I guess those other two male runners must have dropped out. In addition to that award, I also receive an award for being the oldest male participant in all the races. I am not sure that is good.

Now that the race is over, we can get back to exploring Fiji. Not so easy. Turns out that on Sunday, the island closes down. Shops are closed, none of the tours operate, and all the museums, public buildings, and parks close, too. There is no point in hiring Babu to drive us anywhere. We end up spending the day with a long walk along the beach and walking over to a nearby resort (the Outrigger). It is big, it is fancy, it is nice, but a massage costs $120 FJ and breakfast costs $33 FJ. We consider celebrating with a nice dinner at that resort, but I can't convince myself to spend $150 FJ. Instead, we find a local restaurant on the beach, and enjoy a delicious red snapper cooked Fijian style for $30 FJ, including beer.

We are booked to stay on the Coral Coast until Tuesday, but we decide to move into Nadi a day early so we can explore that area of the island. We hire Babu to drive us into Nadi, and make a few tourist stops along the way. Our first stop is at the Sigatoka sand dunes—huge (20–60 meters high) sand dunes along the ocean. We hike about forty-five minutes through the dunes and decide they are not as spectacular as the sand dunes in Colorado. Don't waste your time if you visit Fiji. Next we stop at the Tavuni Hill Fort, a defensive fort built by the Tongan chief Maile Latumai in the eighteenth century and destroyed by the British in 1876. The fort overlooks the Sigatoka River and Valley known as the "salad bowl" of Fiji because most of the vegetables are grown in that area. We continue into Nadi to make stops at the Sri Siva Subramaniya Swami (Indian) Temple, the market, and downtown. Nadi is the second-largest city and is also dirty, congested, and not nice!

On Tuesday we book an ecotour into Koroyanitu National Park. Four native villages donated their lands to the country to form the national park in exchange for government assistance to set up an economy based on ecotours. The native Fijians from those villages guide tourists on hikes into the park and allow them to visit their villages. We are joined on our tour by a honeymoon couple from Cleveland. Our native tour guide escorts us on a hike to a scenic viewpoint above the village of Abaca, where we enjoy panoramic views of the highlands and the Mamanuca Islands.

Then we are "invited" into Abaca. There is an ancient and traditional protocol that must be followed when visiting a Fijian village:

- You must be invited.
- You must bring a sevusevu (gift) of yaqona (kava).
- Your legs must be covered with a sulu or sarong.
- You must not wear a hat or sunglasses in the village.
- You must remove your shoes before entering the bure of the turaga-ni-koro (chief).

- You must participate in a kava ceremony before visiting the village.
- There are other rules, but these are the main ones. Our tour guide brought the kava on our behalf. Since I am the oldest male in our group, I am designated the visiting chief.

After we are welcomed into the chief's bure, the chief and other natives begin the kava ceremony. A young woman takes the kava—ground powder from the root of a kava tree/plant—puts it into a cloth, and passes water through the powder into a large wooden bowl that is made specifically for the kava ceremony. Uh-oh! I see Fijian revenge coming on since they use water from a local stream. This process produces a thick brown liquid that looks like mud. The liquid is narcotic. A European drug company uses the kava root to produce an antidepressant similar to Valium.

The chief blesses the kava and takes the first drink. He then offers a small wooden bowl of kava to the visiting chief—me. Before accepting the bowl of kava I must say "bula," clap once, and accept the bowl with two hands. Then I must drink the complete bowl of kava without the bowl leaving my lips and return the bowl to the chief. I finish by clapping three times and saying "bula" to show that I appreciate the kava. Then the chief repeats the process with all the guests. It is an insult to refuse the kava or not to drink the whole bowl.

Fortunately, the kava does not taste as bad as it looks. It numbs your tongue and mouth. I am the only guest to accept seconds—after all, I am the visiting chief. After the kava ceremony, the young woman escorts us around the village, showing us how they are self-sufficient. They grow vegetables, in addition to harvesting natural plants from the tropical forests. Their houses are built from bamboo. The village has a central kitchen where all meals are cooked. I note that the village has a central generator, and each house has one light bulb—and a TV and DVD. I tell the sports manager that we should move here because it would be cheap retirement living. I won't comment on the look I received, but we both agree that it was the best tour and activity that we enjoyed in Fiji!

After a great farewell dinner at our hotel, we rise early on Wednesday for our flight to New Zealand, where the adventure continues.

Marathon #288—Country #84, SBS

Christchurch Marathon, New Zealand

June 2007

We continue our adventure after running our first marathon of the trip in Fiji.

When we arrive in Christchurch, my friend, Robert, meets us at the airport and drives us to our hotel. The next morning I wake early and run a hard and fast ten miles around Hagley Park in the center of Christchurch. It's very nippy, with temps in the midthirties at 6:00 a.m. I realize that I have forgotten to pack cold-weather gear!

Unfortunately the sports manager does not feel well when she wakes up—she thinks she is experiencing the same symptoms she suffered many years ago when she had a minor stroke. By the time we reach the outskirts of Christchurch, she has worked herself into a tizzy and is suffering anxiety attacks because she is worried that if she really is on the verge of a stroke, there will not be proper medical care available in the remote areas of the South Island. I agree it would be a problem, and it would be safer to turn around and drive back into the city and visit the ER of the Christchurch Hospital. Thus we spend our first day in Christchurch in the ER, where they do every possible test—a CT scan, EKG, blood tests, etc. Happily, all the tests are normal, and the doctors assure us that there's no serious problem and we can continue our journey. We have to stay in Christchurch for the night, so I take another hard, fast run in Hagley Park. We finally start our tour on Friday morning, even though Nicole is still not feeling well. The symptoms seemed to come and go, and after a few days, I notice that she is not eating well. After

I convince her to eat more, the symptoms seem to ease. She later found out when she visited her neurosurgeon in Florida that these symptoms can be caused by long flights and jet lag. She announces that her duties of sports manager for long international trips are finished.

Our first drive and stop is along the Banks Peninsula to the fishing village of Akaroa. It is such a lovely and quaint village that we would have stayed there for a night if it was not so close to Christchurch (only eighty-two kilometers east). We move on and drive south on Highway 1 to Oamaru, a Victorian town with many buildings built out of the local sandstone. We stay the night in Oamaru, and I have a very difficult run in the morning through the hills east of town.

We continue our drive along the Otago Coast with a brief stop to view the Moeraki Boulders—giant spherical rocks on the beach that look like alien eggs. We continue on through Dunedin, turn inland through the Southern Alps to Gore, and reach our destination—Fiordland or the Southwest Coast. We stay in a beautiful little village called Te Anau located on Lake Te Anau. This setting is so beautiful that we immediately know that we want to spend a few nights there. We find a lovely new motel on Lake Te Anau and then look for the tourist center to book a cruise on Millford Sound. By that time we have learned some important facts:

Nothing is cheap in New Zealand.

Hotels are the only reasonable expense. Since it is off-season, we're able to negotiate rates around $100 NZ/night.

Motels do have TVs and phones—some even have Internet access. However, the TV is useless unless you want to watch reruns of *Get Smart* (remember that show?) in prime time. There is no cable TV, but they do have satellite TV. The government restricts satellite TV to three stations: Sky News (either CNN or BBC), Sky Sports, which shows rugby or cricket 24-7, and Sky Movies (like HBO). Most hotels offer Sky News for a premium charge.

Meals are expensive, so we usually buy a muffin at a bakery and a small orange juice for breakfast in our room. The hotels provide free coffee/tea in the room. Dinner entrees ranged from twenty to thirty dollars in a restaurant, so we eat in pubs (like the United Kingdom), which offer specials for about half that. There are no free side dishes. If you want bread you pay for it.

Beer/wine in a pub or restaurant is expensive, so we buy six-packs of beer at the supermarket for about ten dollars and enjoy a beer each day at the end of the drive and limit ourselves to one drink with dinner

Gas is about six dollars a gallon and as high as eight in remote areas.

A friend asked me to check out New Zealand as a potential retirement spot. I believe it would be cheaper to retire in San Francisco!

Back to Te Anau. A lovely town in a beautiful setting! I would love to go back there for a few weeks to hike on the many trails around Te Anau and Millford Sound. We book a cruise on Millford Sound for the following day. It is a long but scenic drive into Millford Sound, so I have to rise early and run through the dark streets of Te Anau at five o'clock. It's friggin' cold! Temps are near freezing, but I need to do some speed work. I probably can't be competitive with the fast Kiwis, but I don't want to embarrass myself with another four-hour marathon!

The cruise is spectacular. The sound is hemmed in by sheer walls of rock that rise four thousand feet. As you leave the dock, the first sights you enjoy are the 5,560-foot Mitre Peak and Brown Falls, tumbling 520 feet into the sea. What amazes me is the vegetation, including trees, growing on the sheer cliffs of rock! Millford Sound is definitely a sight that everyone should see. The sports manager and I agree that Te Anau and Millford Sound are the highlight of the New Zealand tour!

The following day was a short drive (172Km) to Queenstown—the adventure capital of New Zealand! It is located on the edge of the glacial Lake Wakatipu with stunning views of the Remarkables Mountain range. We expected Queenstown to be much larger—it reminds us of a small ski resort town in Colorado. We luck in when the tourist center guides us into a new boutique hotel situated in the hills just off the center of the town with fantastic views of the lake and town—only $125 NZ, including a full New Zealand breakfast! And it's close to a bike path, so I'm able to do another speed workout along the lake. We visit most of the tourist sites including the famous AJ Hackett Bungy jump off the Kawarau Bridge (No, I didn't jump!) and conclude the first day with a scenic drive through the gold-mining town of Arrowtown and along Lake Wakatipu to Glenorchy. That evening we find a nice pub in town that offers delicious lamb shanks as a special.

The next day we set off over the scenic but scary Crown Range Road past the Cardrona Ski Resort to Wanaka as we head to the Westland National Park and the glaciers on the West Coast. We stop at Thunder Creek Falls before we reach Haast Pass. The roads become a bit treacherous as we come around a blind curve or over a hill at 70 kmh to find a single-lane bridge. Fortunately, there is not much traffic, and we only have to stop once for oncoming traffic! We reach an entrance into Fox Glacier in the afternoon and hike about two miles into a forest before we see a paved road going directly into the glacier! Back to the car and drive to the damn glacier! We stay in Franz Josef that evening and the following morning are disappointed to see rain and clouds. We can't even see the tops of the mountains, so we decide there's no point in driving and hiking into the Franz Josef Glacier.

As we continue our tour north along the west coast, the weather clears. We decide to turn back inland and head to Hanmer Springs. Hanmer Springs is called Waitapu (Sacred Waters) by the Maori for the thermal springs. It is a small Alpine village north of Christchurch. We explore the area and find a hotel close to the springs. I can walk over to the springs and enjoy a hot soak. The hottest spring is 41°C—about the same temperature that I keep my hot tub. The legs feel great the next morning when I do my final speed workout in preparation for the Christchurch Marathon.

Instead of driving back to Christchurch, we decide to take a detour to Kaikoura on the east coast. It is known for its whale watching and crayfish. We explore the town and decide to stay for the night to taste the crayfish. Crayfish is the Kiwi version of Maine lobster—and they are proud of it! $100 NZ for a crayfish dinner! We visited a local winery and bought an excellent bottle of Sauvignon Blanc that we took to dinner. I refuse to pay for a whole crayfish but do allow myself $50 for a half, which I enjoy with the excellent wine. It's good but not any better than a $19.95 Maine lobster!

The next day (Friday) we drive back to Christchurch. We park downtown, call Robert to let him know we have arrived, and spend the afternoon touring downtown Christchurch. Christchurch is known as the "garden city" for its many parks and gardens. Founded in 1856, it is the oldest city in New Zealand. There are many beautiful and historical Victorian buildings in downtown Christchurch. The tramway allows tourists to get on and off at eleven stops in downtown Christchurch. We visit Cathedral Square, Victoria Square, Christ's College, and Hagley Park and finish the day by picking up my race packet at City Hall. Then we follow Robert's directions to his home in Halswell, a suburb on the south side of Christchurch. He has a beautiful new home—a surprise for a bachelor who spends all his time working and running. After we settle in, his brother Dave joins us, and we drive downtown for a Thai dinner—lots of carbs!

On Saturday morning the sports manager and I make a final drive tour up into the hills of Banks Peninsula overlooking Christchurch and Lyttelton Harbour. The hills are steep and covered with biking-hiking trails that the Christchurch runners use for training. The views are spectacular! Christchurch on one side and Lyttelton and Sumner on the ocean side. We return the car to the rental agency on Saturday afternoon, since Robert volunteers to drive us to the race on Sunday. Saturday night I treat my support team to a pasta dinner.

Sunday is M-day. There are twenty-five hundred runners in three races—marathon, Half, and 10K—that start together at 9:00 a.m. in front of city hall. The weather is sunny and cool. The course is a half-marathon loop that starts at city hall and follows the Avon River east for about eight kilometers before returning downtown and through Hagley Park in the center of the city. We lucky marathoners get to run the course twice! Robert and Dave have a sister and other family members running the various races and tell me that they would be cheering us along the course. Their mom and dad even cheer me on at one point along the course. I've had some good training runs during our tour and feel that I can run a 3:40. Based on past times in my age group, that's not competitive, but I tell Robert that my goal is to start out at a 3:40 pace and assess the situation at the 30-kilometer mark. If I still have energy in the tank, I might try to push the last twelve kilometers.

I passed five kilometers in 24:49—ahead of pace and ten kilometers in 50:45—still ahead of pace. I slow my pace to reach 15 kilometers in 1:16:58 and the half in 1:49:31. I am right on pace but not sure I can hold that same pace for the second half. When I reach 30 kilometers in 2:35:24, I feel okay and know I can hold that pace for the final twelve kilometers—but I'm not sure that if I push the pace I won't hit the wall. I see Robert at that point taking photos and ask him if there are any old farts in front of me. He replies, "Yes, but they are too far ahead to catch." So I wisely decide to hold the pace and reevaluate at 35 kilometers, which I pass in 3:01:49. I have thirty-two minutes to run the final seven kilometers. I decide to push the pace through Hagley Park since it feels familiar to me. I pass 40 kilometers in 3:28:53, but suddenly my back starts to tighten on me. I've never experienced that problem, and I have to slow down to let the back loosen up. I am able to push the final kilometer, but it isn't enough, and I cross the finish line in 3:40:25! But I am happy with both my time and performance, and I have not suffered any problems with leg cramps!

We return to Robert's for a quick but wonderful hot soak and shower, and then Robert and I decide to go to the awards ceremony or "prize giving," as the Kiwis call it. We can't find the results posted anywhere, so we go into the ceremony at City Hall. I can't believe it. There were twenty-five hundred runners in the races, and half of them are at the ceremony. You would never see that kind of attendance at a US race. Unfortunately, it drags on too long, including the emcee asking Maddog to stand while he announces his accolades and accomplishments! As suspected, I was soundly beat in my AG—finished in fifth place. First place ran a 3:15! A fifty-two-year-old Kiwi ran a 2:32! Those Kiwis are FAST!

As we are leaving the ceremony, a sports announcer for a local radio station asks Maddog for an interview, and that delays us more.

We finally return home in the afternoon, so that Robert and Dave can cook a roast of lamb. Their mom and dad and sister join us for dinner. Dave raises sheep on his dad's farm for a hobby, and he supplies the lamb. It was so tender and scrumptious! I don't understand why we can't get lamb like that in the United States.

On Monday we have a very early flight, and Robert graciously drives us to the airport. We are on our way back to Fiji for four days of R and R before returning home.

Marathon #294—Country #86, Toray Cup

Shanghai International Marathon, China

November 2007

I wanted to run two marathons in Asia to reduce the cost of a trip and found that the Shanghai Marathon was scheduled one week before Macau. And there was no extra cost to add a stopover in Shanghai enroute to Hong Kong. However, it meant having to spend a week in China, but I figured I could find an interesting tour.

I e-mailed a friend in Shanghai and asked for help with a hotel. Linlai used to work with Nicole at Nortel and was happy to help. He checked out hotels and booked one a few blocks from the start line on the pedestrian mall on Nanjing Road, and provided much needed directions on how to get to the hotel from the airport.

I arrive in Shanghai late Friday afternoon (lost one day en route), and it takes more than two hours to travel thirty-four kilometers from the airport to the hotel because of horrendous rush-hour traffic. I am surprised (but pleased) to find Linlai waiting for me in the hotel lobby. I slept on the long flight and want to stay up as late as possible to prevent jet lag, so I agree to let Linlai treat me to a special Chinese dinner. It's a delicious dinner with many local Shanghai delicacies. I have no idea what I'm eating—but it's good. Many times I ask Linlai how I am supposed to eat a certain delicacy. At dinner I ask Linlai for suggestions about a side tour after the race. I mention that I tried to book a tour to Beijing, but it was too expensive. I have always wanted to see the Terracotta Warriors, but I don't think that'll be possible on such short notice Maybe I can travel to Hangzhou—west of Shanghai and located on West Lake. At least I can get out of the city and do some training runs while waiting for the next race.

Linlai promises to check with a friend who is a travel agent.

Linlai insists on joining me on Saturday morning to help me pick up my race packet at the Shanghai Stadium. I tell him that's not necessary, but it turns out to be a good thing, because the location has changed from the details provided on the website. Having a local Chinese guide and translator is useful, although many people in Shanghai speak English.

After successfully getting my packet, I say good-bye to Linlai and set off to explore the city on my own. I walk around the Bund and East Nanjing Road neighborhood. There is a pedestrian mall on East Nanjing Road with lots of shops, etc., and it seems to be a major gathering place for locals. Unfortunately, my blond hair and blue eyes are like a giant friggin' neon sign for hawkers, scam artists, and hookers, and I become so annoyed at being harassed that I avoid that mall for the rest of my stay. I walk down to the Huangpu River to enjoy the views of the Pudong neighborhood across the river with many modern buildings and the Shanghai Tower. By four o'clock, my body clock is demanding that I rest, and I return to the hotel for a short nap before dinner. I wake at eight feeling like crap and make an executive decision: if I go to dinner I will not sleep again that night, so I crawl between the sheets and sleep for another ten hours. I figure that sleep is more important that food, and besides, the flab I have around my beer belly should carry me through a marathon.

I wake at 6:00 a.m. to walk over to the start line at Century Square on the pedestrian mall on Nanjing Road. The race start is well organized except that the twelve thousand runners were not seeded by bib numbers, and there are no corrals for expected finish times. In other words, it's a free-for-all, and I end up in the middle of the pack. The weather is warmer than normal (mid-fifties), so I wear shorts and a T-shirt as the race starts at seven. The start chute is too narrow for that many runners, and it takes about five minutes just to reach the start line. And the course doesn't get any better! The first four kilometers through the city center are scenic but on narrow streets, so we're forced to stay in our pace group and fight for elbow space. At five kilometers, I think the course is going to open up, but instead it dumps onto a single-lane service road for an expressway. The expressway is already clogged with traffic, and we suck up diesel fumes for the next five kilometers. I pass the 8-kilometer marker in 45:40—a little faster than I wanted to start. At ten kilometers, I think we are finally going to get relief from the diesel fumes when we turn onto a major boulevard, but we are forced into a single, coned lane with traffic passing or clogged beside us. Traffic control is bad—bikes, motor bikes, and people are darting across the course in front of us. I bowl over some poor Chinese woman who stepped in front of me unexpectedly!

I pass 18 kilometers in 1:43:54 and a split of 6:20/kilometer (10:08/mile). I have slowed significantly and am already starting to struggle in spite of a lot of spectators along the course cheering and shouting, "Jiayou, jiayou!" I ask a local what that means. The polite translation is "keep going"—the gutter translation is "move your ass faster!" At that point the course climbs up to an elevated expressway that we have to share with congested traffic. Can it get any worse? YES! By the time I pass the half in 2:03:01, it's hot—I am struggling to hold a 6:30 minutes/kilometer pace, and my legs are DEAD! The second half is going to get ugly.

When I reach a water station at 25 kilometers in 2:29:17, there is nothing left in my legs, and I start to walk. At 29 kilometers, we're routed onto another elevated expressway that is straight and long with high walls. It's so boring and depressing that I really want to run the entire section just to get off that raised torture oven. I reach the water station at 30 kilometers in 3:04:20 and a split of 6:59/kilometer. I walk! Then at a water sponge station at 32.5 kilometers, I am forced to walk again. I struggle and play mind games just to make it to the next water or sponge station, where I walk for one minute and continue. At 39 kilometers, we exit the elevated expressway, and I manage to keep the wasted old legs moving to reach 40 kilometers in 4:17:36. I decide to take a long walk at that point so I can run to the finish line, although survival is the most important thing on my mind.

I am thankful to finally see the Minhang Stadium and stumble across the finish line in 4:34:18. I have no idea what caused such a pathetic performance and why I crashed so early in the race. I guess it's a combination of missing the dinner, the terrible pollution during the race, and severe jet lag.

Linlai is supposed to be at the finish line, but I don't see him. I pick up my warm-up clothes and proceed to the finish area to return my chip and pick up a finisher's certificate and award. Slight problem! To receive the certificate and award (a sports bag instead of the normal finisher's medal), it is necessary to turn in one of our two race bibs. The Chinese seem to need physical evidence that an action has been completed. I try to explain that I want to keep both bibs—one for a souvenir of the race and the other for a friend who owns a running store. He posts them on a wall to motivate other runners. No way! No bib—no award! I tell them what to do with their certificate and award! They are shocked.

I finally find Linlai at the finish line, and he volunteers to take a finish line photo and guide me back into the city. I insist that he join me later for a celebration dinner. After a long hot soak and shower, I venture out to explore some more of the city. Shanghai is a very modern and vibrant city, but it's just too big, too noisy, and too crowded for a country boy. I'm glad that I made the decision to get out of the city! Linlai and I meet for a very good dinner in a restaurant overlooking the Huangpu River and the lights of Pudong. I learn that if you stay in Chinese hotels and eat in Chinese restaurants, it is reasonably cheap, but if you stick to Western-style places, the prices are equivalent to big city prices in the United States. Linlai has great news for me over dinner—his friend has arranged a three-day tour to Xian to see the Terracotta Warriors and other tourist attractions in the ancient capital!

Since I will leave on Tuesday, I have one final day to explore Shanghai. I do a self-guided walking tour through Old Town, or Nan Shi, which dates back to the sixteenth century. I start at the Old Stone Gate and walk through back alleys with laundry hanging overhead, past Baiyun Temple and the "wet market" to Dajing Pavilion, which contains the only preserved section of the ancient five-kilometer city walls. Parts of Old Town have been restored and turned into tourist traps!

I also plan to cross the Huangpu River to visit Pudong, but a cold front has brought in fog, and I can't even see the tops of the buildings, so I skip that.

I meet Linlai for a farewell dinner to thank him for his gracious hospitality and go over the itinerary for the tour to Xian. On Tuesday morning, I take the first Maglev train to the airport to catch an early flight. The Maglev train is more expensive than a bus, but it makes the thirty-kilometer trip in eight minutes at 300 kmh.

I arrived in Xian at 11:30 a.m., and I am met at the airport by a private English-speaking tour guide, a lovely young woman, Yao Ming, or "Meggie," as she asks English tourists to call her. We review the itinerary for the day, and since it includes only tourist sites within the city, we decide to use taxis for that day. Taxis are very cheap in China, and that seems like the best option—until I lose a brand-new pair of prescription glasses in one of them. Unfortunately, I don't realize I've lost them until the end of the day. I hope that cabbie enjoys his new pair of expensive high-tech glasses.

Xian is the capital of Shaanxi province in northwest China. Called Chang'an in ancient times, it was the capital city of thirteen dynasties from the Western Zhou (11th century–771 BC) and Qin (221–206 BC) through the Tang (AD 618–907), and it is considered a living history book in China. We start with a visit to the Shaanxi History Museum, which contains artifacts from all the dynasties. Then we tour various sites such as the Big Wild Goose Pagoda, built by Emperor Gaozong of the Tang Dynasty to collect Buddhist artifacts taken from India and Da Ci'en Temple (AD 648). To conclude the day, Linlai has suggested to Meggie that she book me a seat at the Dumpling Dinner and Tang Dynasty Music and Dance show. I'm not in much of a mood for a traditional dinner show after finding my $700 glasses missing, but since the ticket has been booked, I go. I am concerned about a dinner of only dumplings—a local specialty in Xian, but they are quite good. The show is a performance of ancient music and dance from the Tang Dynasty—very interesting—and includes many of the musical instruments I saw at the museum earlier that day! The next day includes sites outside the city, so we decide to hire a private car for the day.

Meggie and the driver pick me up early so we can make a quick stop at the Xian City Wall before leaving the city. The wall was built by Zhu Yuanzhang, the first Emperor of the Ming Dynasty (1366–1644), on the original city wall built during the Tang Dynasty. It stands forty feet high and forty feet wide at the top. The rectangular wall is 13.7 kilometers in length and encircles downtown Xian; it is the most complete city wall in China. A bell tower, used to signal the opening of the city gates each morning, sits in the geographical center of the city. I wish I had time to run the entire wall, because it's impossible to run in the streets of Xian—the roads are too crowded and too dangerous, and the pollution is so thick that I could see it, smell it, and taste it! After walking a short section of the wall, we leave the city to visit the Museum of the Terracotta Warriors—the main reason for the tour to Xian!

The museum is a small part of the Mausoleum of Emperor Qin Shi Huang that began construction in 246 BC. He used seven hundred thousand workers to construct the mausoleum site and killed them all when it was finished to keep the location a secret. It was discovered in 1974 by a farmer, whom I meet at the museum. I didn't realize that it is still an ongoing archaeological site! The museum covers a very large area and is divided into three pits. The first pit is the largest and contains more than six thousand terra-cotta warriors and horses marshaled into battle-line formations to protect the emperor in his afterlife. It is an awesome sight, but I am disappointed that only a small fraction (about 25 percent) of the pit is excavated. The second pit contains four mobile combat units, consisting of a thousand warriors, eighty-nine wooden chariots, and two bronze chariots that were meant to carry the emperor and his concubines around in the afterlife.

The third pit is surmised by archeologists to be a command center for the military who commanded the construction of the mausoleum. It contains sixty-eight warriors, four horses, and one chariot, but no battle formations.

The museum is quite spectacular and amazes a viewer with the obvious wealth of the emperors! It is worth the visit and the smog you will have to endure for a few days! After leaving the museum, we visit Huaqing Hot Springs, which is famed for the scenery and the romantic love story of Emperor Xuanzong (AD 685–762), and his concubine, Yang Guifei, in the Tang Dynasty. A palace, built by King You during the Western Zhou Dynasty, and expanded by Emperor Qin, sits on the grounds with several pools fed by the hot springs.

On the way back to the hotel. I ask Meggie to help me buy a pair of replacement reading glasses so that I can read during the rest of the trip. I am still bummed about losing a brand-new pair of glasses and even more bummed about having to pay another $700 to replace them. That evening, I explore the area of the city close to the hotel. I consider eating outside the hotel but can't find a restaurant with an English menu, so I retreat to the safety of the hotel. Very few staff at the hotel speak English, but at least there is an English menu.

I was hoping to find a place to run on Thursday, but when I get up in the morning and look out the window, I can't see the buildings across the street because the smog is so thick! I refuse to run in that pollution. And Xian is much different than Shanghai. It is not modern, the buildings are the concrete blocks built by the central communist government, the streets are congested with cars, bikes, and people, and there are no rules—it is dangerous and unsafe to run. I decide I don't need to run that badly. Meggie meets me late morning, and we hire a taxi to take us to the last tourist site—Hanyanling, the mausoleum of Western Han Emperor Liu Qi—and then drop me off at the airport. The mausoleum is a joint tomb of Liu Qin, the emperor of the Western Han Dynasty, and his wife, Empress Wang. There are several burial pits containing thousands of artifacts. Compared to the Qin Terracotta Warriors, the pottery figures are one-tenth the actual size and not nearly as impressive.

Finally, I am finished with the tour and the pollution. I ask Meggie bluntly why she lives there. I think the locals are oblivious to it because they don't know anything else and can't do anything aboutit. I arrive in Shanghai around 7:00 p.m. and am met at the airport by a hotel rep. Linlai has booked a hotel near the airport since I have to leave early Friday for Hong Kong. When I arrive at the hotel, I'm a bit disconcerted to discover that no one on the staff speaks English! Any English! Fortunately, my Shanghai tour book has an extensive vocabulary section that I am forced to refer to. With a lot of laughs with and at each other, the staff and I select the necessary words and phrases to check in and arrange a wake-up call and the shuttle back to the airport in the morning. Then the next challenge—dinner.

No English menu, as I expected; it all looks Chinese to me (ha, ha). Rather than try to recognize the Chinese symbols, I make it simple. I look up three words: yu (fish), baifan (steamed white rice), and baiwei (beer). I have no idea what I am going to get, but it turns out to be delicious. And I get to improve my skills with chopsticks eating a whole steamed fish covered in a delicious sauce. The hotel, with dinner and breakfast, cost thirty-three dollars. As I said, you can travel cheaply in China if you are adventurous and stay and eat with the locals.

Now it's time to catch a flight to Hong Kong and move on to the next chapter in the adventure.

Marathon #295—Country #87, Macau

International Marathon, Macau

December 2007

I was heading from Shanghai to Macau via Hong Kong. The Macau Marathon was the initial reason for this trip. When I arrived in Hong Kong, I checked for a direct ferry to Macau that allows passengers to transit through Hong Kong airport without having to pass through immigration. Saves a lot of time and hassle.

I was able to book the next turbo jet hydrofoil to Macau and arrived at 6:00 p.m. The sports manager and I had visited Macau about twelve years ago on a one-day side tour from Hong Kong. I didn't remember much about Macau except that it was a small laid-back country.

It is still small, but everything else has changed. The part on the mainland is now full of gaudy casinos and hotels, and every square foot is occupied! Fortunately, I'm staying on Taipa Island where the race starts and finishes. Although it has a few large casinos and several under construction, there is still some open space, and the streets are not congested (yet). My new four-star casino hotel is located right on the North China Sea, and a room with ocean view costs fifty-five dollars a night with full breakfast. I walk over to the center of Taipa Village. It's small but has several shops, restaurants, and even a Portuguese taverna and an English pub.

I am concerned about not repeating the mistake I made in Shanghai by missing any meals before the race, so I enjoy a nice Chinese dinner with lots of rice (carbs).

On Saturday morning I run four easy miles. I don't normally do that before a race, but since I couldn't or wouldn't run in China because of the pollution, I figure I need to loosen up the legs and remind them what is expected the next day. After breakfast I wander over to the Macau Stadium to pick up my race packet. The marathon website was good and allowed me to preregister, so I can get my packet quickly and easily. Since I have the whole afternoon available, I decide to take a tour since I don't recognize anything. There is one wee problem—the tour is only available in Chinese! No matter—after my final night in Shanghai, I'm confident of my Chinese language skills. Well, that confidence doesn't last long—I can't understand one word the guide says. Fortunately, I have a guide book and a young Chinese family who translates some of the important facts for me. We tour most of the major tourist sites in the city and on Taipa Island. We start on the mainland peninsula, which is only three and a half square miles. Our first stop is Guia Fort (or Mount Fortress) on top of Guia Hill, the highest natural point of Macau, for panoramic views of the city. Right below the fort are the ruins of four-hundred-year-old Saint Paul's Church. The ruins are the most famous structure in Macau, and they're the only thing I remember from our previous visit. Then we stroll through the old city to Senado Square—the city center.

Next stop is the Macau Tower (330 meters high) for panoramic views of the city and country (if you can see through the smog over the peninsula). It also houses the world's highest bungee jump—and no, I do not jump! Our final stop on the mainland is at the Temple of A-Ma, the oldest temple in Macau, dating back six hundred years. It was dedicated to A-Ma, the goddess of seafarers. At the entrance is a large rock, with a picture of a traditional sailing junk engraved more than four hundred years ago to commemorate the Chinese fishing boat that carried A-Ma to Macau. The tour finishes on Taipa Island with a visit to Macau Stadium and Taipa Village. The tour covers about 75 percent of the marathon course, which isn't surprising, since the marathon has to use almost every road in the small country!

On Saturday evening I find an Italian restaurant in Taipa for pasta dinner. I am not going to skip dinner before this race! I am so concerned about repeating the disaster of Shanghai that I even eat a light breakfast on Sunday morning before the race—I never do that before a marathon, but I am going to make sure my glycogen reserves are full! The forecast for the race was warm—18°C at the start and 25°C at the finish. I walk the few blocks to the start line at Macau Stadium at 6:00 a.m. The race starts at 6:30 a.m. on the track inside the stadium. There are two thousand runners in three events: marathon, half, and 10K. Although we start together, the runners spread out quickly after we leave the stadium. At two kilometers, the 10K runners split off, and the others make their first crossing over the Sai Van Bridge to the mainland. The bridge is two kilometers long and fifty meters above the North China Sea. It is the most scenic and toughest section of the course, and we cross it four times during the race!

Once we cross the bridge, there's a short five-kilometer maze through tunnels and overpasses as we pass through the city center. I reach five kilometers in 27:41 and a split of 5:20. At the ten-kilometer mark, we pass by the Macau Tower and head back over the Sai Van Bridge to Taipa. The final loop over the bridge is going to be a bitch! At 17.5 kilometers, the half-marathon runners split off, and I essentially run the rest of the race alone. I pass the half in 1:59:15 and feel good. I am now confident that I won't crash and burn like in Shanghai, but I also know that the second half will be slower because the sun is up and the temps are rising. Sure enough, when I reach the Sai Van Bridge again in 2:51:49, the split is 6:00 minutes/kilometer, and I am starting to fade in the hot sun, but I also start passing a lot of runners in worse shape! The five-kilometer maze through the city is hotter, and I start to struggle as I approach the bridge at 37 kilometers in 3:37:18 and a split of 6:19. I am determined not to walk over that final crossing of the bridge. The one-kilometer climb to the top of the bridge is a bitch, as expected. I have to dig deep and summon up a lot of willpower to keep the tired old legs moving. Only experience and willpower keep the wasted old legs shuffling the final two kilometers until I turn the final corner and see the stadium. Then the old bod provides one last jolt of adrenaline to allow me to cruise across the finish line in the stadium in 4:11:19!

It takes a few minutes and a couple of bottles of cold water to cool down and relieve the dizziness, but I quickly recover. I retrieve my warm-up clothes and return my chip. Uh-oh! Another Chinese snafu! To get my deposit back, I have to return the chip (makes sense) and also a race bib (don't make sense). I try to negotiate to no avail. I will never understand the Chinese thing about wanting a bib back, and I am sure they will never understand the American thing about wanting to keep both bibs. I am not willing to sacrifice a hundred dollars, so I give them their damn bib!

After a long hot soak and shower, I still have an afternoon to explore Macau, so I go back to Old Town to explore the sights at a more leisurely pace. I also need to find an Internet café to send my readers a field report. After a few hours of strolling around old town, I am frustrated by the noise and wall-to-wall people, so I retreat to the village square in Taipa, which is more laid-back and less crowded. I enjoy a few Macau beers and some loud conversation with some (drunken) runners from the United Kingdom at the Portuguese taverna. I need quiet, so I find a nice quiet café to enjoy a celebration dinner by myself. But I have an interesting chat with the owner, who has just moved back to Macau after living in Montreal for twenty years.

On Monday I take a direct/transit ferry back to the Hong Kong airport for the long journey home.

Marathon #302—Country #90,

Dead Sea Marathon, Jordan

April 2008

Planning began for this race/adventure last fall when I started to put together an itinerary for 2008. I figured that it would be nice to run a marathon in Jordan for two reasons:

1) Jordan looked like an interesting country to visit.
2) Since I had already run the highest marathon in the world (Everest), I should also run the lowest (Dead Sea).

My first step was to register for the race, and then I tried to find a package tour to explore the country. That proved much more difficult because few Americans run the marathon and there were no canned English tours. I contacted a German tour operator, Christian, who was very receptive to my joining his group of forty German runners for the race and an eight-day tour of Jordan. I was not concerned that the tour would be in German, because I figured it would get me to all the important tourist sites and I could use a guide book to read about what I was seeing. I also figured (correctly) that many of the German runners would speak English and could provide some translation when needed. I agreed to join the group and meet them at the airport in Amman.

The long direct flight (twelve hours) from Chicago to Amman gave me lots of time to read my tour guide and learn the history of Jordan.

I meet the German group at the Amman airport, and Christian introduces me on the bus. Immediately, one of the runners asks where he and I had met. Only after he states that he is running capital cities in countries do I remember that we met in Trinidad in 2005!

If I tried to describe every interesting site I saw in Jordan I would have to transcribe about forty pages of the tour guide to this report. So for brevity, I will only mention the highlights.

At the citadel, we tour the National Archaeological Museum to view the Dead Sea Scrolls and six-thousand-year-old skulls. Sites visited were the Umayyad Palace and Audience Hall (AD 720), the Colonnaded Street and Temple Of Hercules—Roman (AD 100). From the citadel there are great views of modern Amman and the world's tallest free-standing flagpole (127 meters) and the Roman theater, built in the second century to seat six thousand.

We go to the ancient Roman city of Gerasa (Jerash), which is well preserved. The city is entered through Hadrian's Arch, built in AD 129. Behind the arch is a restored Hippodrome where chariot races are held each day for tourists.

On Thursday we pack our baggage and leave Amman to travel north to the Syrian border and the ancient city of Gadara or Umm Qais, where Jesus was said to have cast the demons out of two people and into a herd of swine. Umm Qais has spectacular views of Syria, the Golan Heights, the Sea of Galilee, Israel, and Lebanon—all in the same view. You can't do anything like that in the United States.

When we return to Amman, the bus stops for a liquor run. Our guide informs us that it is our only chance to buy alcohol for the desert camp where we'll stay after the race. I decide to buy two cans of local beer called Petra—half-liter cans of beer with 10 percent alcohol, equivalent to drinking a liter of wine.

After the booze stop, we follow the route of the ultramarathon/ marathon from the city to the Dead Sea. One of the German runners has a topological profile of the courses. It is hard to believe. The course starts at an elevation of 800 meters/2,600 feet and drops 1,200 meters/4,000 feet to finish at the lowest point on earth, the Dead Sea at 411 meters/1,349 feet below sea level!

The Dead Sea Resorts are located along a stretch of the Dead Sea near the 40-kilometer mark. The tour includes two nights at a five-star resort that is much nicer and more luxurious than the hotels I normally stay at. I could get used to staying at places like that—but not the prices! It means we have a long drive to the start line in the morning but a short walk to the hotel after the race. Christian has already given us our race packets, and only after I check it in more detail at the hotel do I realize that I have a bib for the ultra! I had asked him to reserve bib #90 (country #90) but that bib is colored for the ultra race. We switch the bibs before the race, and they let me keep bib #90 as a souvenir!

The races start at 7:00 a.m. on Friday, but we check in at the start of the ultra by 5:30 to have our bib scanned, which means leaving the hotel by 4:30 a.m. In my haste to get ready, I forget my heart monitor strap. I am flustered and annoyed, because I haven't run a marathon in ten years without my monitor. I will just have to run the race the old-fashioned way—based on pace and how I feel. We leave our warm-up clothes on our tour bus and the race organization buses the marathoners to the start by six. That means a one-hour wait without any toilets or water at the start line. Fortunately, I've taken water with me, and the weather is warm enough (high sixties) that warm-ups aren't needed. There are three thousand runners in all races—but only a hundred in the ultra and a hundred in the marathon. The rest are in the half and the 10K. There are two groups from Germany, one from Italy, and one from France, but only two other Americans in the races. The ultra and marathon start at seven. I am concerned about going out too fast because of the steep descent. There are distance markers every kilometer, which really helps. There are water stations every two kilometers, which we will need because of the heat and dry air.

I pass five kilometers in 24:15. Thinking that's too fast, I try to slow down. I really need to know what effort (i.e., heart rate) I am putting into the sub-five minutes/kilometer (eight minutes/mile) pace, but I screwed up that option/possibility. When I pass the 10-kilometer mark in 50:15 I decide that gravity is doing most of the work. I feel okay, so I decide to stay with the five minutes/kilometer pace for the first half and see what happens. By the time I reach 18 kilometers, the temps have climbed significantly, and I start dumping water over my head/body at every water station to cool down! I pass the half in 1:45:37—the fastest half I've run in the past few years! Now the real test begins as the course becomes flatter. I figure if I can slow down and hold a 5:20/kilometer (or 8:30/mile) pace for the second half, I can finish under 3:45. I am pleasantly surprised to find I've only slowed to a 5:10/kilometer pace for the next ten kilometers, and I started to pass a lot of runners who had passed me in the first ten. They've gone out too fast, their legs are trashed from the steep downhills, and they are struggling.

When I make the turn at 30 kilometers, two hundred meters below sea level, it's HOT! The course is straight as an arrow for the final twelve kilometers, and I can see the series of BAHs waiting for me! I manage to hold the 5:10 pace until I reach the first BAH around the 35-kilometer point. My pace slows to 5:30/kilometer (8:50/mile) pace. When I reached the crest of the second BAH, and my hotel is right there I briefly consider the idea of turning into the hotel and going straight to the pool!

My legs are trashed, I am out of energy, and I am *hot*! But I had reached 40 kilometers in 3:26:07and a split of 6:04/ kilometer (my slowest split of the race). Even if I continue at a 6min/kilometer (10min/mile) pace, I'll still finish under 3:40! I focus on shutting out the pain, the lack of energy, and the heat, and force my wasted old legs to keep moving toward the final BAH and the finish line! When I crest that final BAH, I can see the finish line and the finish clock reads 3:37 and change. I beg the old bod to give me one final jolt of adrenaline and sprint across the finish line in 3:37:48!

Then I struggle to limp down to the beach on the Dead Sea. My legs have started to stiffen and cramp because of the hills, but I manage to make it to the beach and into the sea. What an experience! The salt content (30 percent) is six times greater than the ocean and provides unbelievable buoyancy! It is impossible to swim (or drown), because your body floats so far out of the water that it is difficult to stroke and keep your balance. The easiest way is to float on your back! It is difficult to describe. Remember floating on an inner tube in your youth? Same feeling, but no tube! And don't get any water in your eyes or mouth; it stings like hell and tastes awful!

Many of the bathers, including runners, are giving themselves a Dead Sea mud bath. The spas at the resorts charge a fortune, but all you have to do is scoop the black mud from the bottom. It feels slippery, much like a body lotion, and is supposed to be great for your skin because of all the minerals it contains. I declined!

After my dip (or float) in the Dead Sea, I walk back to the hotel for a cool shower and then explore the resort. I enjoy a pizza under a two-thousand-year-old olive tree! That evening, the race organization hosts a dinner and party at our resort for the runners. I am surprised to see the local (Muslim) runners drinking and dancing and really enjoying the party. Our guide explains that (most) Muslims in Jordan do not abide by the strict interpretations of the Koran. Very few women wear a head scarf.

On Saturday morning, we leave the Dead Sea Resorts to travel south to Petra along the Dead Sea Highway. We do not find the ancient cities of Sodom and Gomorrah that supposedly lie somewhere around the southern edge of the Dead Sea, and we don't stop at Lot's Cave, where Lot and his daughters lived after fleeing Sodom, and where his wife was turned into a pillar of salt.

We arrive in Petra in the late afternoon—in time to enjoy a few beers and make an appointment for a massage at the spa at the Marriott Resort. I tried a Petra beer (10 percent). Thanks to that beer and the massage, my legs feel much better, and I run an easy five miles on Sunday morning through the hills of Petra before breakfast. I am looking forward to the tour of the ancient city of Petra. My research indicates it is one of the wonders of the world. I am not disappointed. There are so many archaeological sites to see in Petra that it would take too much space in this report, so again, I will only mention a few highlights.

When you enter the visitor's center, you begin a long walk to the entrance of the Siq.

The natural beauty of the Siq is spectacular, and along the way are several tombs carved into the walls. As you near the end of the Siq, you suddenly get a peek at the Al-Khazneh, or Treasury, which is the icon of Petra. It was carved out of solid iron-laden sandstone to serve as a tomb for the Nabataean King Aretas in 100 BC but gets its name, Treasury, from the story that the Egyptian Pharaoh hid treasure here while pursuing the Israelites. I stay with the tour group through the Siq but decide to take off on my own so that I can see more of Petra during our short one-day tour of the city.

My biggest disappointment of the day and tour is that we do not have more time to explore and enjoy Petra. It definitely needs two to three days to explore fully. I would definitely qualify Petra as a wonder of the ancient world—on a par with the pyramids of Egypt and the Temples of Angkor Wat! A must-see for wanderlusters!

After leaving Petra, we head south to Wadi Rum, where the desert sparkles and opens up an enchanting landscape of red sands and towering sandstone peaks. This is the region that T. E. Lawrence fell in love with, and where he built a house while leading the Arabs against the Ottoman Turks. We pose for a group photo in front of the jebels, named the "Seven Pillars of Wisdom" by Lawrence. We load into 4x4 trucks for a tour into the desert to see red sand dunes, sixteen-hundred-year-old drawings on the sandstone walls, and enjoy a tea break with a Bedouin tribe. Our drivers then drop us off at a desert camp, where we spend the night with Bedouins. After settling into my luxurious single tent, I sit around a camp fire with the group, drink my two Petra beers, and listen to Bedouin music. Dinner is late, so I open a bottle of Crown Royal that I promised to share with the group. They obviously love Canuck whiskey; I only get three shots before it's gone. After dinner, we continue to share booze and tell stories. I don't know how I made it back to my tent, but I do remember how shitty I feel when Christian opens the flap at seven o'clock and tells me I have thirty minutes to be on the bus. However, my legs don't feel bad. All the pain seems to have moved up to my stomach and head. I think I have a hangover.

We leave the camp at 7:30 a.m. for Aqaba, which is located at the northern tip of the Red Sea—only a few kilometers from Israel and thirteen kilometers from Saudi Arabia. It is a large port city that is also being developed for tourist activities—diving, snorkeling, sailing, etc. I was supposed to do a sail/snorkel trip that afternoon but didn't think my head and stomach could handle rolling seas and the heat. The heat was stifling in Aqaba—temps in the midnineties at ten o'clock in the morning.

Instead, I join another runner to explore the city for a few hours and enjoy a pleasant lunch. There is not much to see in Aqaba other than the ruins of the old city—Ayla—built in the third century BC. To escape the heat, I retreat to the pool at the resort. The pool temp was 72°F. They must use water coolers instead of water heaters—otherwise, I don't understand how they can keep the pool water so COLD! The day in Aqaba is rest time that I would prefer to use in Petra.

On Tuesday, half the group heads back to Amman to catch flights home on Wednesday, and the other half stays in Aqaba to enjoy more water sports and beach time. We arrive in Amman in time for a farewell dinner and to say our good-byes, since we all have different departures on Wednesday.

It was a great trip, and I met a lot of new friends and contacts. And I had a great race and completed country # 90! Now what do I do? Glad you asked. Remember a few adventures/marathons back I mentioned that I had a new goal in mind but was not ready to announce it then? I am ready now!

During the past few months I have contacted many friends/runners around the world to compile a Country Club list—a list of runners who have completed a marathon (or ultra) in a minimum of thirty countries. I have posted this list to my blog and website to make it easier to keep it updated and provide access to the members and readers. One reason for the list was to confirm my position on the list. As I suspected, only one other runner in the world has completed a marathon in ninety or more countries—my good friend and mentor, Wally Herman, who holds the world record, with ninety-nine countries! Wally is a fine gentleman, eighty-three years of age, who still runs fifteen to twenty marathons per year. But he no longer runs international races I have asked him many times to join me on one of my international adventures/marathons to complete #100, but he always declines. He keeps telling me, "I hand the mantle over to you. You need to be the first to reach 100." I believe Wally is afraid to run #100 because of the publicity it might generate, and he is a shy man. Also, I don't think he wants to argue with purists, who may dispute his count because he has also run a few solo marathons in small countries that don't offer an official marathon! Unlike Wally, I am not concerned about their opinions that are biased, and self-centered and their unrealistic rules that don't take into consideration, circumstances and facts, nor do they respect and honor the pioneer runners before them who blazed trails and set goals and records for them to beat. But I was waiting until I reached country #90 to have confidence to accept Wally's offer and challenge, and I now announce, "My goal is to complete a marathon in a hundred countries!"

Of course, as most of you know, my establishing a goal is a problem because it immediately becomes an obsession to Maddog! He is demanding that I complete the goal in 2009 and has already booked six more international marathons/countries in 2008! Let the countdown begin!

Marathon #307—Country #92,

Inca Trail Marathon, Peru

August 2008

I wanted to run a marathon in Peru, and the sports manager and I have always wanted to visit Machu Picchu so why not do both at the same time? When I researched the race I learned that the Peruvian government only permits five hundred hikers per day on the Inca Trail, so the sports/tour agency, Andes Adventures, has to book slots many months in advance. Our son Chris also wanted to see Machu Picchu, and he agreed to join us and run the marathon (his first) with his dad. We booked the trip one year in advance.

Unfortunately, Chris was T-boned by a truck while riding his bike in early June and suffered a broken patella. His leg was to be in a cast for eight weeks, and he had to cancel the trip.

As we made the long flight to Lima I read about the history of Peru, the Incas, and the Inca Trail. At its height the Inca Empire controlled nearly one-third of South America and more than ten million people. It all started in 1438 in Cusco (or Qosqo in the Inca tongue of Quechua). Contrary to popular belief, the word "Inca" does not refer to the citizens of the Inca Empire who are more correctly called "Quechua people." The only true Inca was the ruler of the empire who lived in Cusco.

In 1530 the Spanish explorer Francisco Pizarro arrived and defeated the Quechua people. Today, the majority of Peru's population descends from the native Quechua line. Eighty percent speak Spanish and 16 percent still speak Quechua—the second language of the country.

We arrive in Lima late Tuesday night and are picked up and driven to our hotel in Miraflores—a modern suburb located on the Pacific Coast with lots of great hotels, restaurants, and bars. On Wednesday we take an early flight to Cusco, and check into our hotel near the main square—the Plaza de Armas, located in a valley and surrounded by the Andes Mountains. The topography is barren in that region. Cusco is located at 11,200 feet and has a population of 400,000. The center of the city is compact, and it is easy to walk everywhere. We visit the Plaza de Armas and several other plazas near the city center and then venture up into the San Blas neighborhood, where the artists live and work. I wanted to try *cuy* (guinea pig)—a local delicacy. I had eaten cuy in Equador, and wanted to taste the Peruvian version. Equador grills cuy with lots of spices—Peru bakes it. Equador won the cuy taste test! The sports manager refused to eat cuy. I also tried alpaca several times. It is very common on menus and tastes good. Beer is cheap in Peru, but wine is not. Food is cheap if you eat the "tourist menu" of the day, but cuy costs twenty dollars.

After all that food and cheap beer, I need to run and adjust to the 11,000-foot altitude. But where to run? The streets are narrow and crowded and the drivers are crazy! The hotel suggested I run to the Inca ruins at Sacsayhuaman—but they neglected to say that the ruins were located uphill in the Andes Mountains at 12,200 feet! The first day, I run on the side of the road to the ruins before I discover there's a shortcut via Inca stone steps. I came down the steps to practice/train on the stone steps. The second day, I run up via the steps and continue on to the Inca ruins at Qenco (about 12,500 feet). I am sucking air by the time I reach the ruins but the run back down to Cusco is okay. The steps are steep but wide, and I naively think I am doing fine. Little did I know!

The main group arrives on Saturday—twenty-two people, most from the United States, but a few from the United Kingdom and Australia. About thirteen are running the marathon in one day, five are hiking the marathon trail in two days, three are planning to take the train and hike the final four miles of the trail, and the sports manager (the wisest of all?) plans to take the train all the way to Machu Picchu. We begin our first organized tour of the trip with a city tour. We visited the Plaza de Armas and the Cathedral. When the Spanish conquered the Quechua, they destroyed all the Inca buildings in Cusco and rebuilt their churches and homes on top of the Inca foundations, using the stones from the Inca buildings. On many streets you can see the remains of Inca foundations (the stones are carved to fit perfectly without mortar) next to the sloppy Spanish foundations (stones don't fit, and mortar was used). We visited Qorikancha, the most important temple of the Inca Empire, where the Sun Temple (covered in gold plate) and the Moon Temple (covered in silver plate), were located.

On Sunday we tour the Inca ruins at Sacsayhuaman. Since that word is difficult for tourists to pronounce, everyone calls it "Sexywoman." The remains of a fortress and temple are located on the site. After making a too-long stop at a textile factory, we continue to ruins at Qenco, Puca Pucara, and Tambomachay. We finish the day with a 4.5-mile training run from the village of Yuncaypata to the Plaza de Armas in Cusco. The run starts at 12,800 feet and descends on a section of the trails to 12,000 feet and back up to the Temple of Moon at 12,600 feet. The run is led by our main Quechua guide, Abelardo (a good runner who has no problem with the altitude). I manage to stay close to him and a (hard-core) female ultra runner, Roxanne, from Atlanta, until we reach the Temple of the Moon. After a quick visit to the temple, we continue on a more technical downhill section to Cusco where a few fast and good downhill runners pass me. We are starting to establish the pecking order for the marathon.

On Monday, we travel by bus to the Sacred Valley of the Incas, with a stop in Chinchero to visit a Quechua home and family that makes their own textiles and weavings from scratch. They show us how they wash alpaca and sheep wool in natural soap and dye the yarn with natural colors, etc. I keep telling the sports manager that we should move there so she can learn all those neat ancient skills. I won't tell you her response! After shopping, we visit more Inca ruins located in Chinchero. After the tour, we stop in the middle of a high plain (12,600 feet) and Abelardo leads a second training run on a trail that descends gradually for a short time and then drops steeply past the salt mines at Maras and joins a steep, treachorous dirt trail that descends to the Urubamba River (9,500 feet). We all chase Abelardo and Roxanne again. The run is supposed to be seven miles, but when I pass seventy minutes, hurting because I'm running a sub-ten-minute pace (at altitude), I know that it ain't no seven miles. Turns out to be eight miles, and I am the fourth runner to reach the bus. The pecking order has been established!

After the run, we check into a beautiful hotel in Yucay and get together for a prerace meeting. The race director goes over the course and logistics for the race. There are no race bibs, since the government will not allow a race on the Inca Trail. Officially we are all "fast hikers." All those running the Inca Trail in one or two days will camp on the trail and have to pack one bag accordingly. The rest of our clothes and belongings are to be sent on to Machu Picchu or returned to Cusco. At that point, and with two training runs under our belt, a few runners decide to opt out of the marathon and hike the final four miles of the Inca Trail?

On Tuesday we depart for Urubamba, where half the group chooses to go on a white-water-rafting trip on the Urubamba River. I am in the half that chooses not to raft—I don't want to get wet before the hike to base camp, and I don't want to risk an injury on a raft that could spoil my run. Instead, our half drives to Ollantaytambo, where we visit a Quechua home to see how they live in the same manner as their ancestors. The homes are made of adobe and have one large room only that accommodates all family members (and the cuy). Even the skulls of their ancestors are kept in the home! After the interesting visit, we return to the river to cheer our rafting comrades across the finish line on the Urubamba River. Everyone enjoyed the raft but many are soaked! We have a quick lunch in Ollantaytambo before we go to Piscachucho, where we will start our hike to base camp on the Inca Trail to begin the marathon. Those not running the marathon go back to the luxury hotel In Yucay for another night.

The rest of us start our hike at kilometer 82 of the Inca Trail to base camp. We hike beside the train tracks on the opposite side of the Urubamba River to the Inca Trail. Most of us have decided that we will hike—not run—the six miles to camp because of the fast training run the day before. The race starts early on Wednesday.

We reach the official government checkpoint at Qoriwayrachina, at kilometer 88, where we cross the Urubamba River and enter the Machu Picchu Sanctuary National Park. But not without problems! A few runners have renewed their passports and the permits were issued with their old passport numbers, so they don't match, and the Peruvian officials are not going to let them enter the Inca Trail. After much scrambling and promises to correct the problems, they are finally allowed to enter, and we hike another mile to a base camp at the foot of the Inca ruins at Llactapa (a town on the hillside at 8,592 feet). We arrive just as it starts to rain. Fortunately, our luxury accommodations (tents) have already been set up, and we settle in.

After afternoon tea in the mess tent, I hike up to the top of the hill on the Inca Trail where the race is to start. I want to check out the trail and get a bird's eye view of the camp and the Inca ruins. I was happy that the trail was dirt and the rain had not made it slippery! If only I could have guessed. Read on.

We ate a great buffet dinner including pasta in the mess tent. Some of the marathoners decide they want to get an early start. We have to pass through another checkpoint at around four miles, but it doesn't open until six, so there's not much point in starting before 5:00 a.m. The official start is 6:00 a.m, and since it's already dark, we all go to bed early. As I climb into my sleeping bag, I suffer flashbacks to the Everest Marathon, where I swore I would never spend another night in a tent on a cold mountain! But this is much better—the tent is roomier, and the weather is warmer. I crawl into my bag with two thermal layers on and have to remove one in the middle of the night because I'm too warm. As we settle in for the night, it starts to rain again, and it rains hard, and it rains all night! All I can think is that the trail is going to be muddy and slippery, and there will probably be snow above 13,000 feet. Oh goody!

My tentmate, John—a Brit in my age group—decides to start early so he and I are awakened at 3:30 a.m. The early group starts in a light rain and the dark at 5:10 a.m. By then, I am up, packing my bag to be carried to Machu Picchu, and making final preparations for the six o'clock start. Breakfast is served, but I can't eat before a race. Luckily, the rain stops as we hiked in the dark to the start line. It's cool so I start with two layers. After some photos, the official marathon starts a few minutes early. I carry a backpack with enough water to get me to the first aid station at four miles. The trail crosses the Cusichaca River and climbs gradually out of the Urubamba Valley to Wayllabamba (9,100 feet). The first three miles are nice, soft dirt, and I run at a good pace. Then the trail enters the Llullchayoc Gorge and starts to climb steeply over the next five miles to the top of Warmiwanusscca Pass (Dead Woman's Pass) at 13,779 feet. At three miles the nice, soft dirt, disappears and is replaced with stone paths and stone steps built by the Incas five hundred years ago. The stones are uneven and slippery from the rain, and the steps are even worse! They are steep, narrow, *and* slippery! I reach the aid station at four miles in 51:13. I stop to remove my second layer, fill my CamelBak with enough water to get me to the next aid station at ten miles, take a photo, and continue the grueling, relentless climb up Dead Woman's Pass. We climb thousands of steps straight up the mountain; obviously, the Incas didn't believe in switchbacks or dirt trails. We pass through mossy woods (with mossy steps) and a thick forest before emerging into a large meadow (pampa) at Llulluchapampa at 12,400 feet. It starts to get cold, so I'm not surprised when I soon reach stone steps that are covered with snow and ice. Great. And did I mention that in many places there is a sheer drop of a thousand or more feet off the sides of these steps? I reach the top of Dead Woman's Pass in 2:09:25 where I catch up to my tentmate and another early starter. It's very cold, so we all stop to add another layer of clothing and take photos.

Then they bound off down the stone steps on the other side of the pass. I take one look down and freeze from fear! The stone steps are steep, narrow, covered with ice, and going *downhill*! Climbing uphill on steep, narrow steps is scary, but gravity and altitude kept the pace slow and safe. Going downhill is terrifying! One bad step or slip, and I'll fall a long way down the steps. Did I mention the thousand-foot drop? I don't want to think about that option. I am so terrified of falling that the only way I can make it down the steps is to sidestep—one step at a time, and always leading with my left foot so that my right, dominant side will fall into the steps if I make a mistake! I have to focus strongly on each step and foot plant to prevent a fall and to control my acrophobia. I am afraid that if I look at that drop I'll become dizzy and fall off the mountain! I have to use this method until I'm back below 13,000 feet, where the temps warm up, and the ice melts. At that point, I decide that if I want to finish the race that day, I have to teach myself how to hike down the steps in a normal mode—i.e., like going down the steps in my house. That's a lot easier to say than do, but I manage to get into a somewhat normal pace until I reach more steps that are very steep and narrow, and then it's back to the sidestep routine! It takes me fifty minutes to descend one mile and reach the second aid station at ten miles. I've reached ten miles in 2:59:30. I knew my prerace goal of finishing under eight hours was not going to happen! And I don't care—I am too terrified of the downhill steps to take any risks for the sake of time.

I stop at the aid station to fill my CamelBak with enough water to get to the final aid station at 17.5 miles. The race director told us that there would be bottled water at every aid station. He lied! The porters are boiling local stream water to purify it. That's okay, but the water is still hot when I fill my CamelBak, so I have to drink hot water for the next three hours. Another first for a marathon!

The trail then begins to climb again (lots more steep, narrow stone steps) as it ascends to the top of Runkurakay Pass (13,100 feet). I swear that climb was worse than the first pass. The steps seem to be much steeper and go on… and on…and on…without any relief. I catch and pass a few more runners from the early group as I struggle to the top of the pass while sucking for air.

Near the top, the steps become so steep and narrow that we have to scramble on our hands and knees to get to the top! I stand on the top of Runkurakay Pass at 3:49:33. Then the fear begins again—I have to go down the steps on the other side. Back to my terrifying and slow sidestepping routine for the steep/narrow steps at the top, and I finally ease into a normal pace by the time I reached the Inca fortress at Sayacmarca (12,234 feet). I miss a turn at the ruins and climb up a series of steep steps before I realize there's no trail out of the ruins. I backtrack to the steps. One of the runners I passed is approaching the ruins, and he asks a Quechua porter for directions. I descend the steps and follow a narrow stone path along the perimeter of the ruins. I keep catching up to my fellow runner as we pass through natural and Inca-made tunnels. We join up again at the final water station near the ruins at Phuyupatamarca (Town in the Clouds—11,674 feet) at 17.5 miles. This was the overnight camp for the runners completing the trail in two days. It has taken me 6:08:39 to go 17.5 miles. Maybe I should stay overnight at the camp. The final checkpoint closes at 3:00 p.m.

I stop to fill my CamelBak with enough water to get me to the finish line. Surprise—more hot water! Surprise—very nasty, steep, narrow steps leading down from Phuyupatamarca Pass. They are steep, narrow, and in bad shape. Back to the sidestepping routine. When I finally manage to get down that terrifying stretch of steps. I comment to myself that it can't get any worse than that. WRONG! I reach a rock outcrop of granite that bulges out of the side of the mountain like a big belly. The Incas had carved very narrow steps or toeholds into the granite but time, water, and use had rounded the steps. I look at those steps and say, "I ain't going down there." I look for an alternate route—there is none. I consider quitting, but it's eight miles to Machu Picchu down those terrifying steps or nineteen miles back to the start line. There are no other alternatives. I tried my side-step routine but that requires looking down (to where I would most likely fall and die), and the steps are too rounded and narrow for the side of my foot. So I lie on my belly and cling to the rock outcrop, dig my fingers into the granite, and claw my way down that thirty-foot section of terror. I bet my claw marks will be in that granite for a long time.

The trail seems to get better, with fewer steps after that, and I'm able to make good progress until I reach the ruins at WinayWaya (8,692 feet). The trail passes through the ruins and down another terrifying series of steps inside them. My knees are throbbing and sore, and the only way I can make it down those steps is to sidestep and cling to the walls of the ruins. At the bottom of the steps, the trail has dirt and small stones, and I hike faster (almost jog) until I reach the final checkpoint near 22.5 miles (7:43:09). Abelardo was waiting at that checkpoint to pass us through, and I'm pleased to discover that after the checkpoint, the trail descends gradually and actually has a section of dirt trail? I catch glimpses of other runners ahead of me and hear voices. I started to run easy in hopes of catching them but can't, because they have also started to run. Unfortunately, after a mile, the trail becomes stone paths again, and stone steps as it starts to climb.

I hear footsteps behind me. Abelardo has decided to follow the group ahead and me to the finish line. That works out well for me because I don't have to worry about taking a wrong turn (again). Like a kid in a car, I start asking, "Are we there yet? How far to the finish line?" Since the trail is climbing again, and I expect it to be descending to Machu Picchu, I ask what's going on. Abelardo informs me that the trail climbs around and up the back side of Machu Picchu Mountain to Intipunku, the Sun Gate (8,860 feet), that overlooks Machu Picchu (7,900 feet). I ask, "How far"? Instead of distance, he answers, "About forty minutes." The trail keeps climbing and climbing—more steep, narrow steps. My knees are killing me, but Maddog refuses to stop for a rest in case Abelardo thinks he's a wimp. Finally, I reach a short set of very narrow, steep steps (supposedly built that way for defensive purposes) that climb up to the Sun Gate. The steps are so steep that I have to scramble on my hands and feet, and the last few steps I have to crawl on my hands, feet, and knees to drag myself over the top and through the Sun Gate.

My first look at Machu Picchu! It is awesome. I stop for photos and then ask Abelardo, "How far to the finish line?" He again answers in time—"About forty minutes." I have reached the Sun Gate in 8:30:06. I don't have forty minutes if I want to finish under nine hours and recoup some self-respect

I am determined to break nine hours, even if it means taking some risks. Luckily, that final section of trail to Machu Picchu, known as the Royal Trail, is all downhill and built with larger flat stones that provide better, safer footing, and I jog that final two miles and reach the finish line at the flat rock overlooking Machu Picchu (7,900 feet) in 8:51:23! It is a good thing that Abelardo is behind me because I would have missed the finish line, as many other runners do. He took a photo of a jubilant and glad-to-be-alive Maddog jumping up and down on the flat rock.

I noticed on the final jog down the Royal Trail that I have lots of physical energy left because I have gone so slowly. But as soon as I reach the finish line, I become mentally exhausted. The stress of focusing on every foot plant and every one of the thousands of stone steps and controlling my acrophobia, has totally exhausted me mentally. I ask Abelardo, "How far is it down to the bus that takes us to the hotel?" He tells me, "Ten minutes," and I say that I don't care how long it takes, but I'm going to relax and walk down in a normal fashion!

When we reach the bus stop, the runners from the early group are waiting for the bus. They have finished only a few minutes ahead of me. Everyone complains about sore knees and calves, and a few have bruises and cuts from falls, but everyone is happy and healthy! During the thrilling thirty-minute bus ride down the mountain to Aguas Calientes, I start to question my performance in the race. At first I'm disappointed with my time, but then I remind myself how difficult it was to control my acrophobia and fear of the downhill steps, and how lucky I am to have finished ALIVE and injury-free! I could never have attempted or finished that race five years ago before I started climbing fourteeners in Colorado and learned how to control my acrophobia. No, I should be pleased and proud that I've overcame those difficulties to finish the race!

When we reach Aguas Calientes, our leg muscles have tightened up, and everyone has difficulty getting off the bus and walking to the hotel. The sports manager is waiting at the bus stop to see if I've survived. Unfortunately, our room does not have a tub, so I have to make do with a hot shower before joining my fellow runners for a pizza and beer and to discuss our memorable race.

Thursday is a rest day as we waited for the runners completing the trail in two days to finish. My legs—and especially my knees—are very sore. I haven't been that sore in years. So I schedule a massage with a Thai masseuse who helps a lot, and then I go for a soak in the hot springs of Aguas Calientes. Unfortunately, the hot springs (100°F) were not as hot as my hot tub (108°F).

The runners who took two days have the advantage that they finish less beaten up than us, and get to see/enjoy a lot more of the Inca trail.

Two days later, we take an organized tour of Machu Picchu. Our guide, Abelardo, leads us on a very interesting and informative tour of the ruins. There are lots of steps (surprise) in the ancient city. We visited all the sections of the city—agricultural, residential, and industrial—and the religious temples.

In the midst of a tropical mountain forest on the eastern slopes of the Peruvian Andes, Machu Picchu's walls, terraces, stairways, and ramps blend seamlessly into its natural setting. The site's finely crafted stonework, terraced fields, and sophisticated irrigation system bear witness to the Inca civilization's architectural, agricultural, and engineering prowess. Its central buildings are prime examples of a masonry technique mastered by the Incas in which stones were cut to fit together without mortar.

Archaeologists have identified several distinct sectors that together comprise the city, including a farming zone, a residential neighborhood, a royal district, and a sacred area. Machu Picchu's most distinct and famous structures include the Temple of the Sun and the Intihuatana stone, a sculpted granite rock that is believed to have functioned as a solar clock or calendar.

Historians believe Machu Picchu was built at the height of the Inca empire, which dominated western South America in the fifteenth and sixteenth centuries. It was abandoned an estimated hundred years after its construction, probably around the time the Spanish began their conquest of the mighty pre-Columbian civilization in the 1530s. There is no evidence that the conquistadors ever attacked or even reached the mountaintop citadel, however; for this reason, some have suggested that the residents' desertion occurred because of a smallpox epidemic.

Machu Picchu is believed to have been a royal estate or sacred religious site for Inca leaders, whose civilization was virtually wiped out by Spanish invaders in the sixteenth century. For hundreds of years, until the American archaeologist Hiram Bingham stumbled upon it in 1911, the abandoned citadel's existence was a secret known only to peasants living in the region. The site stretches over an impressive five-mile distance, featuring more than three thousand stone steps that link its many different levels.

On Saturday, we take a train back to Ollantaytambo to visit the Inca ruins overlooking the city. The city was abandoned before completion because of the Inca civil war between the two sons of Huayna Capac. We continue by bus through Pisac to Cusco and return to our old hotel and one final night in Cusco. That evening, the tour agency holds an award ceremony at the hotel in Cusco. No special awards, but every runner receives a finisher's medal, T-shirt, and certificate. To nobody's surprise, Roxanne has won the race—in 6:12, an amazing time under the conditions. I am pleased to learn that I finished in fourth place overall.

On Sunday, we fly back to Lima and take a city tour of Lima. We visit the Plaza Mayor in old colonial Lima as well as the San Francisco Monastery before returning to our hotel in Miraflores one last night. The sports manager and I skip the final tour dinner to enjoy a private seafood dinner and a bottle of Peruvian wine in a small restaurant (we can't face more chicken).

Monday is a very early wake-up call and a long flight back to Colorado.

Another trip filled with amazing experiences. It was the worst, toughest, slowest, most terrifying marathon I have ever run. But I have no regrets and tons of memories.

It is over. I am happy that I finished country #92 ALIVE and injury-free, and now I must focus on more altitude training to prepare for my next marathon in a few weeks in the Himalayan Kingdom of Bhutan.

Marathon #308—Country #93, Bhutan

International Marathon, Bhutan

September 2008

"Where is Bhutan?" you ask. It is a landlocked country in the Himalayas, bordered on the north by China/Tibet and on all other sides by India.

Bhutan's early history is steeped in Buddhist folklore, and Buddhism is still the main religion and cultural influence. The kingdom is ruled by a king who decided to move the country from an absolute monarchy to a democratic constitutional monarchy in 2008 that is committed to improving the GNH (Gross National Happiness) of the country and its citizens. The small population (about 700,000) is friendly and sincere, and you figure if they are serious enough to focus on GNH, then it's well worth a visit.

And a marathon.

I had first considered running a marathon in Bhutan in 2001, when the first and only other marathon was held. But the country is very difficult and expensive to visit. The number of tourists is restricted (fewer than twenty thousand per year) and all guests (except those from India) must be invited and escorted by a Bhutanese travel agency at all times. There is a tourist tax of $250/day included in the tour package that can only be purchased from a Bhutanese agency! Bottom line—it is not cheap to visit Bhutan. However, in my quest to run one hundred countries, I felt that now was the time. I had better visit Bhutan when I had the chance because there might not be another marathon. And I am not getting any younger! When I mentioned my trip to some other runners/friends only one—my good friend Frank (aka—the MadMonk) expressed interest and actually booked the trip. He agreed to share a room with me.

Maddog and MadMonk arrive in Bangkok in midafternoon after thirty-two hours of travel time and are totally wiped out from jet lag. Wisely, we have arranged a two-day layover to recover from jet lag and explore Bangkok.

Our families send us frantic e-mails warning us that the prime minister of Thailand has declared a state of emergency. We've heard the same news on the BBC news channel, but our hotel is located on the outskirts of the city, and we haven't noticed any turmoil or problems in the streets. We book a city and temple tour for the afternoon and decide to visit the Grand Palace on our own during the morning. We don't see any problems when we arrive in the old section of Bangkok, but there are lots of police and military armed with machine guns.

Later that day, we tour the old city of Bangkok and visit (too) many Buddhist temples. Again, we don't see any political protests? But most of the protests seem to occur at night, and we are in bed by eight o'clock. Since we have a (ugly) 4:30 a.m. departure for Bhutan the next day, we enjoy a great seafood dinner and go to sleep. Five hours later, we get up and head to the airport. Our Druk Air flight connects via Calcutta, India, and arrives in Paro about eight in the morning on Sept 4. We are finally in Bhutan!

A tour guide from the travel agency that organized the marathon and trip meets us at the airport. We soon learn that Khandu will be our dedicated guide (and babysitter) for our entire stay in Bhutan. There is one other runner in our group—a lovely young woman from Germany. Corinna only decided in the past few weeks to run the marathon. We are amazed to learn that a tour guide is dedicated to each group or individual guest who arrives on different dates or has a different length of stay Khandu checks us into a hotel in Paro, and I watch in amusement as MadMonk lets some young Bhutanese women carry his luggage to our room. After breakfast and checking out the grounds of the Hotel Gangtey Palace—an old palace that has been converted to a hotel—Maddog and MadMonk decide to do a run. Paro is the second largest city in Bhutan with a population of 9,000 (no error in the zeroes). The town and surrounding area are rural, which is perfect. We couldn't run in Bangkok because of the traffic and pollution, and we need to run! We run down the mountain and through the town. The roads are narrow, with no shoulder, but there is very little traffic. The biggest problem? Dogs—hundreds of stray dogs lying around the roads in town and outside the town. Fortunately, they aren't mean or aggressive—they just lie in the middle of the roads and force cars and people to go around them. I can't believe that they won't move for cars. They would be dead in minutes in the United States. After our much-needed run and endorphin kick, we enjoy a nice (vegetarian) lunch at the hotel.

After lunch, Khandu takes us on a guided tour of the National Museum in Paro. The museum used to be a watchtower for the Paro Dzong (fortress) but was renovated in 1968 to house the National Museum. At the end of an interesting tour we ask Khandu to drop us off to explore the town and do some shopping. Khandu is hesitant about leaving us alone, because he is supposed to babysit us 24-7, but he soon realizes that's not going to happen. We walk back to the hotel in time for dinner (vegetarian, of course)! Since the hotel has no TV, telephone, or Internet, we go to bed early to prepare for a tough hike the next day.

The next morning after breakfast, we walk down the hill from the hotel to the Taju Elementary School before starting the day's activities. We have brought school supplies that we want to give to Bhutanese kids. What better way than to donate them to a school? We arrive at an opportune time—the kids are assembled in the schoolyard for morning assembly. We watch as the kids stand quietly at attention in their school uniforms while a few classmates read short essays, and then everyone sings the national anthem. After the assembly is dismissed, many of the kids approached us politely to ask who we are and where we are from. I thought, "I sure wish we could send our kids from the United States (and <insert the name of your country>)to Bhutan for a few years to learn a lesson in humility and discipline." We find the principal and explain that we want to donate some school supplies to the kids. He gladly accepts our gifts and explains that he will use them as prizes or rewards for good grades. Our good deed done, we return to the hotel to prepare for the day's activities.

The itinerary calls for a long tough hike up to Taktshang Goemba, the most famous of Bhutan's monasteries, miraculously perched on the side of a sheer cliff three thousand feet above the floor of the Paro Valley. The name means "tiger's nest." It is said that Guru Rinpoche flew to the site of the monastery on the back of a tigress, a manifestation of his consort Yeshe Tsogyal, to subdue the local demon, Singey Samdrup. He then meditated in a cave for three months. The only way up to the Tiger's Nest is to walk, ride a horse, or fly on the back of the magic tiger. I was concerned about the MadMonk and his poor back, but Khandu assures us that although the trail is steep, it's soft dirt up to the top of a chasm, where it becomes necessary to climb many steps built into the side of the cliffs to get to the monastery. MadMonk decides he can make it to that point. Because of my excellent training on fourteeners, I forge ahead on the steep trail and leave the group. Khandu is no fool—he stays with the lovely young woman, and Madmonk trails behind. I wait at several points for Khandu and Corinna to catch up and take photos. MadMonk catches up to us at a cafeteria located at 9,700 feet while we're enjoying a tea break. We continue to the top of the chasm at 10,362 feet, where there is a small temple, and you're eyeball to eyeball with the monastery—except it's on the opposite side of a chasm. The only way to get to the monastery is to descend about two hundred meters on stone steps built into the sides of the sheer cliffs to a waterfall that drops 3,000 feet to the valley floor and then ascend about a hundred meters on more stone steps on the opposite cliffs to the monastery. I go into the temple, light a butter lamp, and say a prayer (you can easily guess what my prayer was). MadMonk refuses to go any farther because of his delicate back and severe acrophobia, so I forge ahead. My recent terrifying experience on the stone steps of the Inca Trail prepared me well for this pilgrimage. I don't find the steps or the sheer drop that terrifying, and I quickly make it to the monastery. Maybe I should run the Inca Trail again next year. Nah, not a chance in hell!

There are four temples carved and built into the side of the cliff. We are permitted to visit three of them, including the cave where Guru Rinopche meditated. I make a donation, but my wish at the sacred cave is never fulfilled, so I am not converting to Buddhism! No photos are allowed inside the monastery, so you will have to make the visit and wish on your own. We agreed with the MadMonk that we will all meet back at the cafeteria for lunch, so I hustle back there while Khandu and Corinna meditate to join him. When I arrive—no MadMonk. When Khandu finally arrives, he informs me that one of his fellow tour guides has found the MadMonk (alone) at the car and called Khandu. The MadMonk has broken two important rules. First, when you are on a mountain you always, *always* stay at the agreed-upon meeting place until your group joins you, and second, in Bhutan, you do not go off on your own without your tour guide—especially in unknown and risky situations! Fortunately, Khandu has arranged for his friend to drive the MadMonk to a restaurant while we eat lunch at the cafeteria. When we finally pick the MadMonk up at the restaurant, I am really pissed off, and I tell him bluntly and emphatically how foolish he has been. By the time I finish my tirade, he understands that he has screwed up!

It has been a long tough hike, so we return to the hotel in Paro for a short rest before Khandu takes us to the Paro Dzong for a guided tour. The Rinchen Pung Dzong was built in 1644 to defend the Paro valley from invasions from Tibet. Like all dzongs, it was built to house government offices at one end and a Buddhist temple at the other. Inside the entrance to the dzong was a very colorful painting of a wheel of life depicting the six stages of life that humans go through as they progress to either heaven or hell! Khandu tries to explain the various stages and meanings, but unless you have a basic knowledge of Buddhism, it is difficult to grasp. We soon realize, as we visit many more dzongs and temples, that a basic knowledge of Buddhism would be very helpful when visiting Bhutan since so much of their life and culture is derived from that religion.

At the end of the dzong tour, Maddog and MadMonk once again ask Khandu to drop us off in town so that I could take photos of the town and locals.

We depart early for the capital, Thimpu, to join up with the other guests who will be running the marathon. On the outskirts of Paro, we stop at the Tamchhog Lhakhang, a six-hundred-year-old temple owned by the descendants of the Tibetan bridge-builder Thangtong Gyalpo. The traditional iron bridge at the temple was built using some of the original iron chains forged by Thangtong. We continue on to Chhuzom, known as the "confluence," at the juncture of the Paro Chhu (river) and the Wang Chhu, where there are three chortens built in different styles: Bhutanese, Tibetan, and Nepali. There is also a police checkpoint at Chhuzom. I ask Khandu why, and he explains that the road to Thimphu is treacherous. Often cars do not make it to the far end, and this way, the police can look for them. I'm sorry I asked!

However, we make it to Thimphu, the capital of Bhutan, and the biggest city in the country with a population of 90,000. They are proud of the fact that it is the only capital city in the world without a traffic light, although there is one traffic cop at the main roundabout in the center of the city. We check into a modern hotel in the city center, where we are supposed to meet up with the rest of the runners. Khandu informs us that the rest of the day was free until we join up with the other guests at three o'clock for a bus tour of the marathon course. He asks if he can drive us anywhere. We all agree that we would like a short drive/tour around Thimphu to get the layout of the city.

As we start our drive around the city, Khandu suggests that we drive out to the Motithang Takin Preserve to see Bhutan's national animal, the takin, a cross between a goat and a cow. This becomes a contentious point for me. One of my chief complaints with the tour and tour agency is the lack of a formal itinerary and lack of information. Because I was expecting a short tour of the city I do not bring my camera. Fortunately, Corinna brought her camera and promised to send me some photos of the takins! After seeing the takins, we drive back into the city and go to the only Italian restaurant in Bhutan for lunch. I order a pizza with lots of pepperoni and meat—my second-best meal in Bhutan! Thimphu is small and compact so the tour is short, and I decide to go shopping for souvenirs. I saw a unique Bhutanese musical instrument in the shops in Paro but decided to wait till Thimphu where I expected there would be better selections and prices. Much to my surprise and chagrin, I cannot find the instruments in Thimphu. I return to the hotel to meet the other guest runners, including an old running friend and fellow Country Club member, Andy Kotulski, who is running his seventy-sixth country. Andy and I have just met recently when we ran the Estes Park Marathon, the "Highest Paved Marathon in the World." We are curious how this marathon course will compare to Estes Park.

There are fifteen guest runners—thirteen running the marathon and two running the half—and three spouses who are not running. We load onto a bus and begin our tour of the course.

Again I don't bring a camera because I believed it to be strictly a tour of the course. The course starts in downtown Thimphu near the National Stadium (elev. 2,320 meters/7,650 feet) and climbs gently along the right bank of the Wang Chhu (river). At seven kilometers it crosses the Dechencholing Bridge to the left bank, and at 7.9 kilometers the two courses (marathon and half) diverge. The marathon course begins to climb the first BAH (badass hill) to 2,508 meters/8,276 feet, past some water towers, where it turns north and enters a pine forest, where there's a series of short BAHs until it reaches the Begana Bridge at 15 kilometers. The course then climbs another BAH through oak forests to a turnaround point near the Cheri Goemba (monastery) at 17.9Km and 2,583 meters/8,524 feet. We stopped at the monastery for a photo op—except for Maddog, who has no camera! The course then loops back over the Begana Bridge and past a large gold-painted petroglyph of Chenrisig on a rock beside the road.

The course continues to retrace the route back to the BAH at the water tower and down to the bridge at Dechencholing, where it rejoins the Half-marathon course. It then turns into an army base and passes the queen mother's palace as it climbs up into the mountains overlooking Thimphu from the west. At 32 kilometers, the course climbs the final BAH—five kilometers long and reaches an elevation of 8,200 feet before descending back into the city and the finish line. As the bus chugs and strains up that final BAH, I comment to the group that the hill will be an "absolute bitch" tomorrow. Andy and I agree that the course looks much tougher than Estes Park because of the number of BAHs. I finished Estes Park in 4:13 but feel I'm in much better shape for this race, so my target remain four hours, but I expect to finish between 4:00 and 4:15.

The itinerary calls for a pasta dinner and party that evening, but again there's a serious lack of information. I've learned my lesson and carry a camera, but they neglect to advise us that the party will be held outside. It's cold at 7:00 p.m., and most runners have not dressed properly, so it's difficult to enjoy the wonderful dancers and singers who are entertaining us with traditional songs and dances. Luckily, we moved inside for the prerace dinner and another surprise! The pasta and rice are served *cold*! Now, I do admit that I am rigid in my prerace diet requirements. I always, always eat hot spaghetti bolognese and will not deviate from this proven routine. I hate cold food, so I refuse to eat any of the pasta dinner. I want to leave and go back to the Italian restaurant for hot food but don't want to be rude. So instead, I return to the hotel hungry and eat a Power Bar for my prerace dinner, hoping that the huge pizza I ate for lunch will carry me through the race.

The races start at 6:30 a.m. but Khandu drives us to the start line at 5:30 a.m. so we can enjoy the opening ceremony—a traditional Marchhang ceremony to invoke the deities for the protection and good luck of all runners. Khandu becomes our de facto sports manager, and promises to follow us around the course, so I give him my backup camera to take photos along the course. In addition to the fifteen guest runners, there are more than a hundred local runners. The races are treated as two separate events. There's no doubt that the locals would kick our butts. The locals don't pay an entry fee (most would not enter if they had to pay), and are eligible for cash awards equivalent to two months' salary (paid from the $300 entry fee charged to the guest runners). There are no awards for guests! For our $300, we get a race T-shirt, a finisher's medal, and a certificate! And the results are kept separate.

The weather is nice at the start—cloudy and temps in the low fifties. The race starts on time, and the locals take off like rockets. Also one guest runner takes off very fast—a young man from Norway. I let him go, figuring that the hills and elevation will soon slow him down.

I run with some local and guest runners for the first seven kilometers. After I cross the Dechencholing Bridge, a young German runner passes me, and I decide to let him go but keep him in sight. As we start climbing the first BAH I was determined to run the entire hill. However, as we approach the top of the BAH near the water towers, my legs are churning madly, but they feel like they're moving in slow motion. I figure I can power walk faster and easier than I'm supposedly running.

I am correct, but I am also concerned that I'm setting a bad precedent very early in the race We turn onto the side road and enter the pine forest. As I cross the Benang Bridge over the Wang Chhu at the 15-kilometer point, I meet the three local leaders of the race. That means they have a six-kilometer lead on me at that point, and I know I won't see them again! I start the climb up the BAH to the turnaround point at Cheri Goemba, and I'm disappointed that I have to start power walking again. As I approach the turn point, I meet the young Norwegian and then the German runner and time my split to the turn point. I calculate that the Norwegian has a six-minute lead and the German about a four-minute lead. I remember the distance at that point (17.9 kilometers), and I'm not concerned, because I figure—I hope—the hills and elevation will slow them down.

The return leg down the BAH and back to the bridge is easy, and I'm able to haul ass! However, once I cross the bridge I'm faced again with the series of short BAHs. The gold-painted petroglyph takes my mind off the BAHs and pain for a few minutes, and soon I reach a water station—the only station that knows what the distance is—23.3 kilometers. I look at my watch—2:05! A sub-four-hour finish is not looking good, because the second half has a lot of BAHs and elevation changes, but I keep on pushing the pace. A few minutes later, I hear a loud commotion, and a tribe of twenty or thirty monkeys emerges from the forest and crosses the road in front of me. I don't want to threaten their territory, so I stop immediately and retreat while they cross the road. A few minutes later, I meet the MadMonk coming in the opposite direction and hope that he has an opportunity to see the monkeys. (He did).

Soon I reach the main road and the top of the BAH at the water towers. I'm looking forward to that BAH this time—a two-kilometer steep descent! I haul ass, hoping that I might close within sight of the youngsters ahead of me. However, when I reach the water station where the course rejoins the Half

(26.9 kilometers), there's no sign of the youngsters. I won't catch them unless they crash on the final BAH. I climb into the mountains west of the city and enjoy some nice views of Thimphu (when I wasn't grimacing with pain). And finally, I reached the section of the course I was dreading—the final BAH that climbed steeply and relentlessly for five kilometers. It did not take long for my prediction to come true. After one kilometer of climbing and running, my legs again feel like they're moving in superslow motion? That BAH *is* an absolute bitch! I develop a strategy to walk for thirty seconds and run for two minutes, and managed to maintain that cycle except on a few very steep sections, where it becomes walk thirty seconds and run thirty seconds! I'm becoming concerned that I might not finish under 4:30 with all the walking I have to do.

I reach a water station near the top of the BAH. No water! That doesn't upset me as much as the fact that the volunteer has no idea what the distance is or how far it is to the finish line. I need to know that so I can determine how hard I need to push the pace. I decide to push the pace to the top of that BAH/absolute bitch. When I finally crest that BAH, a support car comes by and gives me a bottle of water. I ask, "How far to the finish line?" The answer is useless: thirty minutes. For whom? I look at my watch—it's just under four hours! If he's correct, I'll be lucky to finish under 4:30.

Maddog screams at me, "That is not acceptable!" I agree, and we decide that I have to push the pace, all out, to the finish line. If I crash, at least I'll go down in flames trying. I figure it's four or five kilometers to the finish line, and all downhill. I haul ass and soon am pleasantly surprised when I make a sharp turn at a large stupa. I remember that stupa is approximately two kilometers from the finish line. I look at my watch—about 4:05! I'm now confident that I can finish under 4:15 and qualify for Boston. That final mile is a very steep downhill, so I stretch out my stride and use gravity to fly down that hill. I reach the bottom of that BAH and downtown Thimphu at 4:10 and can see the finish line on the other side of the Wang Chhu! I look at the bridge. The sidewalk is crowded with pedestrians who may impede my path and my speed, and there's no traffic control on the bridge. I decide to take a chance and charge down the middle of the traffic lane forcing (and trusting) cars to avoid me. I make it across the bridge safely and beg the old bod to give me one final jolt of adrenaline so I can sprint up the final, short and steep hill. I cross the finish line in 4:13:23!

The youngsters are waiting at the finish line. The Norwegian finished in 4:01 and the German in 4:08. I'm not disappointed—they're half my age, and I've finished in third place (among the guest runners). And it turns out that I am the only runner (including the locals) who finished that tough course with a BQ (Boston Qualifying) time. I am pleased! I wait at the finish line for the first guest female to finish (from Hong Kong) in 4:33. Then I decide I might as well walk back to the hotel for a long hot shower since the MadMonk won't finish for another two hours. After a much-needed shower, I meet several of my fellow runners in the hotel lobby. Everyone agrees with my course assessment—it was tough and that last BAH was an absolute bitch. Andy and I agree that it was much tougher than Estes Park, but the strange coincidence is that I finished in the exact same time as Estes Park, and Andy finished exactly one hour behind me—the same as Estes Park.

Most runners are going to lunch at the hotel, but I can't eat after a race, so I walk, back to the finish line to wait for the MadMonk. The race director has assigned two teenagers to accompany him through the second half, and he was in constant contact with the volunteers. When he reaches the stupa near the finish, I walk backward on the course to escort him to the finish line. He finishes in 6:53:26. He's a very tired puppy, but he has survived! He's the last guest to finish, but *not* the last runner. A local couple, Japanese expats living in Bhutan, finish five minutes later. The race director, Penjo, calls all guests to reassemble at the finish area for the awards ceremony. The cash awards are presented to the local winners, and all the guests received a finisher's medal and certificate.

Later, I visit handicraft shops in the hopes of finding my musical instruments, but no luck. I'm not concerned, since we'll return to Paro, and I can buy them there. The following day, most of the groups part ways and continue on their different tours. We're scheduled to drive to the Punakha Valley. Although it's only seventy-six kilometers, it's a four-hour drive because it's necessary to drive over a pass at Docha Lu (3,140 meters/10,362 feet) and then descend to Punakha (1,250 meters/4,125 feet). We make a short stop at Simtokha to take photos of the Simtokha Dzong, built in 1629. Then we begin a long drive that is tough on Khandu and scary for his guests! The road is paved but is a narrow, single lane, and it can be a challenge when you meet another vehicle. Both cars must swerve onto the shoulder and there are no guardrails to prevent a car from plummeting three thousand feet off the side of the mountain. However, in a few hours we safely reached Docha Lu, where there's a large array of prayer flags and a collection of 108 chortens built in 2005 to commemorate the loss of life caused by the flushing out of Assamese militants in Southern Bhutan. As usual, the chortens are shrouded in rain clouds. A few hours later, we had descended safely to Punakha Valley and check into a hotel in Wangdue. Due to the low elevation of Punakha Valley and the warm climate, the valley is fertile and provides two crops of rice and tropical fruit such as oranges and bananas. The scenery is spectacular, with terraced rice fields climbing up the sides of the mountains.

After a short rest and lunch, we drive up the valley to visit the Punakha Dzong, one of Bhutan's most impressive dzongs. It sits at the confluence of the Mo Chhu (Mother River) and Pho Chhu (Father River). Punakha was the capital of Bhutan for more than three hundred years, so the dzong was the seat of government power. After visiting the dzong, we're scheduled to visit a monastery that requires a short hike. However, Corinna is suffering from a sprained ankle and can barely walk, and the MadMonk was still exhausted from the marathon, so we rebelled and tell Khandu that we will take photos from the road! We decide to head back to the hotel to rest, use the Internet, and drink beer!

The following morning, we want to do a short run, so we leave the hotel at six o'clock and head south on the highway. About two kilometers from the hotel, we reach a police checkpoint. I explain that we're jogging and want to run another five kilometers past the checkpoint. The guard looks at me like I'm crazy and says, "Okay, have a good day, sir!" After turning around I meet many kids walking to school. They're very friendly and curious, wanting to know where I'm from, etc. I really enjoy talking to the kids!

After breakfast, we're scheduled to visit our last dzong—the Wangdue Phrodrang Dzong on the edge of Wangdue at the confluence of the Punak

Tsang Chhu and the Dang Chhu. But first, we ask Khandu to drive us to the Wangdue Elementary School, where we will donate our final school supplies. We arrive as the morning assembly was being dismissed and get to talk to a lot of the students. Then we find the principal, who gladly accepts our gifts. Needless to say, we feel quite pleased with ourselves when we leave the school.

Then it's on to the dzong. The Wangdue Dzong was built in 1638 and is the most authentic dzong we visited. Most of the architecture and buildings are original. Also, we arrive at an opportune time. There are many local Buddhist laymen practicing dances for an upcoming festival in the courtyard, and we're invited into a building to watch Bhutanese women rehearsing songs and dances for the festival. And then we're invited into the temple to watch some student monks performing a ceremony, and last invited into a classroom where students are being taught.

That's the best visit of a dzong—either because of the above activities, or maybe because it's the last. By now, we're completely dzonged and templed out, so we head back to Thimpu and the long scary ride over Docha Lu pass. We arrive in Thimphu in time for lunch—you guessed it, another vegetarian lunch! However, by then I've resolved that I don't want to see or eat any more rice or green vegetables for at least three months! I refuse to eat any more stir-fried vegetables. Instead, I order a big plate of french fries—hot, greasy chips made from scratch with fresh potatoes. They are wonderful! The third-best meal I've eaten in Bhutan!

We then continue our drive back to Paro. When we reach Paro, I insist that Khandu drive us to a few handicraft shops, so I could buy my musical instruments—a Bhutan guitar, handmade in the shape of a dragon, a great addition to our kids' collection of unique musical instruments from around the world. I also insist on one more stop—to buy a birthday cake! After we check into the same hotel, Corinna enjoys a hot stone bath while Maddog and MadMonk enjoy a Thai massage before dinner. Then I go to the bar to gorge myself on peanuts and Bhutanese beer, knowing that it's unlikely that I can or will eat any (vegetarian) dinner! But I do enjoy the birthday cake after we sing "Happy Birthday" to celebrate Khandu's twenty-eighth birthday.

I believe Khandu is happy to be finished with his babysitting duties as he drops us off at the Paro airport the next morning for our flights to Bangkok to begin our thirty-two-hour journey home.

Marathon #310—Country #95, Defis

Du Chott, Sahara Desert, Tunisia

November 2008

Although this trip and marathon turns out very well, planning and booking the trip was one of the worst nightmares I ever experienced in all my travels! I located a tour agency in Paris that was organizing a tour and marathon in the Sahara desert. I contacted them and quickly negotiated a package to join a French tour/running group in Tunisia. And then the nightmare began! The tour operator insisted on payment before making any arrangements (reasonable), but demanded payment in cash! Attempts to wire the funds and send a bank draft both failed, and the agency's (arrogant and uncaring) attitude was "Not my problem. No money, no trip!" I desperately searched for an alternative rather than risk losing more money trying to send money to the uncaring and unprofessional agency, and fortunately, I found another tour agency in Paris offering a similar marathon package in the Sahara at the same time. I contacted that agency, and they worked hard to develop a tour package around the flights I had already booked to Tunisia and accepted payment by credit card. The staff of Hypervacances were professional and a pleasure to work with.

Now I had to train for a marathon in the desert. Fortunately, I had run a previous marathon in the Sahara (Algeria) and knew what to expect. Thus, when I returned from a marathon in Nicaragua in early October, I trained for two weeks on the beaches on Longboat Key to get my legs and ankles accustomed to running in the soft, uneven sand. I also confirmed quickly that my trail shoes offered the best support for running on sand. I was ready!

My modified tour package has me arriving in Tozeur in Southern Tunisia one day before the main group arrives from France. Philippe, the tour operator, picks me up at the airport. He speaks very limited English, so we communicate in French! He informs me that one of his staff speaks good English and will arrive on Monday evening with the main group. Since Monday is a free day for me, I wake early and enjoy an easy ten-mile running tour of Tozeur and the palmeraie. Tozeur, like all towns in southern Tunisia, is located on an oasis, and has the second-largest palmeraie in the country with 250,000 date palms. The dates are being harvested. By the end of the run, I'm familiar with the layout of the town and the main roads through the palmeraie, and later that day I explore more of the town on foot.

By the time the main group arrives, I am ready to move out of our three-star hotel; the TV and A/C didn't work. When I complain, the manager explains that the wind has damaged the satellite system (and he isn't optimistic or concerned that it would be fixed soon), and they've turned the A/C off for the winter. The TV I'm willing to live without, because it means I'll get no political/election BS from the United States for one week, but the A/C is a bigger issue. It's still hot during the day, and the rooms have no windows to open to let cool air in at night! I'm hoping that the main group will also be upset, but neither of these problems get fixed during our week-long stay.

When the main group arrives Monday evening, I am relieved to meet Jean Marie, who does speak good English, so I can learn more details about the itinerary. On Tuesday we'll visit the desert in 4x4s, and he asks me to join him in his 4x4. For the first few days I stick close to Jean M, because few members of the tour group seem to speak English. My French is okay for basic conversation, but not good enough to understand lots of details. On Tuesday morning our 4x4 caravan heads out into the Chott (salt lake) el-Gharsa. There are two large salt lakes—Chott el-Gharsa and Chott el-Jerid near Tozeur covering five thousand square kilometers. The caravan stops so that we can ride quads (ATVs) on the salt beds. The next stop is Ong Jemal (Neck of the Camel)—a rock formation that looks like a camel and overlooks

Chott el-Gharsa and lots of sand dunes. Close to Ong Jemal is Mos Espa—a very well-preserved *Star Wars* film set. Then we head into some massive sand dunes to surf the dunes in our 4x4s. That's a lot of fun, but some of the 4x4s are driven by race staff who are not experienced in the desert, and we spend a lot of time digging and pulling 4x4s out of sand dunes! There is a technique to surfing sand dunes that I learned from Bedouin drivers in the UAE a few years ago, and the French drivers do not know it!

After enjoying lunch at a Bedouin camp, we participate in camel races. That's lots of fun and serves as a good way for the group to meet and bond. A few people even start talking to the ugly American in French and English! Jean M informs me that some of the dunes we've been surfing are on the marathon course, and on the way back to the hotel we drive the final ten kilometers of the marathon course into Nefta—another oasis town. During happy hour I meet a few couples/families from the French Riviera (Nice and Cannes) who invite me to join them for dinner. We become good friends during the week, and invite each other to visit our homes.

On Wednesday we load into the 4x4s again for another trip into the desert—only this time, Philippe changes all the groups to force people to meet others in the group. We drive along a causeway that separates the Chott el-Jerid and provides a spectacular view of the Chott and salt piles, which look like snowfields. We stop at the small oasis village of Bechri, where winds have sculpted the sand into rugged and magnificent natural shapes and sculptures. Then we continue south through Kebili into the Southern Sahara to Es-Saiba where we encounter a sirocco—a sandstorm! The Bedouin call it *la neige de sable*—"the snow of sand." I suck in enough sand to coat my lungs with a permanent sand filter and will not have to worry about digestion for a while! I pray that the weather will be better on race day.

We quickly leave Saiba to drive to Douz—the gateway to the Southern Sahara and the Grand Erg Oriental—the largest sand sea in the Sahara. Douz has the largest palmeraie in the country with half a million palm trees. We eat lunch in Douz, but the sirocco is also blowing there, and we ingest lots of sand along with our food. After returning to the hotel, it takes me thirty minutes to wash sand out of every orifice of my body.

Thursday is a free day for the group, so I decide to make an easy seven-mile training run through the palmeraie before spending the rest of the day walking around Tozeur to take photos. Tozeur is famous for its amazing traditional brickwork that is unique to that area of Tunisia. I spend a few hours touring and taking photos in Ouled-el-Hadef (the old quarter) where the brickwork and doors are spectacular.

Since most meals are included in the tour package, I figure lunch on my free day is the best opportunity to enjoy a camel steak. It was delicious—better than any buffet meal I ate at the hotel! After lunch, I finish my tour with a visit to the Belvedere Rocks—an outcrop of rocks with the head of Aboulkacem Chebbi (a famous Tunisian poet) carved into one end. Steps carved into the rocks provide a spectacular view of sunsets over the palmeraie and the Tozeur golf course.

On Thursday evening the rest of the tour group arrives—mainly hardcore runners who have signed up just for the races! I'm eager to find out how many more runners have arrived and how many are running the marathon. Most of the guests in the initial tour group are not runners and joined the tour to play in the desert. I have not met one person running the marathon. When I pick up my race bib (#95!) Jean M informs me that there are 115 runners—twelve in the marathon, thirty in the Half, and more than seventy in the 10K.

Friday is another group activity—a hike into the Jebel en-Nebeg Mountain Range near the Algerian border. It sounded interesting, so I decide to participate, even though it's the day before the race.

We arrive in Chebika at the foot of the mountains at ten o'clock, and it's cold and raining. We start off in a canyon below the ruins of old Chebika and past a spring-fed stream and brilliant blue pools. Then we start to climb into the mountains. After crossing two ranges, I start to wonder if I've made a wise decision The views are awesome, but it is not an easy hike—and much longer than I expected.

Finally (three hours later) we see our destination in a canyon in the distance—Tamerza—and start our descent into a magnificent canyon. It reminds me a lot of the SIQ in Petra, Jordan. At the end of the canyon, we emerge into the oasis at Tamerza with the green palmeraie and a waterfall—a very contrasting and spectacular view! We enjoy lunch in Tamerza while being entertained by some locals jamming with drums and flutes. A fun time—only hope it hasn't messed up my legs too badly.

There is a prerace meeting on Friday evening (in French), followed by a pasta dinner. I get together with Jean M, who laid out the marathon course, to clarify some specific details that I need to prepare for the race. I am ready!

Saturday is race day!

The races are scheduled to start at 8:00 a.m., so we're bused out into the desert near Nefta to a location close to a highway where the final ten kilometers, which we had driven a few days before, begins. The weather was nice—sunny and in the high fifties at around eight—and no siroccos! I expect the marathon to start at eight, but instead, they run a few fun races for the kids. I am concerned about the delay and missing the cool morning temps, but it's fun to watch the kids participate with their parents and all the runners cheering them on. The marathon/half/10K finally starts at 8:45 a.m.

Although there are water stations every 2.5 kilometers, I wear a water belt for safety (I want a supply of water with me at all times) and to carry a new compact camera with the intention of taking photos along the course (if the race isn't competitive).

There are two loops/courses—a 10K loop and a half-marathon loop. We all run the same course to the 4.5-kilometer mark, where the 10K runners turn left for the shorter loop. I let the 10K runners surge ahead and lead the way. Jean M warned me that the course is difficult and not to expect to finish under five hours! From what I've seen of the course, I agree and figure five hours is a reasonable goal.

The course was laid out with quads that left a track, which is also marked with blue plastic bags. At first everyone runs in the tracks made by the quads, thinking that they've compacted the sand and made an easier path I soon learn that it's easier to run off the tracks on the virgin desert. The desert has a thin crust on the surface. The quads broke through the crust, and the tracks are soft and deep! However, on the hard crust, the footing is much better and faster!

As we reach the turnoff point at 4.5 kilometers for the 10K runners, I think I might be lonely until four runners pass me and continue on the half-marathon course. There are two females and two male runners, and one male looks like he's in my age group. They're running just a wee bit faster than me, so I decide to drop in behind and follow them. A pattern quickly emerges. I catch up to them at each water station, where everyone stops to drink water and leave the cup at the station (environmental rules). It takes them about thirty seconds to drink their water, take off again, and build up another short lead on me. I also stop at each water station, even though I'm carrying a full bottle of water—don't know why.

When we reach a water stop at 9.5 kilometers (52:15), we turn into the desert toward the Chott el-Gharsa. The next five kilometers of the course cross a series of small sand dunes they call "dunettes." That's tough running! The dunettes are only one to three meters high, but they're continuous—like running a washboard! It was difficult to maintain any kind of rhythm, and I soon find myself falling farther behind the group of four. After a few kilometers, they've increased their lead to about 250 meters, and although I can see ten kilometers across the desert, I have difficulty finding them in the dunettes.

I need to close the lead and push the pace! I pass both females in the next two kilometers, and the young male runner as we approach a water station at 14.5 kilometers (1:26:16). Only the old fart remains ahead of me, and when he sees me closing the lead, he pushes his pace and increases his lead again. At that point the course leaves the dunettes and runs across the Chott el-Gharsa. On this section of the course, it's easier and faster to stay in the quad tracks since they have compacted the soft lake surface. We reach the next water stop at 17 kilometers (1:36:47), where the course leaves the Chott and starts into a series of huge BASDs (badass sand dunes)! They're the same ones we surfed a few days before and range from ten to twenty meters in height! I'm not sure how to run those BASDs, so I try to run in the quad tracks like the old fart ahead of me. Disaster! I quickly sink up to my knees in sand! I move out of the tracks and looked for an unused (virgin) route up the BASDs. I learn that if I stay on the crust, step softly, and move my feet quickly, they barely sink into the sand, and I can climb those BASDs quickly and easily! Descending is trickier, because gravity and momentum cause the foot plant to be heavier, and it's necessary to turn my feet over faster to prevent them from sinking into the sand once I break through the crust. Using this desert strategy, I catch up to the old fart at the top of the final BASD. He takes off like a scared rabbit.

He has a slight advantage—he knew I was running the marathon, but I wasn't sure if he was. I don't want to waste energy trying to pass a half-marathon runner, so I decide to follow him to the (Half) finish line (21-kilometer point). If he's running the marathon, I'll need a better strategy than just chasing him. I decide that in the second half I'll start using my water bottle and skip the water stations, which will save me several minutes. I follow the old fart into the water station at the half-finish line in 2:03:03! Damn—that's a lot faster than I thought possible for this course! And I finally get a look at his bib (#2). He is running the marathon! I skip the water station and continue through the finish line to begin the ten-kilometer loop. I'm not surprised when he charges by me around 22 kilometers. This SOB is not going to give up! I decide to run a smooth, easy pace, drink water from my bottle every fifteen minutes, and follow this worthy competitor through the first section of the ten-kilometer loop. It's easier to follow him than trying to follow the quad tracks and spot the blue course markers. Once we return to the chott and the BASDs, I can take the lead.

When he reaches the first water station on the 10-kilometer loop, he makes his first mistake—he skips the water stop. Hydration will be important by the end of the race! When we reach the next water station at 25.5 kilometers (2:31:40), he's forced to stop for water. I pass him. This is the point where the ten-kilometer loop turns into the desert and start into the dunettes for the second time. I am happy when he comes charging by me again to take the lead through the dunettes, because it's easier to follow him than to follow the course.

When we leave the dunettes and start across the chott for the second time, he makes his second mistake. He runs a tangent or shortcut across the chott! Initially I follow him but quickly realize the surface is too soft and requires a lot of energy and effort to run, so I move back to the quad tracks. I run farther but expend less energy. When we leave the chott and start up the BASDS for the final time, he has increased his lead to 250 meters, but I use my proven desert strategy and look for virgin routes up and down the BASDs. I catch him again at the top of the final BASD. I expect him to take off again, but this time he runs with me for the next kilometer back to the start point.

I'm going to ask him what age group he's in so we can determine if it is necessary to kill each other over the final 10 kilometers, but then I think, "No, I don't want to know. He has pushed me through this course faster than

I thought possible, and he is hurting me, but he isn't killing me! If I find out we are in different age groups, I will probably slow down!" It's better if I believe he's in my age group, and I have to beat his ass! We reach the water stop at 32 kilometers in 3:11:11. We both stop for water, but he gains a logistical advantage when there are no bottles of water readily available to refill my water bottle. By the time I refill my bottle and look up, he has established a lead of 250 meters! He has thrown the gauntlet down! It is clear that he is not going to give up, and it's going to be an ugly and painful pissing match for the final ten kilometers.

I'm not concerned for two reasons. We drove the final ten kilometers a few days before, and I know it's a 4x4 track used by all the tour groups to drive back into Nefta. It is firm and compact, and that section of the course will be more like a road race—my preference and strength! The final ten kilometers will come down to guts and willingness to accept pain! I have all the confidence in the world in Maddog's willpower and ability to accept pain.

Let the pissing match begin!

I lower the hammer and begin the chase. My heart monitor starts beeping wildly to warn me that it had exceeded 90 percent max. I ignore it and continue to push the pace. But each time I close the lead to 100 meters, that SOB responds and pushes harder! He has earned my respect, but Maddog is pissed and even more motivated to bury his ass! We dig deeper and push harder, ignoring the frantic beeps of my heart monitor (now at 95 percent max), and we're rewarded when we notice that the old fart starts to fade around 34 kilometers. At 34.5 kilometers, he makes his final—and fatal—mistake! He skips the water station! It is now noon, and the sun is getting hot. Hydration will be critical over the final seven kilometers. Sure enough, he soon fades, the lead closes, and I pass him around 36kilometers. I'm sure that he'll try to stay with me, so I accelerate when I blow by him to discourage that. I never let up or look back, for fear he will consider it a weakness.

When I passed the water station at 36.6 kilometers (3:42:34), I'm hoping that he'll be wise and desperate enough to stop for water. I continue to push the pace and don't look back until Jean M comes by in a quad. I stop to refill my water bottle and steal a glance back. I have a lead of 250 meters, but the old fart is still coming after me. Jean M informs me that I have about three kilometers to the finish line, and I'm in fifth place. I now have a full water bottle and a good lead for the final push. When I reach the palmeraie and make a left turn at 40 kilometers, I steal another glance over my shoulder—my lead has increased to five hundred meters. I know I have him! I look at my watch—just over four hours. Damn—if I hold a fast pace, can I finish under 4:15?

The final two kilometers through the palmeraie are on a firm service road shaded by palm trees, so I allow myself to slow just a wee bit to ease the pain level and quiet my heart monitor! When I reach the end of the palmeraie and start up a short steep hill into Nefta, I see a course marker indicating a sharp left turn, and it reads, "*Arrivee a 100 m.*" I glance at my watch—4:12. I decide to sprint up the hill and the final hundred meters. All is going well until I reach the top of the hill and change my momentum to make the hard turn. My right hamstring cramps and locks up! I try to ignore it and limp across the finish line, but the cramp/pain is so severe I'm forced to stop fifty meters before the finish line to stretch and massage the leg for one minute to ease the pain enough to limp/drag the leg across the finish line at the Hotel Caravanserail in 4:13:27!

Needless to say, I am happy—ecstatic—with my race, one of my best and most satisfying race performances in a long time! I am fifth overall, and my time of 4:13 qualifies for Boston. In fact, I'm the only runner in the marathon (including the Tunisian, who won in 3:37) who finishes that tough desert course with a BQ time!

I limp around the finish area to wait for my friend/competitor to finish in 4:18. I finally ask him his age. Shit—only fifty-two! But I don't care. I thank him for pushing me to a fast finish. I am not sure he shares my appreciation. We wait for the winning female to finish in 4:37 before we enjoy a long hot shower and a nice BBQ lunch at the hotel—accompanied by a few cold Tunisian beers, of course! After lunch, all runners are bused back to our hotel in Tozeur to rest and prepare for the awards ceremony and postrace party on Saturday evening.

The evening starts with an awards ceremony that's well organized and begins with awards presented to the kids for the fun run. Since I did not finish in the top three, I have to be satisfied with an award for winning the Master's Division. It's a lovely ceramic plate, handmade by a local artisan. I like those kinds of awards. Following the ceremony we enjoy a great postrace dinner and party with champagne, beer, wine, and dancing. It's my farewell dinner with my new friends.

On Sunday morning, we're bused back out to the Jebel en-Nebeg Range near Degache for a short hike into a canyon. The tour staff has driven 4x4s into the canyon and set up a stereo and PA system so we can listen to classical music in the canyon (with amazing acoustics) while sipping champagne for a final toast to friends and a great week! I have to pack and leave for the airport after the hike since I'm flying back to Tunis. I've decided that since I've come all the way to Tunisia I might as well visit Tunis for a few days.

The main tour group leaves Monday, so I figure I'll be alone on the flight to Tunis, but the winner of the marathon, a doctor from Tunis, is also on my flight, so we enjoy a long discussion about the race and marathons.

I arrive at my hotel in Ville Nouvelle in time for a late dinner. I eat nothing but seafood for the three days I'm in Tunis—a whole grilled fish with a bottle of wine costs less than twenty dollars—and I'm sick of buffet food! Tunis is the capital of Tunisia, with a population of two million. What a difference from Tozeur. The traffic and streets are so busy there is no way I can run. I decide my legs deserve a few days to rest!

Tunis dates back to the eighth century BC when the Phoenicians founded the city of Carthage on Byrsa Hill. At the end of the third Punic War in 146 BC, the Romans destroyed Carthage, and on top of the ruins they built the third-largest Roman city outside of Italy. In the fourth and fifth centuries, Carthage was ruled by the Vandals (Vikings) and the Byzantines, before being captured by the Arabs in AD 695. The Arabs destroyed the Roman city and used the building materials to build a new city in Tunis in an area called the Medina. In the nineteenth century, the colonizing French built Ville Nouvelle (new town). Medina is now a listed UNESCO World Heritage Site.

On Monday, I walk through the Port de France into the Medina, and following the advice of my guide book, I wander aimlessly among the souks (markets) and back alleys of the old city. I visit the Zaytouna (Great) Mosque, the Place de la Kasbah, and other tourist sites during my walking tour. I'm not worried about getting lost, because I could always ask for directions to the Mosque or the Port de France! After many hours of wandering and getting lost, I finally have enough harassment by the souvenir hawkers and scam artists and decide to retreat back to Ville Nouvelle to visit the few tourist sites in that section of the city. Avenue Habib Bourguiba—the main boulevard—is lined with shops, bars, and cafés. Most of the bars and cafés have outdoor patios. It seems strange to watch the locals sipping coffee and water at the outdoor patios. A strange Islamic law forbids alcohol outside. It is permissible to drink a beer inside the café, but everyone smokes, and the bars are not pleasant to sit in.

I'm supposed to meet up with a German friend (travel agent) who is escorting some clients to the Sahara Desert, but somehow we've mixed up our dates and never do connect. However, he has kindly arranged for a private, English-speaking guide to take me around the sites outside of Tunis for one day. After a hard and exciting day of tours, I return to the bars and cafés of Avenue Habib Bourguiba to relax and enjoy a few cold Tunisian beers and a delicious seafood dinner. It is time to go home.

Marathon #314—Country #99,

Tiberias Marathon, Israel

January 2009

This marathon and country were included in a list I prepared at the beginning of 2008 because I wanted to find English-speaking countries for #99 and #100! At the time, all was peaceful in Israel.

Imagine my surprise when war broke out a few weeks before the race. I contacted the tour company to ask if the war in Gaza would affect the marathon and tour plans. They said no and would make any changes necessary for safety. The sports manager and I decided to go, because the marathon and tour were not near Gaza, and there was no way to substitute another race/country before #100, which was planned for February. Many of our family and friends expressed concern and advised us not to go, but I responded, "Maddog was faster than a speeding bullet." Thus, we departed for the long flight to Tel Aviv.

We arrive in the late afternoon on Tuesday, and quickly receive the second surprise. Very few people in Israel speak English, and all signs/information are in Hebrew. I had made a false assumption that their close ties with the United States would mean that most would speak English. Wrong.

We have to find our own way to Tiberias. The guide book stated that it's necessary to take a bus from the airport to the Central Bus Terminal in Tel Aviv to catch an express bus to Tiberias. What it doesn't tell us us, however, is that the buses were local—even the express bus! It's an interesting trip. It's the end of the workday, and soldiers are getting on or off the buses at various locations, carrying their rifles and submachine guns! By law, they must carry their guns at all times. It seems strange, but we feel very safe on the bus. Other than that, we don't see any signs of the war in Gaza—except for a bus driver who listens to the news on the radio, complete with the sounds of shooting.

Shortly after we arrive at the hotel in Tiberias, we meet up with two friends, fellow members of the 100 Marathon Club UK. Roger and Peter had also planned this trip/marathon a long time ago to join me for #99 and were not about to change their plans for a "little problem" in Gaza. We agree to meet for breakfast and tour the city in the morning. Tiberias is located on the western shore of the Sea of Galilee. It is one of the four holy cities of Judaism and also a tacky holiday resort. There are not a lot of tourist sites to visit, but we stroll past the Greek Monastery and Leaning Tower, El Bachri Mosque, and the Southern Wall. We stroll along the Alon Promenade to the sea level measurement—a visual display of the current sea level of the Sea of Galilee (213 meters below sea level). We then head to race registration to pick up my race packet.

I am concerned because the website for the race is poorly organized/managed, and the race staff did not respond to e-mails. All of us were forced to ask the tour agency to register us for the race because of problems with the website. I e-mailed several times to request bib #99 with the obvious explanation but received no response. I even had the tour agency call the race committee with my request. Thus, I'm not surprised when I learn that my race number is *not* #99! I ask to speak to the race director, and his excuse is that I had asked for two race numbers (99 and 100), and they could only give me #100. I am pissed, but it's too late to fix the problem. Later that day when we go to the pasta dinner, they won't let us in. Roger had specifically asked what coupon or ticket in our packet was required for the pasta dinner, but when we present that coupon they inform us that we need a different one. By that time, I'm so frustrated and annoyed with the incompetence and uncaring attitude of the race organization that I don't even care if I run the race. I just want to run the race to count #99 and get out of there! Fortunately, our hotel package for the race includes meals, so we return to the hotel for a much better meal than we probably would have gotten at the race dinner.

Thursday is marathon day. The race starts at 9:00 a.m. There are seven hundred runners in the marathon. The weather is sunny with temps in the high forties. I had a special T-shirt printed for the race that read "Country #99" on the front and "John's 99th Country" on the back. That T-shirt elicits some comments and conversations with a few runners before and during the race, but very few runners speak English. Roger and I have always been closely matched and competitive, and although neither of us would admit it, as usual each of us intends to beat the other. I decide to go out at a 5:20/kilometer (8:30/mile) pace, since we both feel that a 3:45 finish will be the best either can do (in our current shape), and that time will hopefully be competitive in the race.

The race starts in the center of town and comprises a 21-kilometer loop south and then north to Ein Gev on the east side of the Sea of Galilee before returning to Tiberias. Fortunately, the race and course are better organized/managed than the prerace events. There are distance markers every kilometer that help me to monitor and manage my pace and water stations every three kilometers. The two-lane highway is closed to traffic, and there is excellent police control at intersections. I pass the five-kilometer mark in 26:15, slow a wee bit up a long steep hill at eight kilometers, and reach ten kilometers in 52:50. I have left Roger behind, but I know he's chasing me.

I reach 16 kilometers in 1:24:45 as the lead pack of Kenyans blows by me on the return loop. The winner finished in 2:08, so it's a fast race! I pass the turnaround at the Half in 1:51:47—almost right on pace. I don't think I'll be able to run the second half that fast, but I still feel good and figure I'll try to hold that pace as long as possible. I meet Roger two minutes later, which means I have a four-minute lead, but I know that he'll come after me in the second Half. I couldn't slow down. I pass the 25-kilometer point in 2:12:28 and later learn it was around that time when Muslim extremists in Lebanon fired five rockets into Israel about ten kilometers north of the marathon course. I am so focused that I don't hear a thing, but Roger later said that he and the pack he was running with heard explosions, and a few of the local runners commented, "That is not good."

I reach 32 kilometers in 2:49:32—I have fifty-five minutes to run the last ten kilometers. I think about trying to push the pace harder but wisely decide to wait till 35 kilometers before making any change to my pace. Good thing, because when I pass 34 kilometers in 3:00:41, my split has slowed to 5:36, and I'm starting to tire! It's time to summon Maddog. He can accept the level of pain necessary to push the pace back below 5:20. We start playing the old mind game: "Just run the next kilometer in 5:20, and we will reevaluate." It is much easier to lie and fool yourself to accept pain for one more kilometer than admit that you have to do it for eight. At the end of each kilometer, you just continue the lie for the next one. I pass the 40-kilometer mark in 3:32:58 and a split of 5:26. But I am hurting, and the pain level is high. Only when I pass 41 kilometers in 3:38:18 am I confident that a sub-3:45 finish is in the bag, because I am confident that Maddog can push the pace for the final kilometer on willpower alone. I cross the finish line in 3:44:39.

As I walk around the finish area trying to recover, Roger finishes in 3:48. He has tried to catch me, as I expected, but he just couldn't make up the four-minute lead I had at the Half. We figure Peter will finish in close to six hours, so we decide to go back to the hotel for a shower and return to cheer him across the line. Ninety minutes later, Maddog, Roger, and the sports manager wait at the finish line as Peter finishes in 5:44. We find race results posted at the host hotel to confirm that I have finished in fourth place and Roger in sixth place in our age group. We are both pleased with our times and performances and acknowledge that both of us ran faster than expected because of our friendly competition. However, we are a little disappointed/surprised that 3:45 wasn't competitive. Third place finished one minute ahead of me—Damn!—I could have pushed the old bod for one more minute had I known.

Later, the four of us enjoy some celebration beers at a local restaurant before a farewell dinner. We plan to start a seven-day tour the next day, and Roger and Peter are returning to Tel Aviv to tour and visit relatives.

Although I'm not happy about the race committee's failure to provide bib # 99 for this special race, I am happy to have finished marathon #314 and country #99! That ties the world record held for a long, long time by my good friend and mentor, Wally Herman, who is eighty-three and still running. I still consider Wally to be the world champion until somebody passes him. The sports manager and I will meet Wally and his lovely wife, Marie, for pasta dinner next weekend in Miami before Wally and I run the Miami Marathon. That will be my final tune-up before I run country #100, Tahiti, in February.

We are ready to begin a one-week tour of Israel. I've always wanted to visit Israel with its many historical and biblical sites.

But first, before I begin the stories (or "fairy tales") of our tour, I must state this disclaimer: my stories are my recollection of the stories/tales related to us by our tour guides, which are supposedly based on historical facts and the Bible. I accept no responsibility for the accuracy or truth of these tales. Let us begin.

Our guide, Ezra, picks us up at 8:00 a.m., and we join three English-speaking couples (Wales, New Zealand, and Australia) for a short drive along the Sea of Galilee to Capernaum. According to Christian belief, the village of Capernaum was the home base of Jesus during the most influential period of his Galilean ministry. He preached at the synagogue and healed the sick, including Peter's stepmother. He stayed in Peter's house. Then we continue along the Sea of Galilee to the Mount of Beatitudes, where Jesus preached to his disciples in his Sermon on the Mount. We continue into Northern Israel to the ancient city of Safed, founded in the second century BC. The labyrinth of cobbled streets is lined with medieval synagogues and an artist colony.

From Safed we drive through the Hula Valley and across the Jordan River into the Golan Heights. As we climb the Golan Heights, Ezra points out the minefields on both sides of the road. Instead of spending time and money to clear the mines, the Israeli government allows the farmers to graze their cattle in the mine fields. If a cow steps on a mine, there is instant, cheap hamburger available. We then drive west back through the Hula Valley to the Banias Nature Reserve, which is one of the sources of the Jordan River. Ezra points out that the six-day war with Syria was all about controlling the water from the Jordan River, and Israel will never give up that control. We hoped to visit a waterfall but the guards were locking up the gate at three o'clock to make an early escape for Shabbat (sunset Friday to sunset Saturday). So we drive on to Kfar Giladi near the Lebanon border, where we stay for one night at a kibbutz. Ezra warns us not to leave the compound, since we're so close to Lebanon. He warns us not to climb the mountain behind the kibbutz, because Lebanon is on the other side. We obey and go to the bar in the kibbutz. I want to do a training run on Saturday morning but decide my legs need an extra day's rest (read chicken or smart, but I'm not running that close to the border with the risk of rockets flying).

After breakfast, we drive south and west along the Lebanon border to the Mediterranean Sea. This region contains a lot of orchards and vegetable farms. We stop in the ancient city of Akko—more than five thousand years old. It has a natural port that was captured and used by the Crusaders in the eleventh century, and it has changed hands many times. There are ruins dating back before the Crusaders, and fortifications built by the Crusaders are still intact and original. We visit Crusader City and Knight's Hall, and then stroll through the Arab market to the port, passing the El Jazzar Mosque and the Khan El Omdan. I suggest that you allocate at least two days to visit the city. Our visit lasts only three hours before we continue south to Haifa. Since it's Shabbat, not much is open, and we enjoy a falafel—pita bread stuffed with spicy meat and vegetables—at a local fast-food stand. It's strange, but no matter where we eat lunch—at a fast-food stand, restaurant, or cafeteria—it always seems to cost 100 NIS (shekels) (twenty-five dollars) and dinner costs 200 to 300 NIS. Nothing is cheap in Israel, and most of the food/meals suck—very little variety or flavor.

On Sunday I enjoy a pleasant twelve-mile run along the Sea in Tel Aviv and discover a network of trails that allowed runners/bikers to go more than a hundred kilometers without having to worry about traffic. As I run, I shout my normal "good morning" to all I meet. They look at me like I'm crazy. Israelis are not very friendly! There are not a lot of tourist sites in Tel Aviv, so we do a self-guided walking tour.

On Monday morning we join twelve new tourists and the tour guide, Avi, for the start of the next tour. We experience the first minor change in the itinerary caused by the problems in Gaza. The tour was supposed to drive south along the Sea to Ashkelon and then head west to the Dead Sea. However Ashkelon is close to Gaza, and the tour agency considers the city and highway unsafe. Good thing, because Hamas fires fifteen rockets into Ashkelon. There are no objections.

At Beit Ha'arava we turn south along the Dead Sea. We make a brief stop for an obligatory factory tour—only this is one of the few times it is welcomed. The Ahava factory manufactures (expensive) cosmetics from minerals in the Dead Sea that are therapeutic for the skin. Nicole uses the product, and surprisingly, the factory prices are 50 percent less than US prices. I tell her to load up, because it's probably the only bargain we'll find in Israel. We continue on to Masada.

Masada is a historic site that I have wanted to visit since seeing the movie twenty years ago (Peter O'Toole). Masada is a desert mesa that rises high and alone above the Dead Sea. It was fortified in 103 BC, and Herod built a palace and more fortifications as a potential refuge against a Jewish revolt. In AD 66 a small band of Jews revolted and captured Masada. The Romans sent eight thousand soldiers and set up eight camps at the base of Masada. Over a period of three years, the Romans built an earthen ramp up to the fortress walls, and prepared to breach the fortress. Rather than allow their families to be captured and put into slavery, the men burned their homes and chose ten men by lots who killed everyone, and then nine of the ten were killed by the final zealot who killed himself. It has become Israel's symbol for a "they'll never take us alive" attitude and the term "Masada complex" is a part of modern-day Israeli parlance. We ride the cable car to the top instead of walking up the snake path. Avi shows us around the fortress, including Herod's palace, the synagogue, cisterns, and a two-thousand-year-old bathroom! It's very interesting, and the views of the Dead Sea from Masada are awesome.

After leaving Masada, we continue to Ein Gedi Beach for a "float" on the Dead Sea (the lowest point on earth at 420 meters below sea level). We decline, since I've already enjoyed that experience after running the Dead Sea Marathon in Jordan last year. Nicole and I sit and enjoy a beer while some of our companions float and roll in the Dead Sea mud. Then we drive back across the Judean desert and mountains to Jerusalem. As the bus climbs up into Jerusalem, traffic is slowed by a security checkpoint. The twenty-foot wall was not completed at that point. It's a chain-link fence with barbed wire, and on the other side, a group of Palestinian youths are throwing rocks at the cars. They never bother with our bus, but it's the one time during the trip that I feel nervous.

Our hotel is in West Jerusalem near the central bus terminal. Although there is a shopping mall next door, it is not a good location. There's only one restaurant in the area other than the hotel, which only has the usual bland (expensive) buffet dinner. We are quickly introduced to security measures in Jerusalem. It is necessary to pass through a security check to get into any major building—hotel, shopping mall, supermarket, restaurant, bus terminal, museums, public buildings, and most tourist sites! The check can be as simple as a security guard with a wand to check your bags, or the same security used at airports. What a pain in the ass. I don't know how the locals can stand it, but as inconvenient and annoying as it is, it makes us feel safer.

I planned to run the next morning, but at six o'clock it is too friggin' cold (midthirties), too dark, and too hilly! But the real reason I don't run is because I'm concerned about running into a wrong neighborhood and finding myself in trouble. I easily convince myself that my legs would appreciate a sabbatical or rest until I return home. In two days I only see two people jogging in Jerusalem.

The first day of touring in Jerusalem is the least hectic. We start with a visit to the Israel Museum, which included the Shrine of the Book where the Dead Sea Scrolls are kept. There is a huge scale model of Jerusalem as it was in AD 66, which Avi uses to describe the layout of the city and what we will see the next day. Close to the museum is the Knesset—the home of the Israeli Parliament. Next we visit the Hadassah Medical Center to view the twelve stained-glass windows created by Marc Chagall for the synagogue. Each window depicts one of the tribes of Israel. Then it's on to Yad Vashem, the Holocaust Museum. It contains many photos, videos, and artifacts from the Holocaust, but we had visited the death camps in Auschwitz, Poland, which were much more graphic and shocking. However, I notice that there are many people crying.

After lunch, we drive to the West Bank and Bethlehem. The first thing we see is the massive, ugly twenty-foot wall separating Jerusalem and Israel from the West Bank. You have probably seen them on TV.

We have to leave the bus, walk through an entrance in the wall, pass security, and join another bus and guide in Bethlehem since the city is in Palestinian territory and control. We drive through Bethlehem to the Church of Nativity. We entered through the Door of Humility (must have been short people) into a Greek Orthodox Church. We were quickly educated in the hierarchy of religious sites. Three or four religions or faiths share every religious site in the Holy Land. The Greek Orthodox Church enjoys the dominant position and location (usually right over a religious site) because the Turks gave it to them several centuries ago when they controlled the Holy Land. The Catholic Church usually holds the second-best location followed by the Armenian Orthodox and Lutheran churches. There is a lot of dispute about control, and Avi explains that only a few weeks ago, riots and fights broke out in Manger Square between the various factions. Anyone want to bet that it is all about the huge amounts of money spent by pilgrims? Anyway, back to the tour. We descend steps below the Greek Orthodox Church into caves to visit the Grotto of Nativity—the spot where Jesus was born. A few feet away is the Grotto of the Manger where his crib was kept. Well, blow my mind—my Sunday school teacher and Christian teachings always depicted the manger as a stable with animals. Saint Catherine's Church, built next to and attached to the Church of Nativity, is where the Christmas Eve broadcasts originate.

We return to the Wall and leave Bethlehem. That evening Avi offers to take us on an optional (read, more money) night tour of Jerusalem to see the Old City and tourist sites lit up. It is interesting, but friggin' cold! We had not packed for weather that cold and had to layer several T-shirts under a light spring jacket. Each time we stop, we get out, look, and run back to the bus to warm up. Other than seeing the main tourist/religious sites lit up, the best part of the tour is a walking tour on the pedestrian mall on Ben Yehuda Street in the city center. It contains many shops, bars, and restaurants—what we've been missing and looking for in the area where our hotel is located! We are definitely going back there for our last night in town!

Wednesday is the final day in Jerusalem, and the final and most hectic day of our tour. We start by entering through security at the Dung Gate, and visiting the Western or "Wailing" Wall. Then we pass through security to gain access to Haram Ash-Sharif or Temple Mount. This is one of the most religious—and disputed—sites in the world. The Jews consider the large slab of rock protruding from Mount Moriah as the foundation stone of the world. It was here that God gathered earth to form Adam, Abraham nearly sacrificed his own son, Isaac, and where Solomon built the First temple and placed the Ark of the Covenant. For Muslims this is the place where Mohammed ascended to heaven to join Allah and is Islam's third-holiest site! Temple Mount is located in the Muslim section of Jerusalem and is controlled by the Muslims. The Dome of the Rock that is the symbol of the city covers the slab of stone sacred to both the Muslim and Jewish faiths.

We exit Temple Mount through the Gate of the Cotton Merchants into the souqs of the Arab Quarter. Avi guides us through the souqs to Via Dolorosa (Way of Sorrows)—the route that Jesus is believed to have taken from where he was pronounced guilty to carry his cross to Calvary. There are fourteen stations along the route dedicated to holy events and places such as where he received the cross, where he fell for the first time, etc. The last five stations are inside the Church of the Holy Sepulchre built over the site where he was nailed to the cross, and the final station is the Tomb of Jesus.

Many of the sites had churches of one or more faiths built over them. By the end of the Via Dolorosa we are confused about what we've actually seen.

We leave the Old City and drive to Mount Zion to visit the Tomb of King David, the Room of the Last Supper and Dormition Abbey, on the site where the Virgin Mary died. By that time we're totally confused by the many, many religious sites or churches for almost any event. About the only site we do not see is one dedicated to where Jesus took a Holy crap. Sorry—give me a break—but that is the way I feel! But we still aren't finished. On to the Mount of Olives to visit the Church of All Nations and the Garden of Gethsemane where Jesus was arrested. The garden still contains olive trees over two thousand years old. The final stop is the Tomb of Virgin Mary. Once again I'm confused, because I swear we have already visited two other places where Mary was buried! I need a drink and time to sort out this confusion. The Mount of Olives also provides fantastic views of the Old city—especially the East Wall and the Golden Gate. The Muslims sealed the Golden Gate in the seventh century to prevent the Jewish Messiah from entering Haram! Kind of makes you wonder what they were smoking back in those days.

Avi returns us to our hotel to pack and get ready for the trip home. Since we have a very late flight, we take a taxi to Ben Yehuda Street to stroll along the pedestrian mall, purchase some last minute souvenirs/gifts, and enjoy a farewell dinner at El Gaucho, an Argentinean restaurant that serves Argentinean beef. It's the best meal we've eaten in Israel.

After touring both Jordan and Israel, traveling up and down both sides of the Dead Sea, and observing the desolate land of that region, I now understand why it is called the Promise(d) Land. I promise never to go back!

Marathon #316—Country #100, Moorea

Marathon, French Polynesia Islands

February 2009

I DID IT! I accomplished my goal of breaking the world record!

It seems like a long time ago (April 2008) when I announced that I was going after the world record of completing a marathon in ninety-nine countries. There were times when I thought Maddog was being too aggressive and obsessive in demanding that I accomplish this goal before I turned sixty-five (in March).

Now we have come back full circle to the "Fast Forward" chapter at the beginning of the book. But this is not the end of Maddog's adventures.

Postscript—Expanding the World Record Since #100

If I thought Maddog would be content with one hundred countries and a new world record, I was wrong!

New goals kept fueling his obsession. The new and primary goal was to once again complete a marathon in every country in Europe. I thought I had accomplished that goal in Bosnia in 2005. However, the Country Club decided to include the Isle of Man and the Channel Islands to the approved list of countries. Thus I had three more countries to run in Europe—plus Kosovo, which had declared independence in 2008. That new goal was finally achieved in Kosovo in 2014 to reestablish that world wecord!

Then there were other continents with uncompleted countries, and new world records to achieve. I have now completed marathons in every country in Europe, North America, South America, and Oceania. Asia and Africa will probably remain unfinished goals, because there are countries on those two continents that are unsafe to travel to.

I now hold eight world records for marathons, and I have completed 376 marathons in 125 countries (as of June 2015)—*and I'm still counting*!

I have not included any adventures after country #100 in this book. Nor have I included any of my 240+ domestic marathons (except marathons #1 and #200) in this book for the sake of brevity—and to save you from boredom.

However reports and photos of all 376 marathons and 125 countries are available online. As mentioned earlier, I started writing race or trip reports after each race in 1999, after moving to England. For the next six years, I would e-mail those reports to family and friends. In 2005, when I ran the Sophia Marathon in Bulgaria, a young sports journalist, Elenko, kindly assisted me in setting up a blog, www.maddogwallace.blogspot.com, so I could post the reports to the Internet. Later, I uploaded all my previous reports to my blog in chronological order.

Photos of my races experienced a similar process. I did not own a digital camera until 2004 when I created a photo website @ www.maddog.smugmug. com. I uploaded all my race photos after that date. But that left more than twenty years of race photos undocumented. In 2012, while I was recovering from a health issue and was bored, I decided to gather all my old paper photos and color slides, sort and edit them, and have them converted to digital by a professional firm. I got back several CDs of photos that had to be sorted, catalogued, and uploaded to the albums on my website. Then I spent several weeks compiling photos into two chronological photo journals: one for domestic and one for international marathons. These journals or albums provide a quick overview of my races. I also created photo albums for each country that help to understand the sights referenced in the race reports.

And for readers of my blog or photo website who want a quick and easy way to view Maddog's adventures, my son Chris created Maddog's Marathon Map @ https://www.zeemaps.com/map?group=768435. This map provides markers on a world map indicating the location of each of my marathons. When one points to a marker, or to a marathon in the chronological index on the side of the map, it brings up a photo and brief summary of each race and adventure.

These websites have been kept updated for all countries and marathons completed after country #100 in February 2009 and are the best sources to follow Maddog's adventures. It is unlikely there will be a sequel to this book!

The Country Club

While I was pursuing my first major goal of completing a marathon in every country in Europe, I started to recognize the same runners at many races around Europe. Most of us became friends and would arrange to meet at races in Europe and around the world. We often shared rooms and expenses and always shared new adventures. I started to form the idea of founding a club for crazy people like us.

During those early years, when we enjoyed an informal club relationship, we would have lively discussions about two important questions:

What defines a marathon?

What is a country?

What defines a marathon has been established by many running clubs around the world, but the definition is not consistent. The second question had not really been addressed, because most running clubs were not interested in countries. And I found that whenever my friends and I discussed the subject, the discussions were lively, then became heated, and often ended in arguments. I concluded the reason was because each person had an opinion based on a) emotion, b) politics, and c) religion. No wonder it was impossible to reach a consensus.

As the years and Maddog's accomplishments progressed, rather than continue to argue with other runners and clubs about these questions, I decided it was time to form a club, which I named—appropriately—the Country Club, for runners who share a passion for travel and running marathons in countries around the world. At first, rules and guidelines were established but not written down. Finally, in February 2014, we developed a website, www. countrymarathonclub.com where we published our rules and a formal list of countries approved by the club. How did we create this list? Let me explain how we define a "country."

Some running clubs and travel clubs use the UN list as their list of countries—period! The UN list is a "political list" of countries. The Country Club is a sports/running club, and thus figures that a political list such as the UN list is a good starting point to define a country, but sports must also be considered.

The Country Club looks at member lists of major international sports federations such as FIFA, IOC, IAAF, Commonwealth Games, etc., and these lists have more importance than the UN list in determining a country for the purpose of a sports club or sports event.

For example, England, Scotland, Wales, are not recognized as countries by the political UN. However they are members of FIFA and can win the World Cup—one of the biggest sporting events in the world.

Similarly Guam (a US territory) is not recognized as a country by the UN political list but is a member of the IOC and can win Olympic gold medals against most of the countries on the UN political list.

Puerto Rico and the USVI (US territories) are members of the IAAF and IOC and compete against the USA and many members of the UN political list in international sports events sponsored by the IAAF and IOC.

There are many territories of Great Britain/United Kingdom that have self-autonomy and compete against Great Britain in the Commonwealth Games. The Country Club recognizes these territories as countries.

And in a few cases, the Country Club and other running clubs have granted exceptions: e.g., Antarctica and Vatican City. Many runners run a marathon in Antarctica to complete the seven continents. Most clubs believe it is only fair to let runners count Antarctica as a country, even though it doesn't pass any of the above criteria. Vatican City does not meet most of the above criteria but is also accepted as a country by most clubs.

Thus, it is not a simple question and does not have a simple answer. Certainly there is no common answer that everyone or every club would agree to, but I believe the Country Club has selected criteria that make the most sense for a sports club and runners!

Similarly, the definition of a marathon varies among runners and clubs. The Country Club tries to comply with the majority of rules established by other running clubs, but some of those rules are impractical when applied to marathons in Third World countries. Some countries and clubs do not have the technical expertise and budget to comply with many of the newer rules (primarily about having websites or calendars on the Internet). Also, in many small countries the field of runners can be very small—often fewer than ten starters and fewer than five finishers. In such cases, the Country Club will review a marathon and grant an exemption if it is warranted. I believe the Country Club provides the best and fairest venue for runners trying to complete marathons in countries around the world.

Membership is free and available to anyone who qualifies (must have completed thirty countries). We have grown from our initial membership of fewer than ten to more than sixty members today.

Maddog's List of Countries and Marathons

Date	Marathon #	Marathon	Location	Country	Country #	Continent	Time
9/19/1982	1	Silver State	Reno	USA	1	NA	3:28:24
5/1/1988	21	Vancouver	Vancouver	Canada	2	NA	3:08:43
8/20/1988	27	Rio de Janeiro	Rio de Janeiro	Brazil	3	SA	3:05:49
4/22/1990	51	London	London	England	4	Europe	3:11:20
10/21/1990	52	The Original	Athens	Greece	5	Europe	3:38:40
2/17/1997	110	The Last	King George Island	Antarctica	6	Antarctica	3:59:58
2/22/1998	123	Old Mutual	Capetown	South Africa	7	Africa	3:52:21
3/8/1998	124	China Coast	Hong Kong	Hong Kong	8	Asia	3:46:39
8/30/1998	130	Noosa	Noosa Heads	Australia	9	Oceania	4:12:46
11/15/1998	132	Cozumel	Cozumel	Mexico	10	NA	4:19:26
5/13/1999	133	Prague	Prague	Czechoslovakia	11	Europe	3:43:31
6/12/1999	134	Stockholm	Stockholm	Sweden	12	Europe	3:37:55
6/27/1999	135	Tallinn	Tallinn	Estonia	13	Europe	3:39:15
7/4/1999	136	Paavo Nurmi	Turku	Finland	14	Europe	3:39:00
8/15/1999	137	Middelkerke	Middelkerke	Belgium	15	Europe	3:39:41
8/29/1999	138	Moscow	Moscow	Russia	16	Europe	3:37:45
9/4/1999	139	Oslo	Oslo	Norway	17	Europe	3:25:47
9/19/1999	140	Wachau	Wachau Valley	Austria	18	Europe	3:47:12

9/26/1999	141	Edinburgh	Edinburgh	Scotland	19	Europe	3:34:40
10/3/1999	142	Budapest	Budapest	Hungary	20	Europe	3:48:30
10/17/1999	143	Amsterdam	Amsterdam	Netherlands	21	Europe	3:37:33
10/25/1999	144	Dublin	Dublin	Ireland	22	Europe	3:37:32
10/31/1999	145	Snowdonia	Lanberis	Wales	23	Europe	3:43:21
11/21/1999	146	Monaco	Monte Carlo	Monaco	24	Europe	3:33:35
11/28/1999	147	Lisbon	Lisbon	Portugal	25	Europe	3:28:39
12/5/1999	148	Calvia	Mallorca	Spain	26	Europe	3:29:24
1/1/2000	149	Rome Millennium	St Peter's Square	Vatican City	27	Europe	4:17:00
1/14/2000	150	UAE	Dubai	UAE	28	Asia	3:58:24
1/17/2000	151	Malta	Sliema	Malta	29	Europe	3:54:24
2/11/2000	152	Egyptian	Luxor	Egypt	30	Africa	3:49:38
2/27/2000	153	Pafos	Pafos	Cyprus	31	Europe	3:48:37
3/4/2000	154	Gibraltar	Gibraltar	Gibraltar	32	Europe	3:59:10
3/7/2000	155	Casablanca	Casablanca	Morocco	33	Africa	3:59:15
3/18/2000	156	Steinfurt	Burgsteinfurt	Germany	34	Europe	3:41:12
3/26/2000	157	Turin	Turin	Italy	35	Europe	3:38:41
3/31/2000	158	San Marino	San Marino	San Marino	36	Europe	3:57:00
4/9/2000	159	Paris	Paris	France	37	Europe	3:45:12
4/30/2000	161	Wroclaw	Wroclaw	Poland	38	Europe	3:57:57
5/10/2000	162	Andorra	La Vella	Andorra	39	Europe	3:58:00
5/21/2000	163	Copenhagen	Copenhagen	Denmark	40	Europe	3:49:14
10/15/2000	165	Eurasia	Istanbul	Turkey	41	Europe	3:47:12
10/21/2000	166	Lausanne	Lausanne	Switzerland	42	Europe	3:39:07
11/26/2000	167	Panama	Panama city	Panama	43	NA	3:48:00
12/2/2000	168	Costa Rica	San Jose	Costa Rica	44	NA	3:45:00
2/26/2001	172	Sahara	Tindouf	Algeria	45	Africa	4:33:58
4/14/2001	174	Nagano	Nagano	Japan	46	Asia	3:32:40
6/9/2001	177	LGT Alpine	Vaduz	Liechtenstein	47	Europe	4:46:02
6/22/2001	178	Lake Myvatn	Lake Myvatn	Iceland	48	Europe	3:34:12
10/21/2001	184	Luxembourg	Echternach	Luxembourg	49	Europe	3:38:23
10/28/2001	185	Ljubljana	Ljubljana	Slovenia	50	Europe	3:40:35

12/8/2001	188	Reggae	Negril	Jamaica	51	NA	3:47:41
1/20/2002	191	Bermuda	Hamilton	Bermuda	52	NA	3:51:52
3/24/2002	194	Thailand Temple	Bangkok	Thailand	53	Asia	3:35:18
3/29/2002	195	Angkor Wat	Angkor Wat	Cambodia	54	Asia	3:54:50
4/7/2002	196	Bali Mar	Candi Dasa	Indonesia	55	Asia	4:08:00
10/5/2002	202	Bucharest	Bucharest	Romania	56	Europe	3:31:57
10/13/2002	203	Zagreb	Zagreb	Croatia	57	Europe	3:39:36
12/1/2002	205	Barbados	Georgetown	Barbados	58	NA	3:44:48
5/17/2003	209	Riga International	Riga	Latvia	59	Europe	3:43:52
8/31/2003	211	Panevezys	Panevezys	Lithuania	60	Europe	3:27:25
10/5/2003	212	73rd International Peace	Kosice	Slovakia	61	Europe	3:31:30
10/19/2003	213	Belgrade	Belgrade	Serbia	62	Europe	3:28:41
10/26/2003	214	Podgorica	Podgorica	Montenegro	63	Europe	3:20:48
12/7/2003	217	Cayman Islands	Georgetown	Cayman Islands	64	NA	3:33:43
1/13/2004	218	Mumbai	Mumbia	India	65	Asia	3:50:55
7/3/2004	226	Minsk	Minsk	Belarus	66	Europe	3:27:00
7/7/2004	227	Moldova	Chisinau	Moldova	67	Europe	3:50:55
7/18/2004	228	Rivne	Rivne	Ukraine	68	Europe	3:38:50
11/5/2004	235	Skopje	Skopje	Macedonia	69	Europe	3:49:11
11/7/2004	236	Lake Ohrid	Lake Ohrid	Albanaia	70	Europe	3:53:06
2/27/2005	238	CLICO	Port of Spain	Trinidad & Tobago	71	NA	4:29:37
5/2/2005	241	Belfast	Belfast	N Ireland	72	Europe	4:17:13
7/16/2005	246	Torshavn	Torshavn	Faroe Islands	73	Europe	3:38:52
10/8/2005	250	Sofia	Sofia	Bulgaria	74	Europe	3:52:18
10/15/2005	251	Jesenji	Bihac	Bosnia	75	Europe	3:51:59
11/21/2005	252	Everest	Mt Everest	Nepal	76	Asia	7:43:38
8/5/2006	268	Nuuk	Nuuk	Greenland	77	NA	3:34:06

10/8/2006	273	Underground BA	Buenos Aires	Argentina	78	SA	3:58:23
10/10/2006	274	Colonial	Colonial del Sacramento	Uruguay	79	SA	3:51:39
11/19'06	276	Marabana	Havana	Cuba	80	NA	4:02:27
3/18/2007	283	Seoul International	Seoul	Korea	81	Asia	3:46:28
4/1/2007	284	Santiago	Santiago	Chile	82	SA	3:50:19
5/20/2007	287	Fiji	Coral Coast	Fiji	83	Oceania	4:02:26
6/3/2007	288	Christchurch SBS	Christchurch	New Zealand	84	Oceania	3:40:25
10/7/2007	290	Guayaquil	Guayaquil	Ecuador	85	SA	4:47:28
11/25/2007	294	Shanghai International	Shanghai	China	86	Asia	4:34:18
12/2/2007	295	Macau International	Macau	Macau	87	Asia	4:11:19
1/1/2008	296	St Croix International	St Croix	USVI	88	NA	4:11:46
3/30/2008	301	Kuala Lumpur	Kuala Lumpur	Malaysia	89	Asia	4:14:02
4/11/2008	302	Dead Sea	Amman	Jordan	90	Asia	3:37:48
5/4/2008	303	42K en la Cuidad	Caracas	Venezuela	91	SA	3:57:21
8/5/2008	307	Inca Trail Marathon	Machu Picchu	Peru	92	SA	8:51:23
9/7/2008	308	Bhutan	Thimphu	Bhutan	93	Asia	4:13:23
10/5/2008	309	Q50 Finca Las Nubes	Matagalpa	Nicaragua	94	NA	4:52:34
11/1/2008	310	Defis Du Chott	Tozeur	Tunisia	95	Africa	4:13:27
11/22/2008	311	Srefidensi	Paramaribo	Suriname	96	SA	4:02:16
12/14/2008	312	La Guadalupe	Ponce	Puerto Rico	97	NA	3:53:38

12/21/2008	313	Taipei	Taipei	Taiwan	98	Asia	3:56:57
1/8/2009	314	Tiberias	Tiberias	Israel	99	Asia	3:44:39
2/7/2009	316	Moorea	Moorea	French Polynesia	100	Oceania	4:12:41
12/6/2009	321	Singapore	Singapore	Singapore	101	Asia	4:43:41
2/14/2010	325	Bahamas	Nassau	Bahamas	102	NA	4:14:04
5/23/2010	329	Andina	Paipa	Colombia	103	SA	4:27:01
8/8/2010	334	Maraton Bicentario	Asuncion	Paraguay	104	SA	4:28:01
9/26/2010	335	Accra International	Accra	Ghana	105	Africa	4:56:05
10/3/2010	336	Maya	Amatitlan	Guatemala	106	NA	4:25:36
3/27/2011	343	Guam	Agat	Guam	107	Oceania	4:36:11
6/18/2011	345	Dili Peace	Dili	East Timor	108	Oceania	4:47:15
6/26/2011	346	Manila	Manila	Philippines	109	Asia	4:51:16
8/14/2011	347	Isle of Man	Ramsey	Isle of Man	110	Europe	4:55:13
10/2/2011	348	Jersey	St Helier	Isle of Jersey	111	Europe	5:19:55
12/4/2011	351	HBN Law	Willemstad	Curacao	112	SA	5:43:23
3/3/2012	355	Saipan	Saipan	N. Mariana Is	113	Oceania	5:03:02
6/2/2012	358	BlueSky	Apia	Samoa	114	Oceania	4:51:05
8/26/2012	360	Guernsey	St Peter Port	Guernsey	115	Europe	4:46:20
5/12/2013	361	St Kitts	Basseterre	St Kitts	116	NA	5:27:39
9/1/2013	364	Da Nang	Da Nang	Vietnam	117	Asia	6:05:45
12/8/2013	367	End of the World	Placencia	Belize	118	NA	5:11:15
1/5/2014	368	Let's Go Haiti	Cap Haitien	Haiti	119	NA	5:02:00
3/2/2014	370	Kilimanjaro	Moshi	Tanzania	120	Africa	5:17:50
5/25/2014	372	Kosovo	Pristina	Kosovo	121	Europe	5:20:35
1/30/2015	373	Muscat	Muscat	Oman	122	Asia	5:32:26
2/6/2015	374	Bahrain	Manama	Bahrain	123	Asia	5:18:35
4/12/2015	375	Punta Cana	Punta Cana	Dominican Republic	124	NA	5:28:47
6/28/2015	376	Victoria Falls	Victoria Falls	Zimbabwe	125	Africa	5:47:43

About the Author

John "Maddog" Wallace was born in 1944 and raised near Ottawa, Canada. He and Nicole have been married for forty-eight years. The family moved to Reno, Nevada, in 1979, where he ran his first marathon in 1982. They are both retired and currently reside in Sarasota, Florida, and have two sons and three granddaughters.

He has run 376 marathons in 125 countries. He has completed a marathon in all fifty states plus DC twice, and four US territories; all thirteen provinces and territories of Canada, and all seven continents.

He has completed a marathon in every country in Europe, North America, South America, and Oceania, and he has completed a marathon in at least eight countries on every continent—except Antarctica, which only has one country.

Health issues and age have slowed him down the past few years, but he still continues to follow his passion to travel and run marathons around the world.

Acknowledgments

I wish to thank all my family and friends, who encouraged and pushed me to write a book about Maddog's marathon adventures.

I wish to thank the following people:

Wally Herman, a friend and mentor, and a true pioneer in marathon running. He provided guidance and mentoring in the "old days," when marathons were difficult to find. When I was close to breaking his world record of ninety-nine countries, which he held for many years, he offered his blessing and told me, "I am happy that it is you who will break my record."

Nicole Wallace, wife and best friend for forty-eight years, and sports manager for the past thirty-four years. She has supported me through all my races and was my travelling companion to many marathons and countries. Her enthusiasm only started to wane when the marathons became more remote, the countries became smaller, poorer, and harder to get to, and toilets became holes in the floor or ground.

Malcolm Anderson, a friend and successful author of four books: *A Marathon Odyssey, The Messengers, The Cayman Islands Marathon*, and *The Marathon Maniacs*. While interviewing me for *The Messengers*, he suggested that we should write a book on Maddog's marathon adventures. He completed more than half of the book before work commitments forced him to hand the project back to me for completion. Without his efforts and support, this book would never have happened.